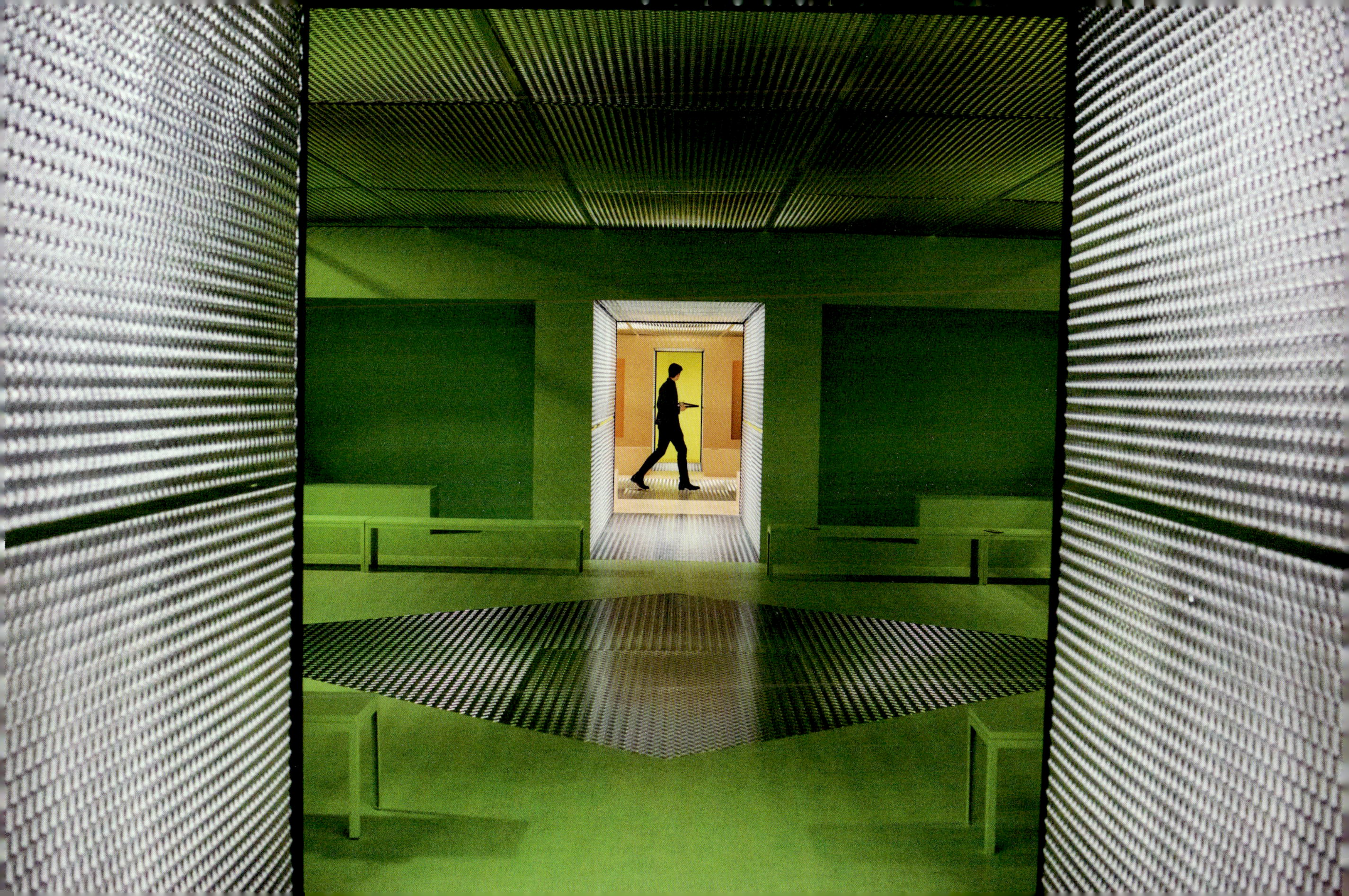

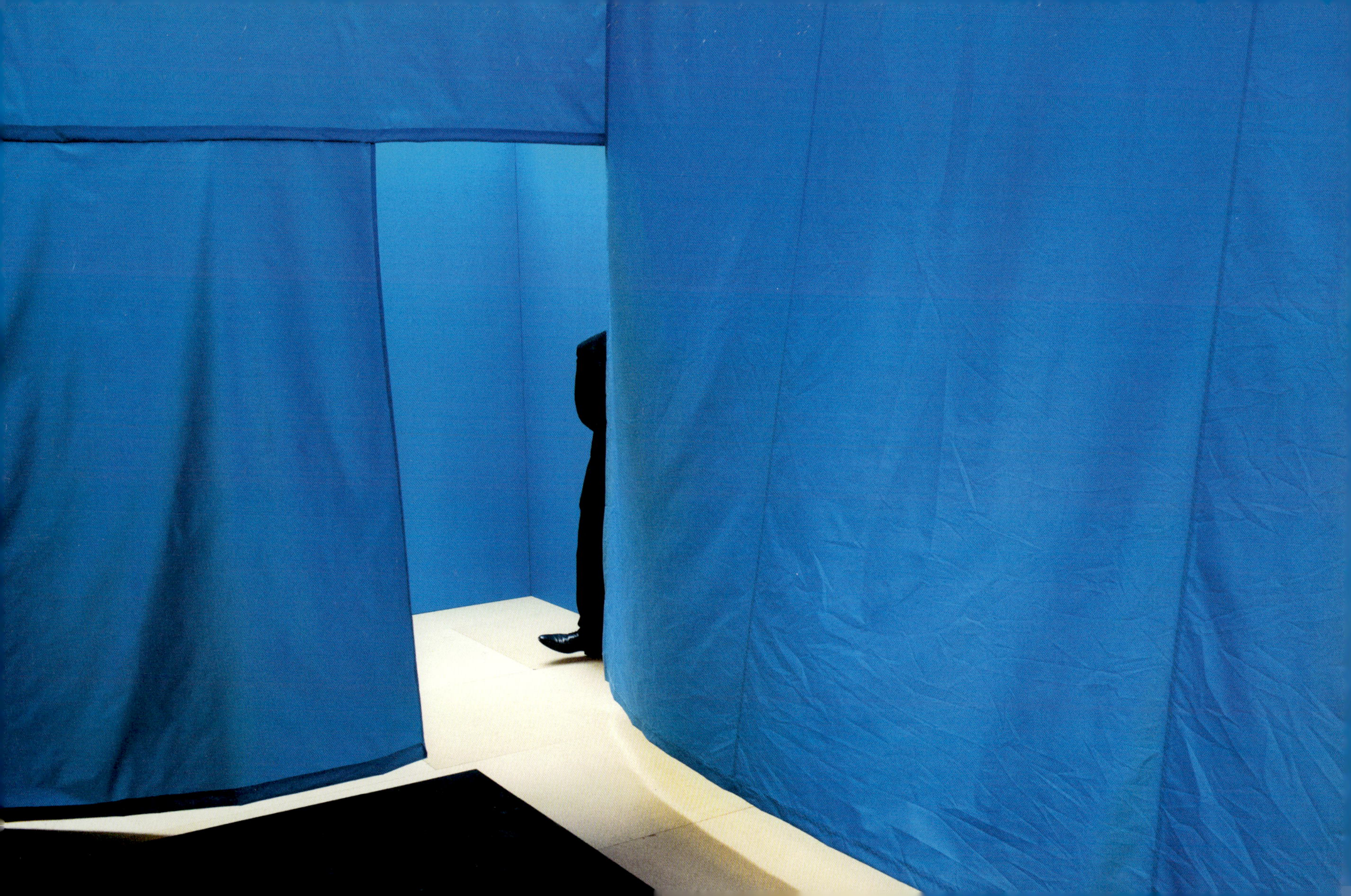

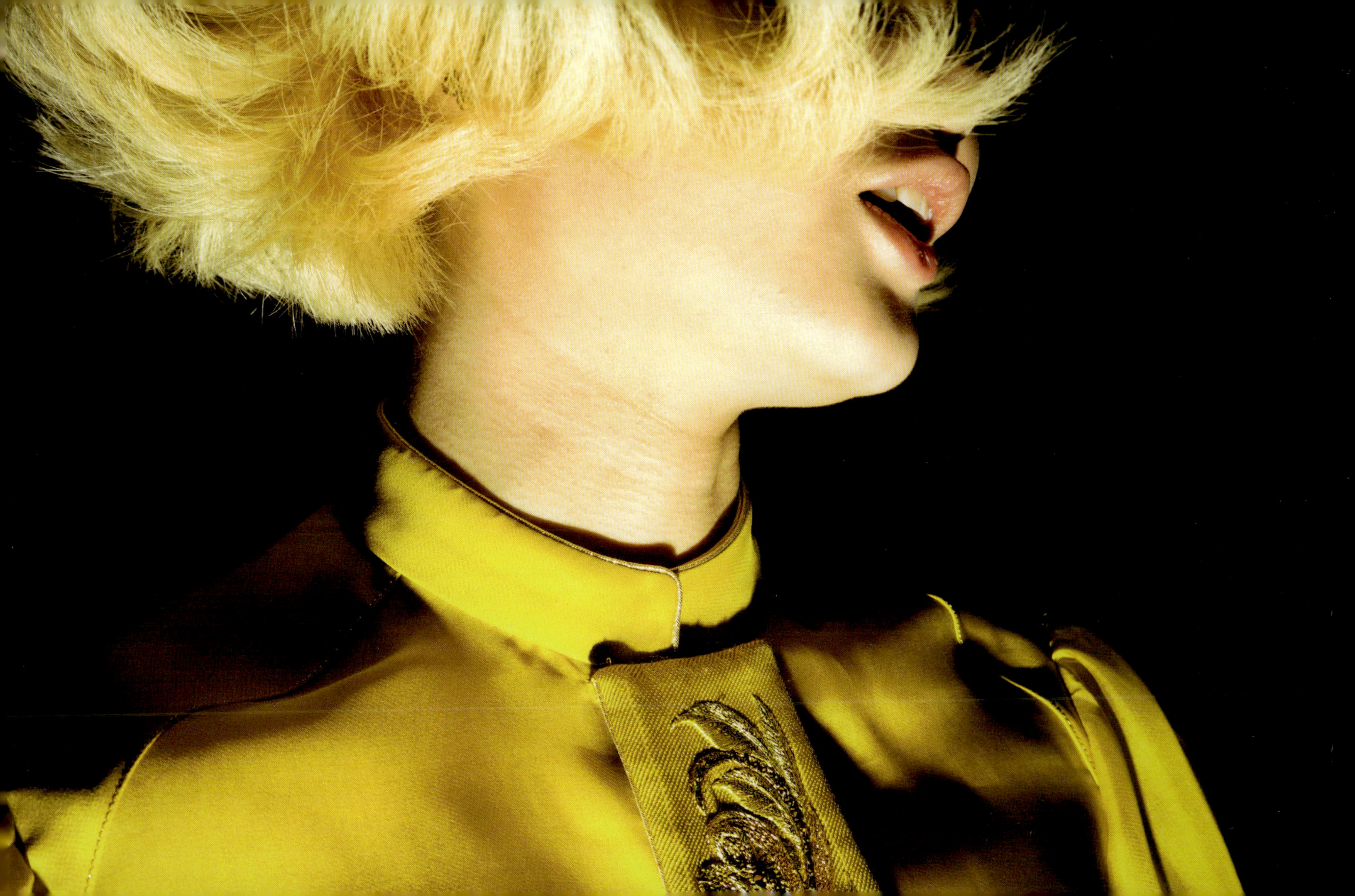

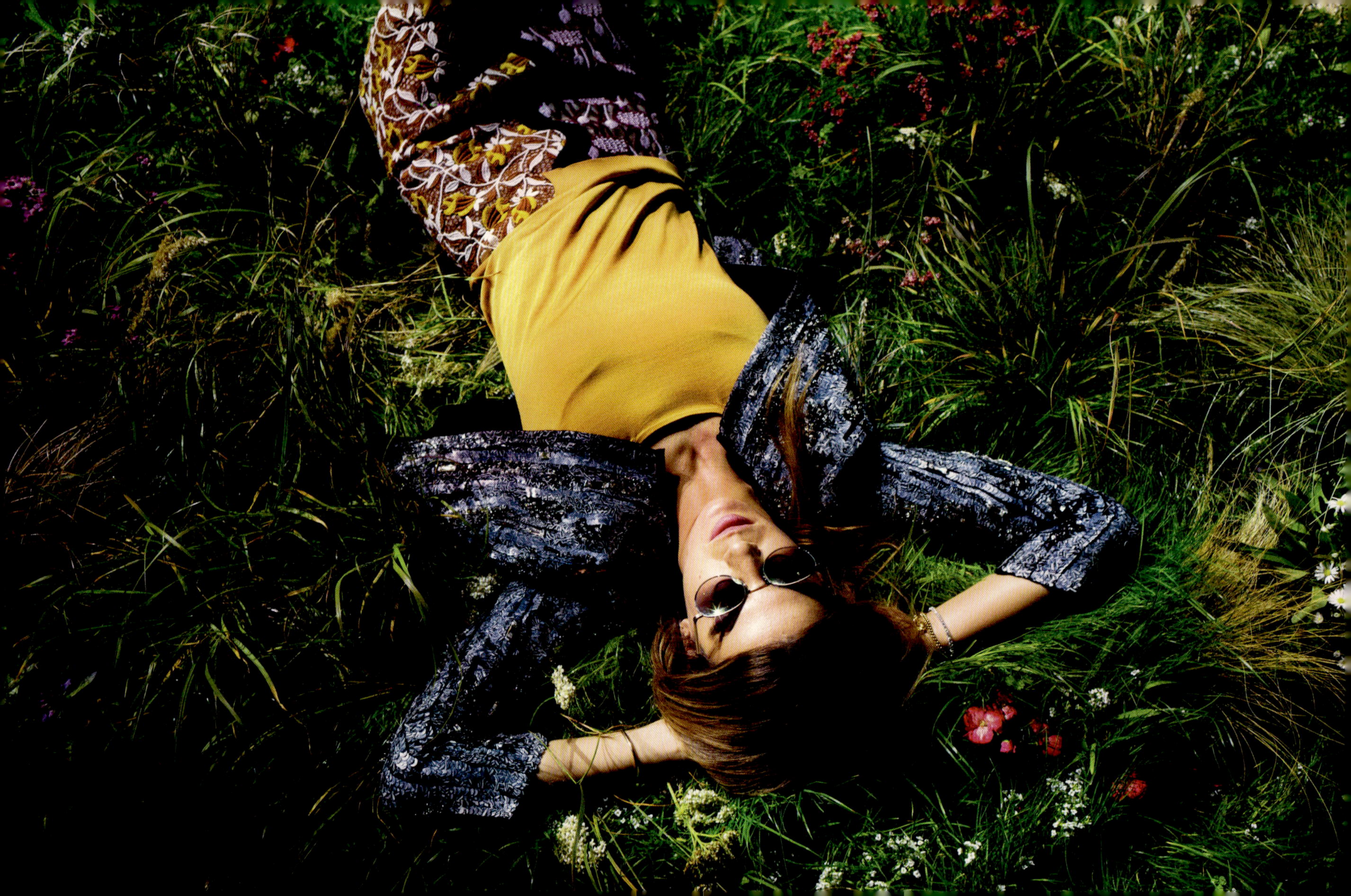

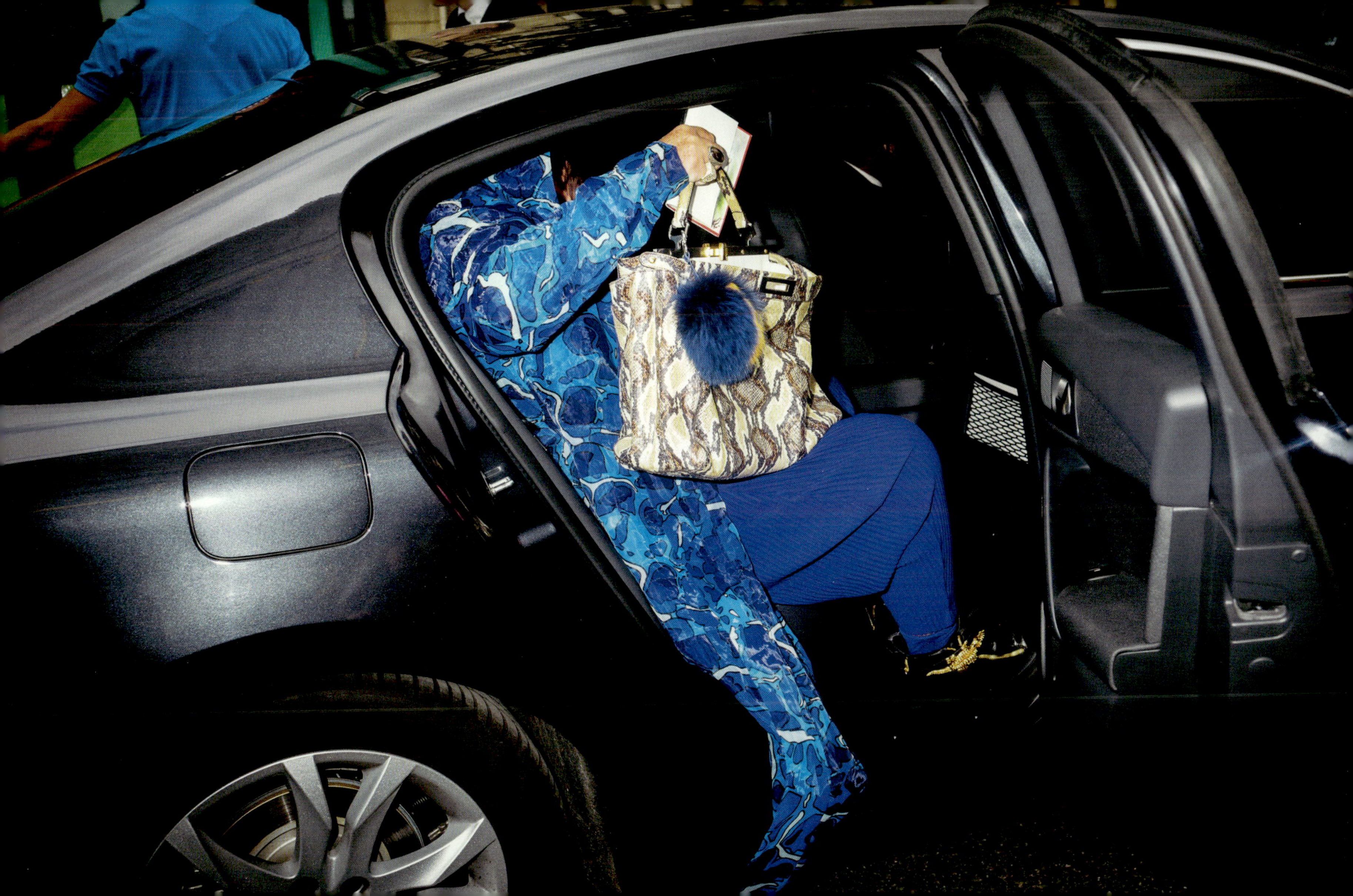

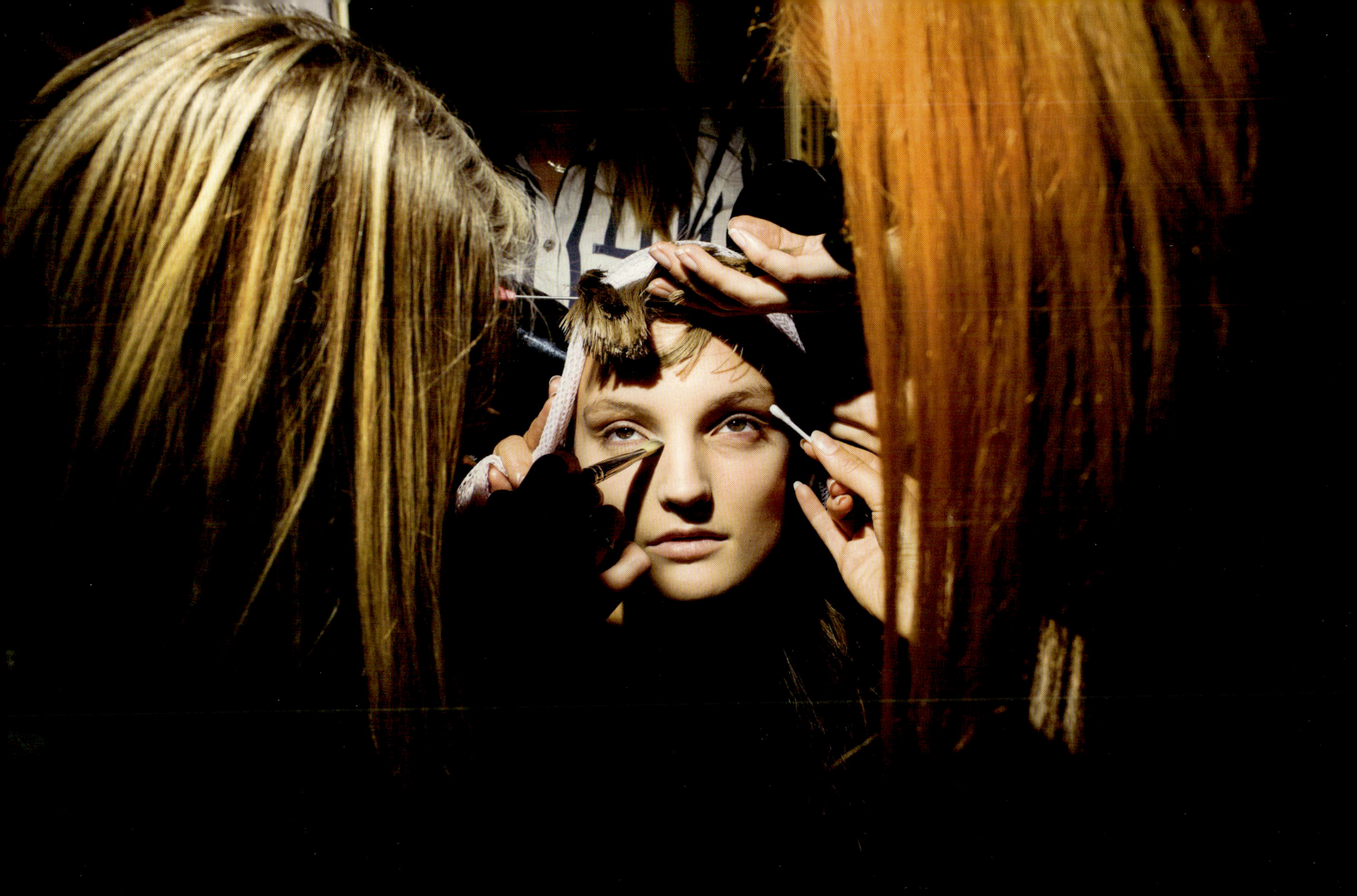

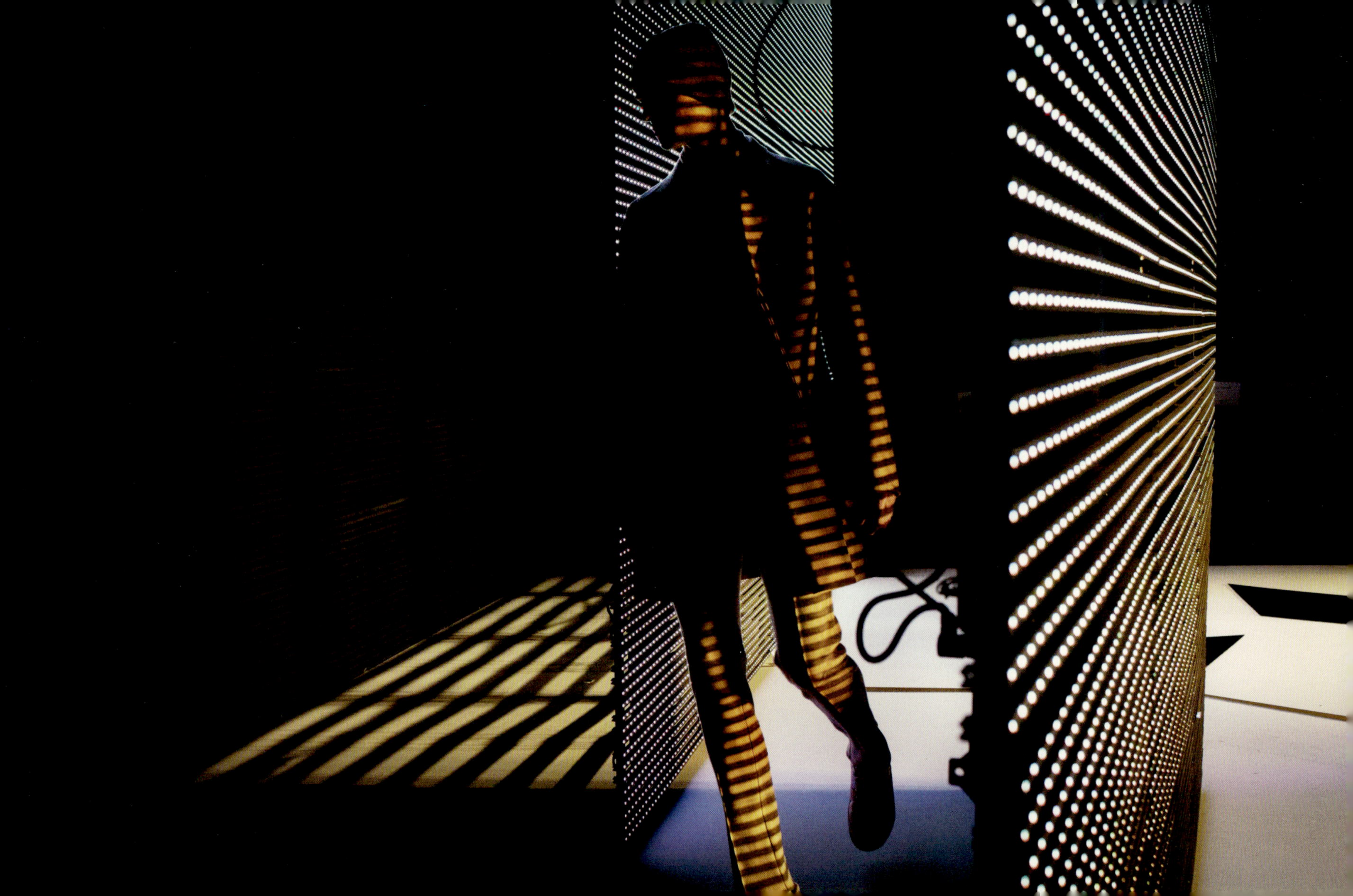

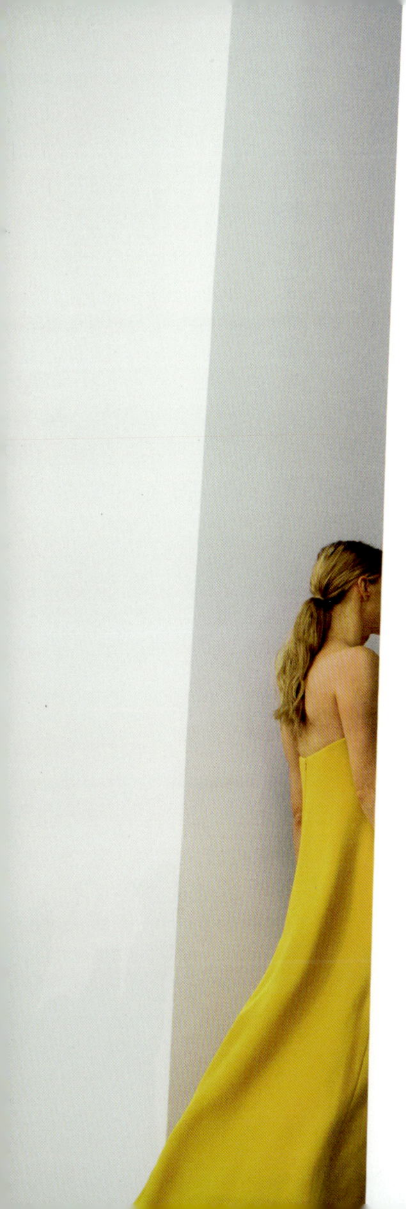

OUT OF FASHION

PHOTOGRAPHS BY LANDON NORDEMAN

DAMIANI

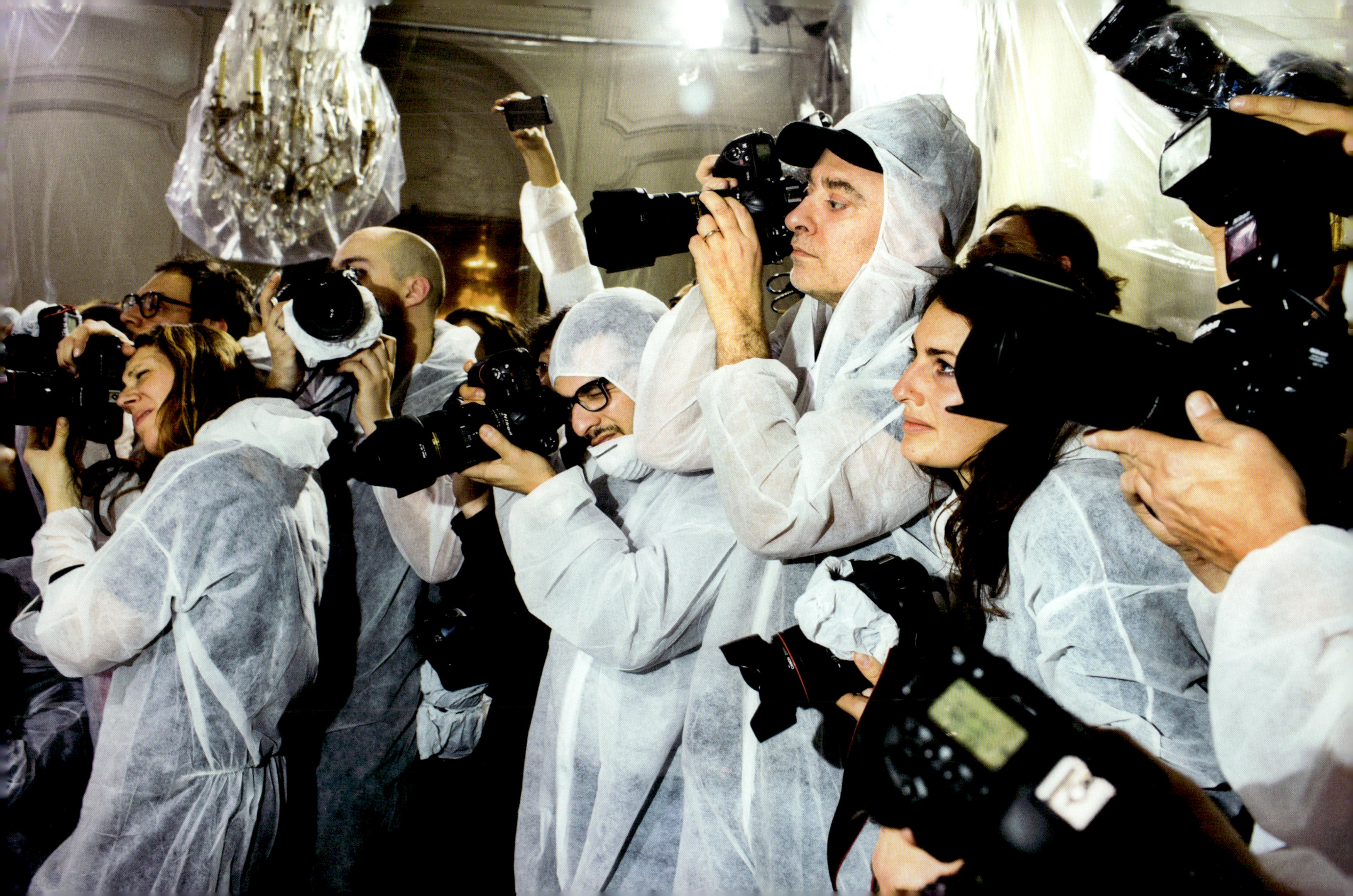

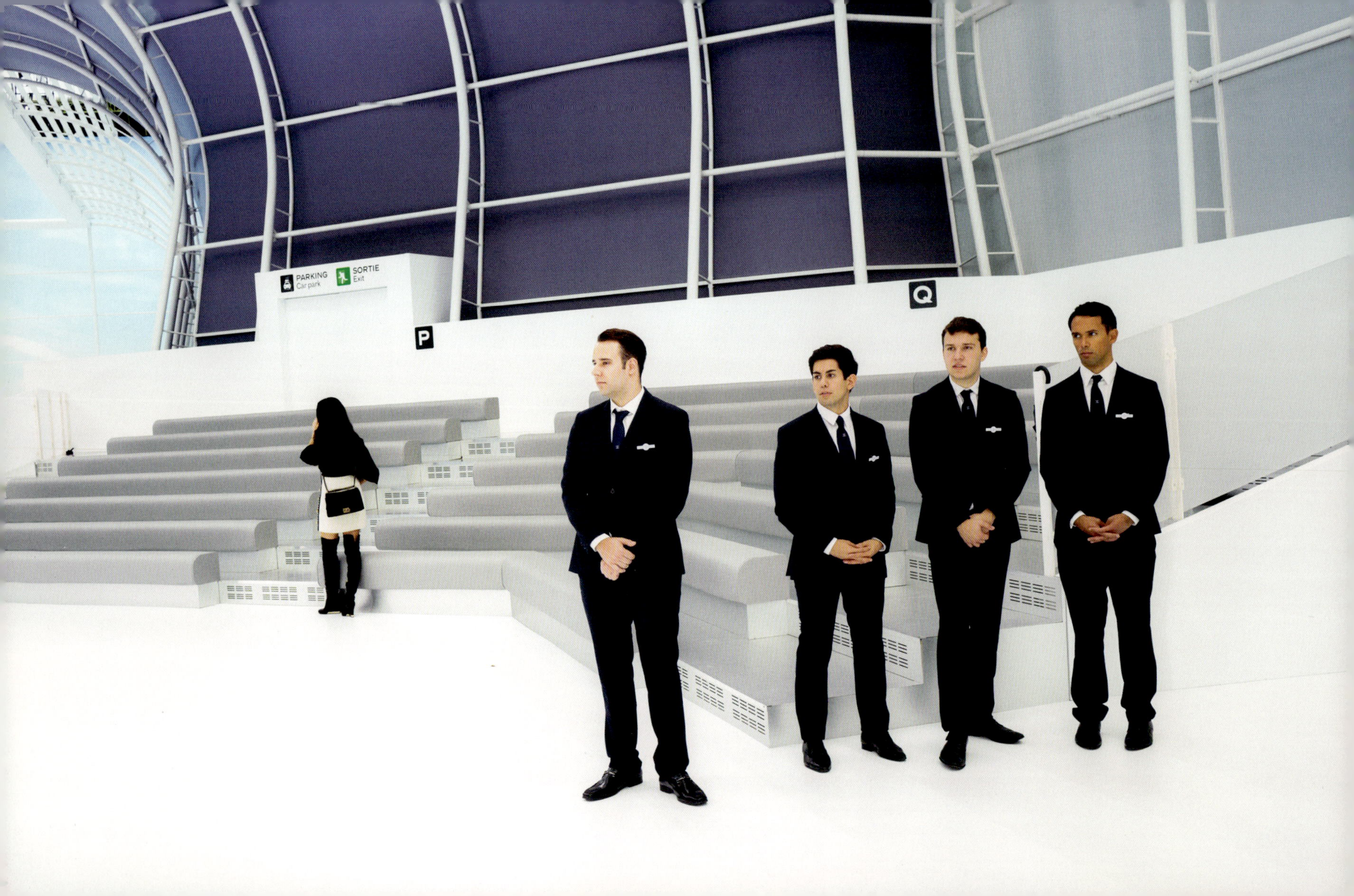
PARKING
Car park
SORTIE
Exit
P
Q

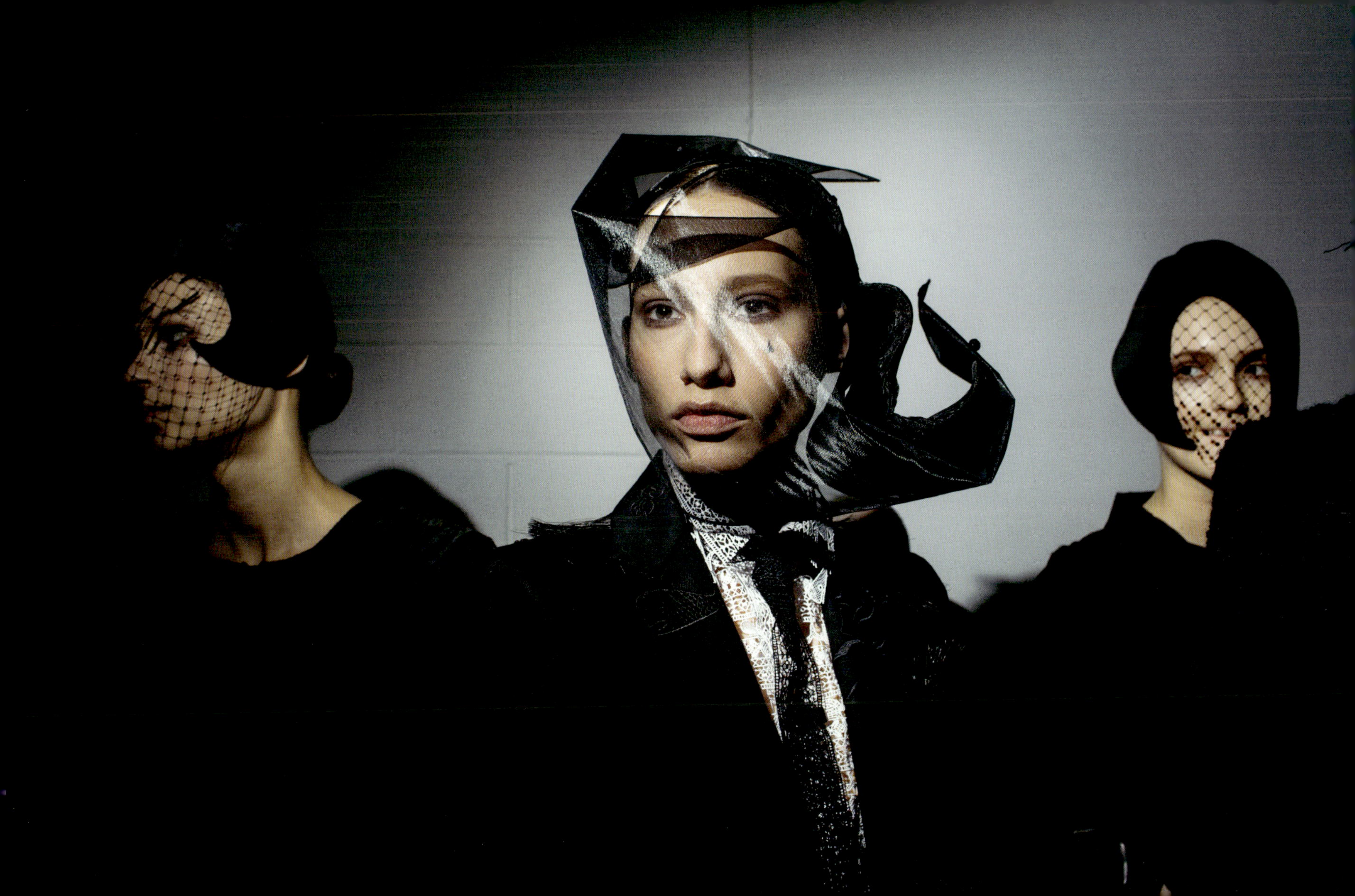

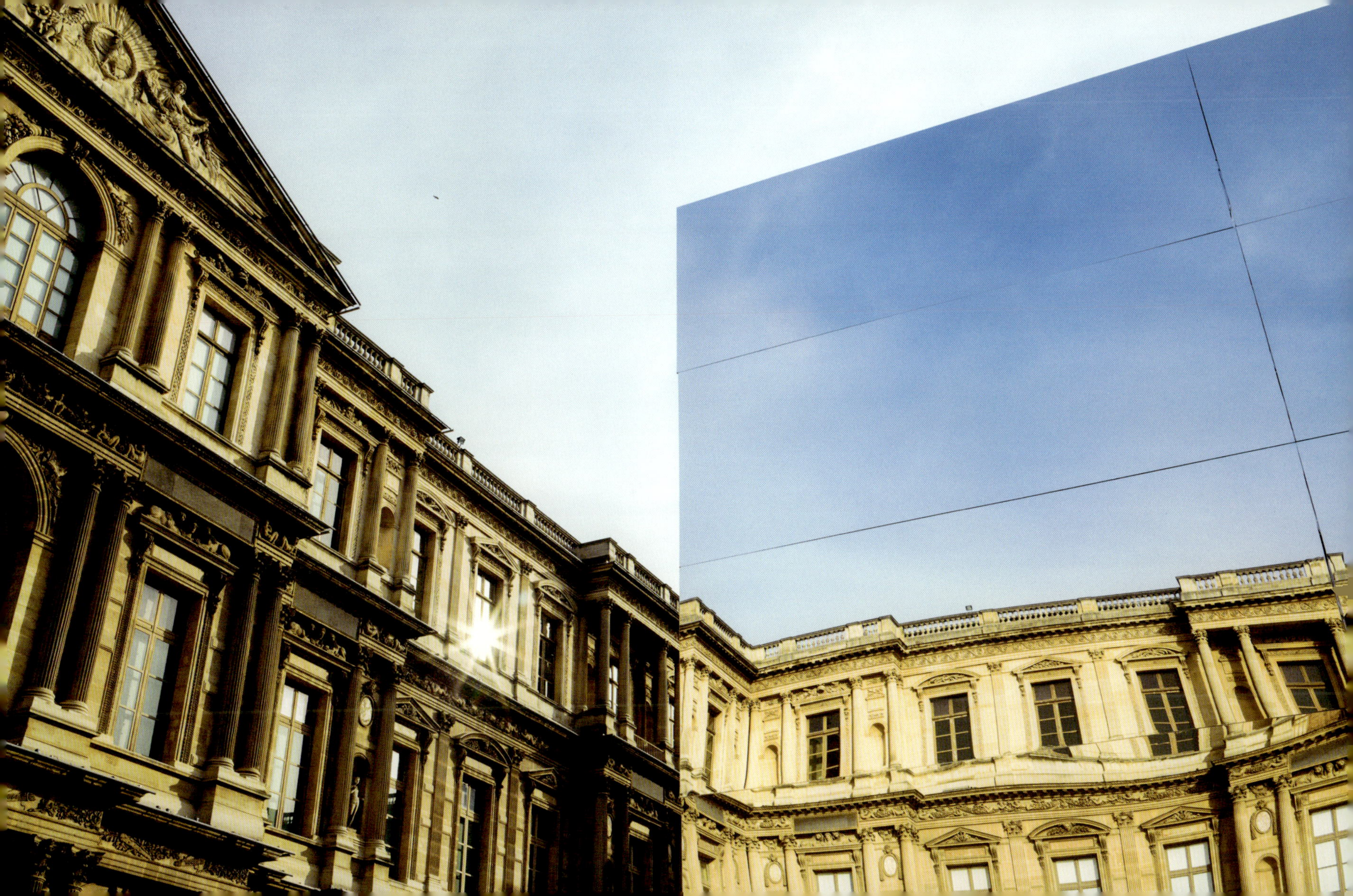

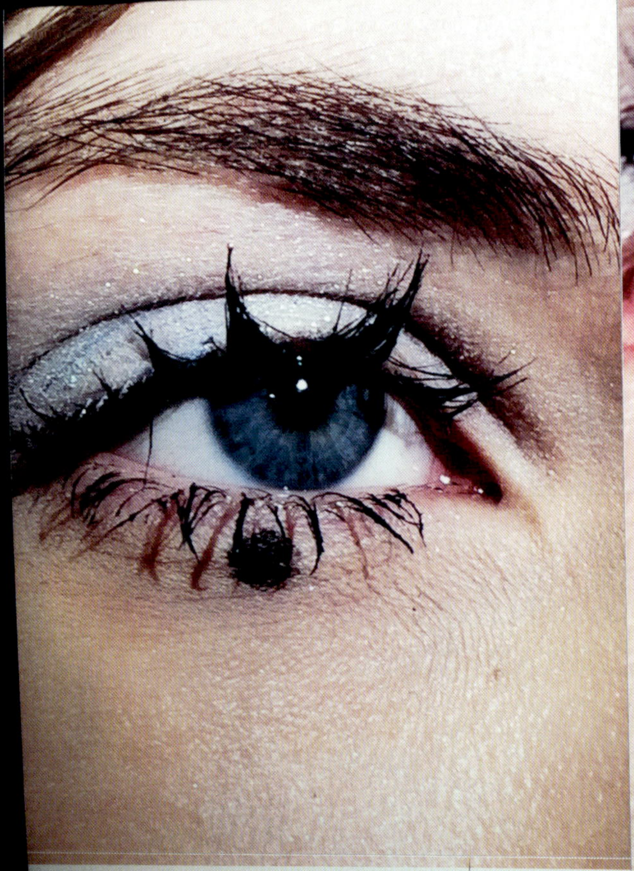
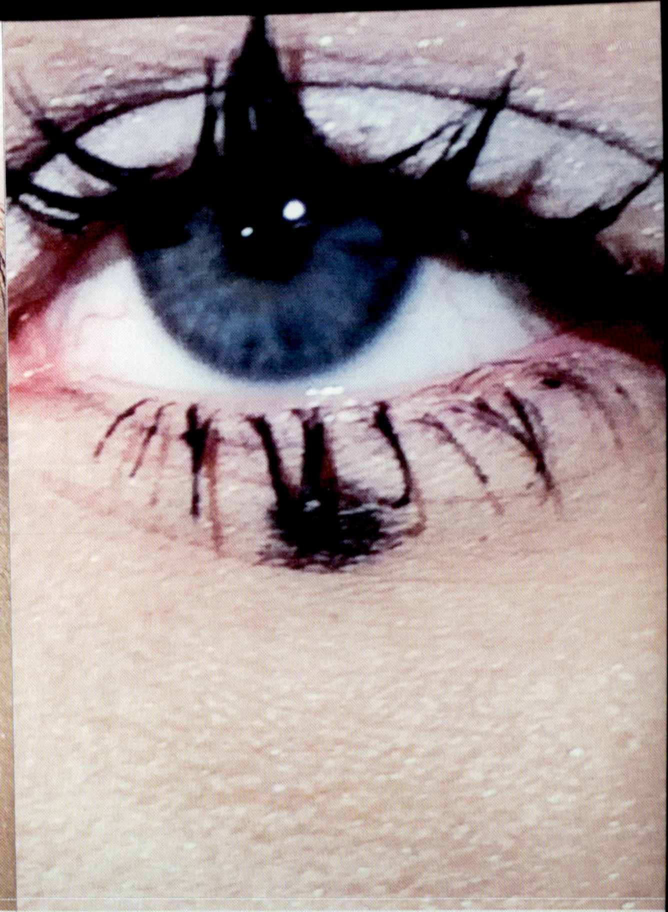

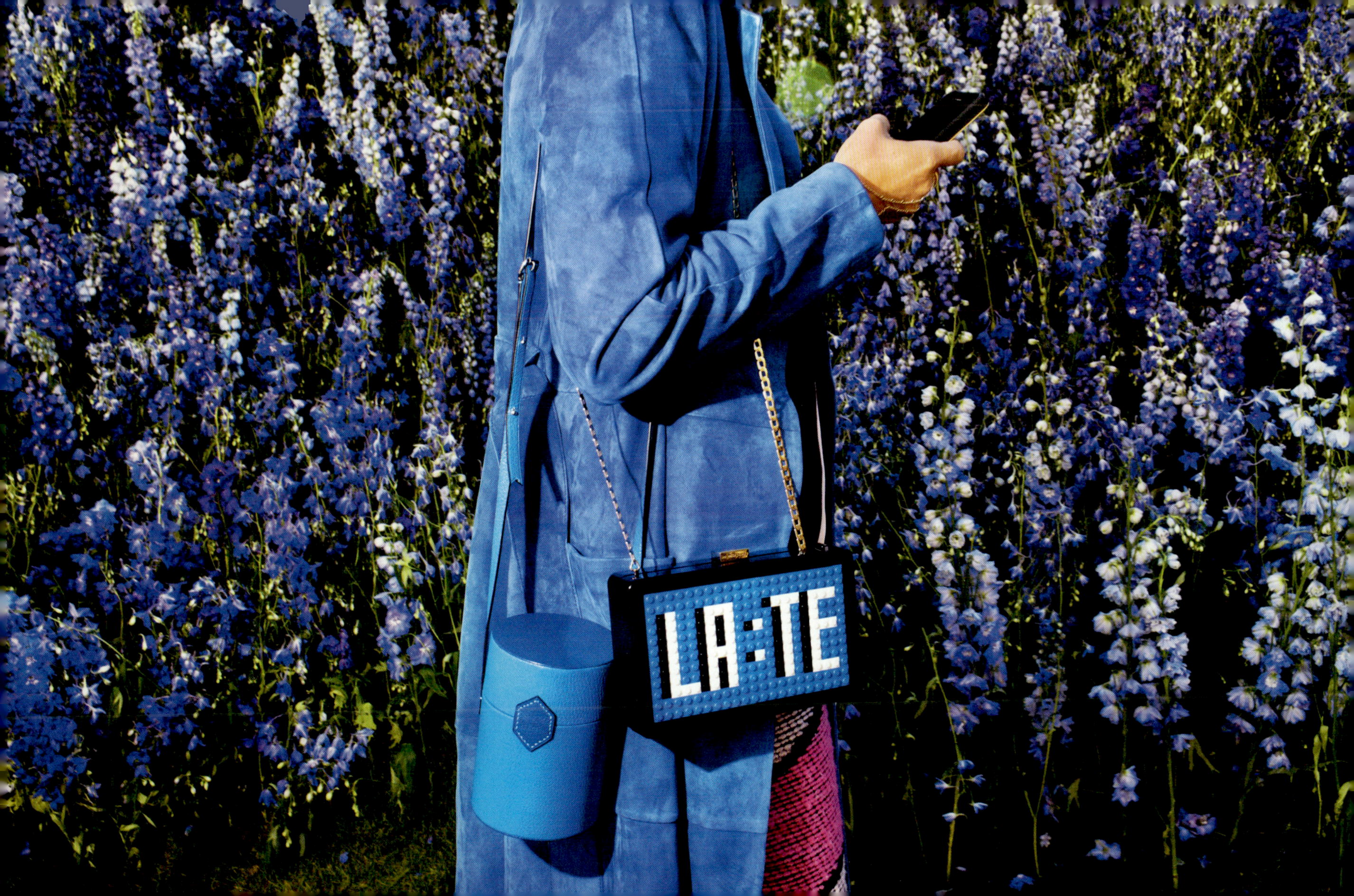
LA:TE

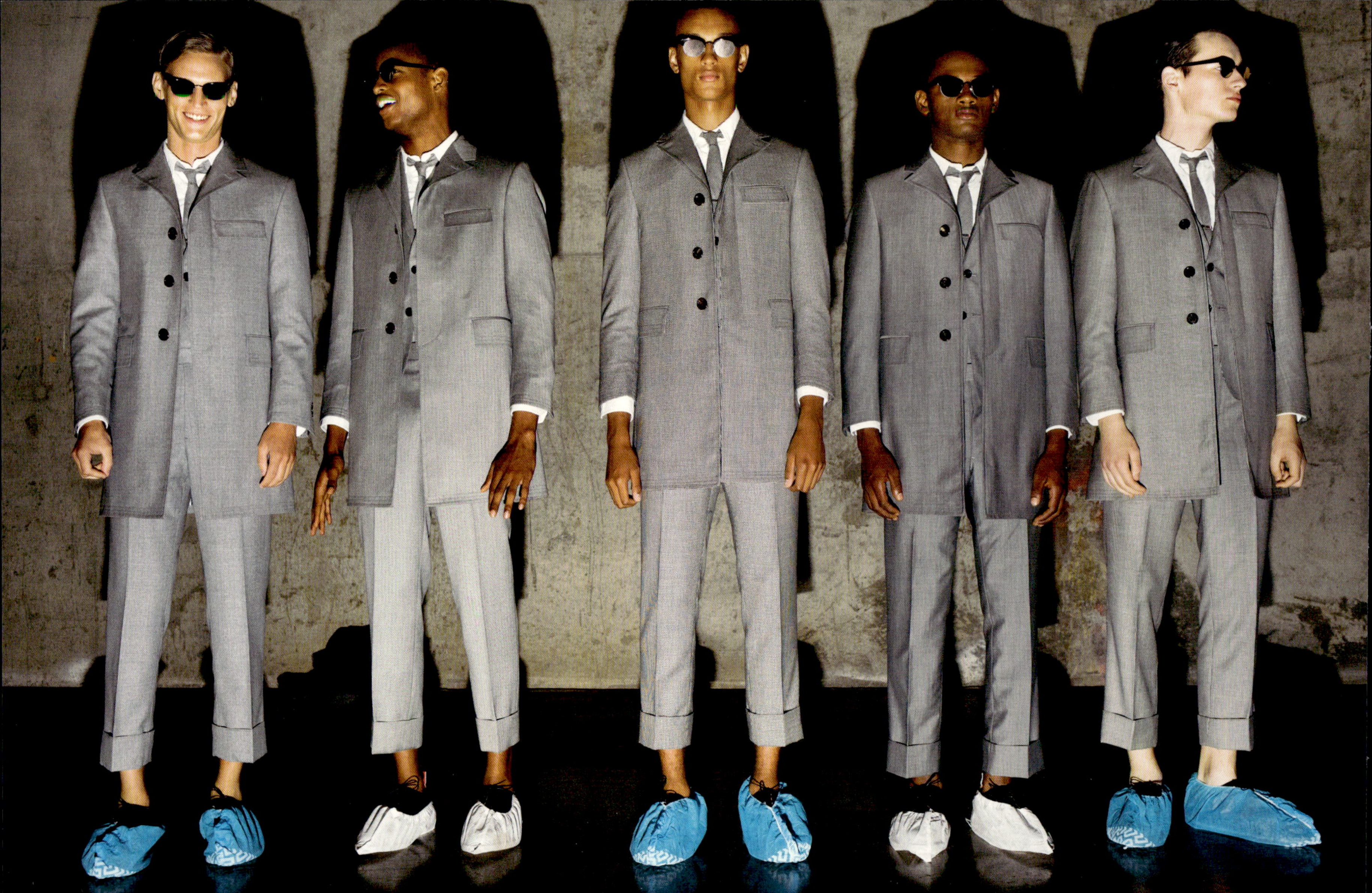

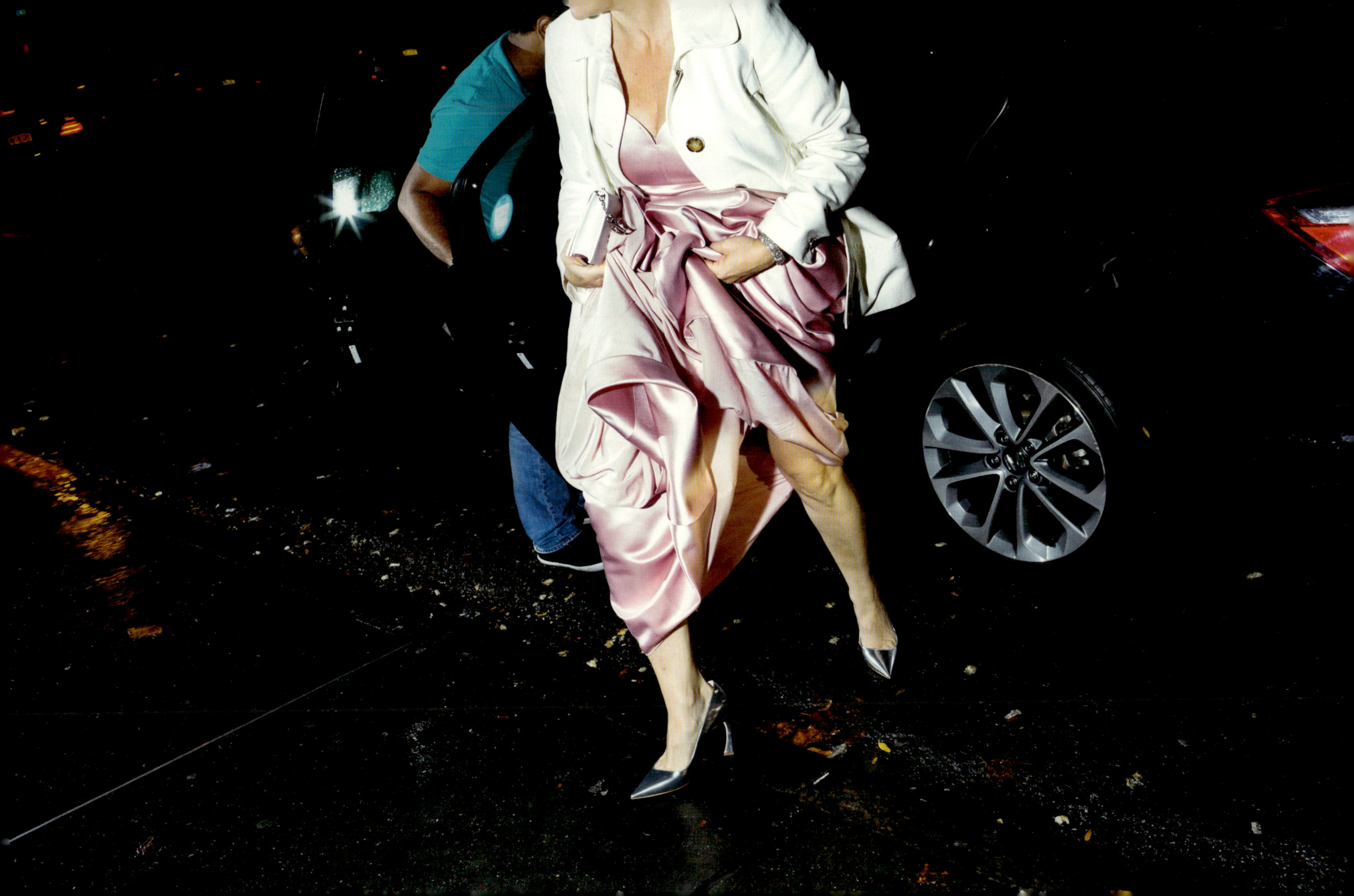

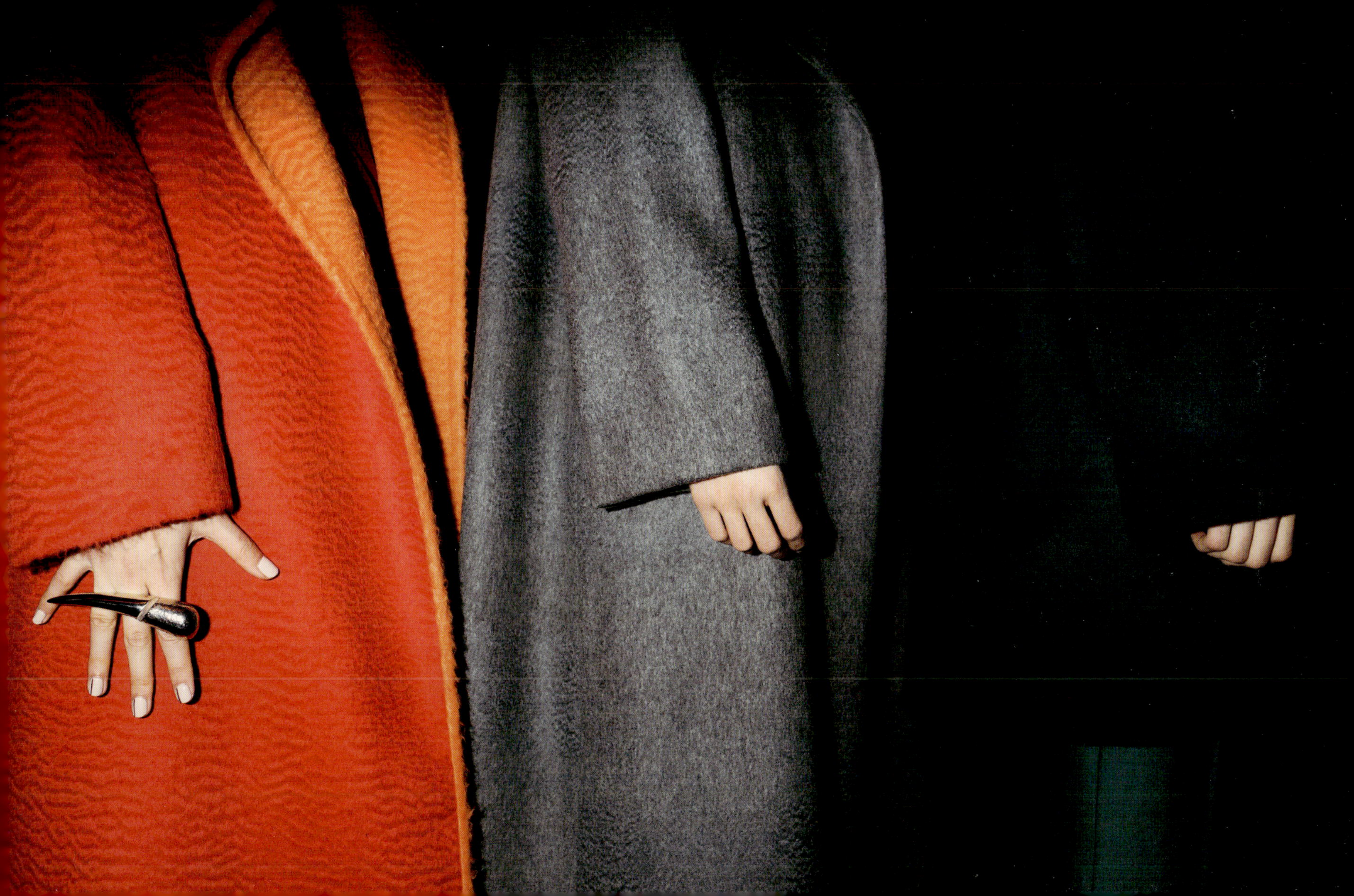

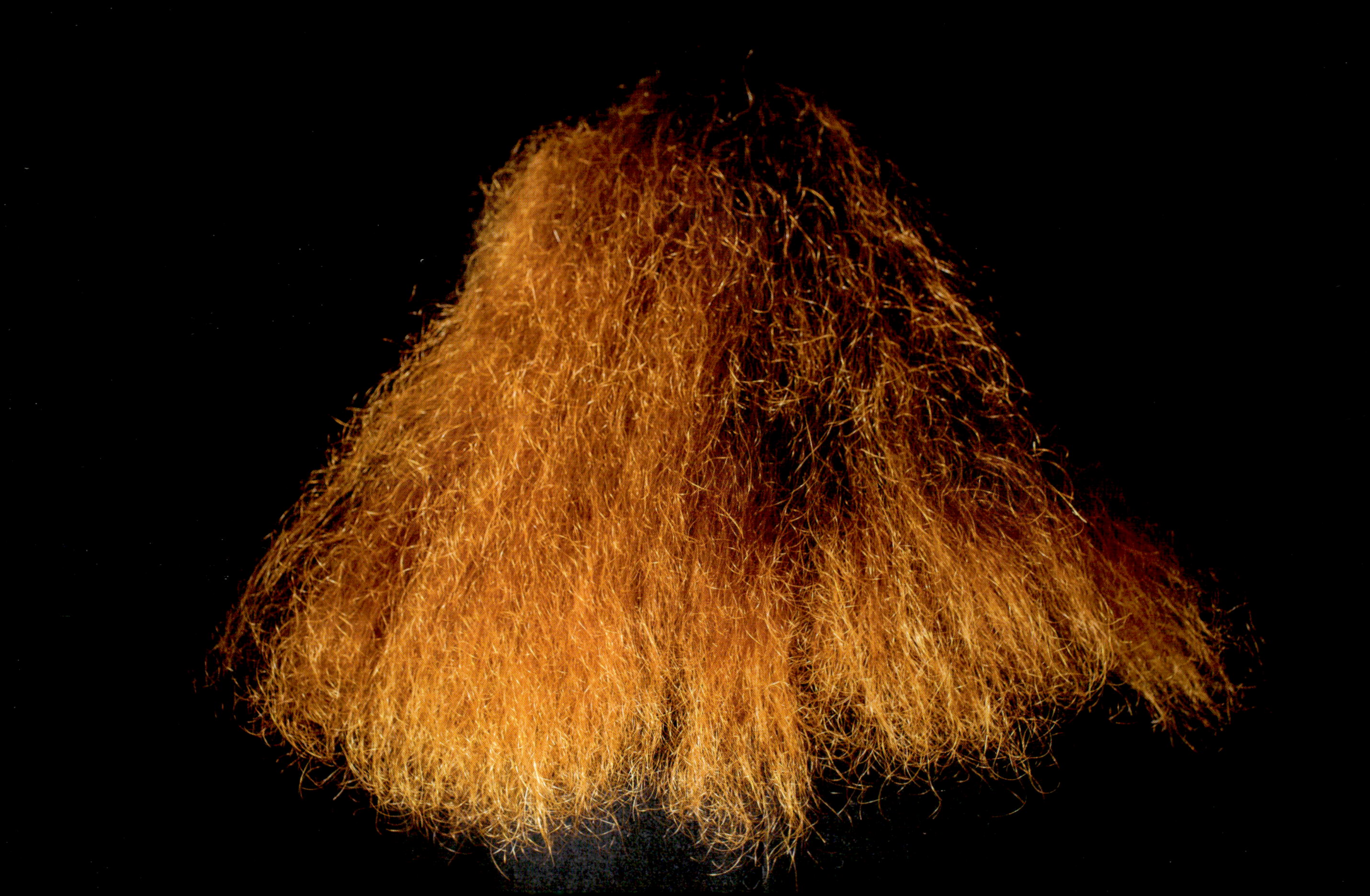

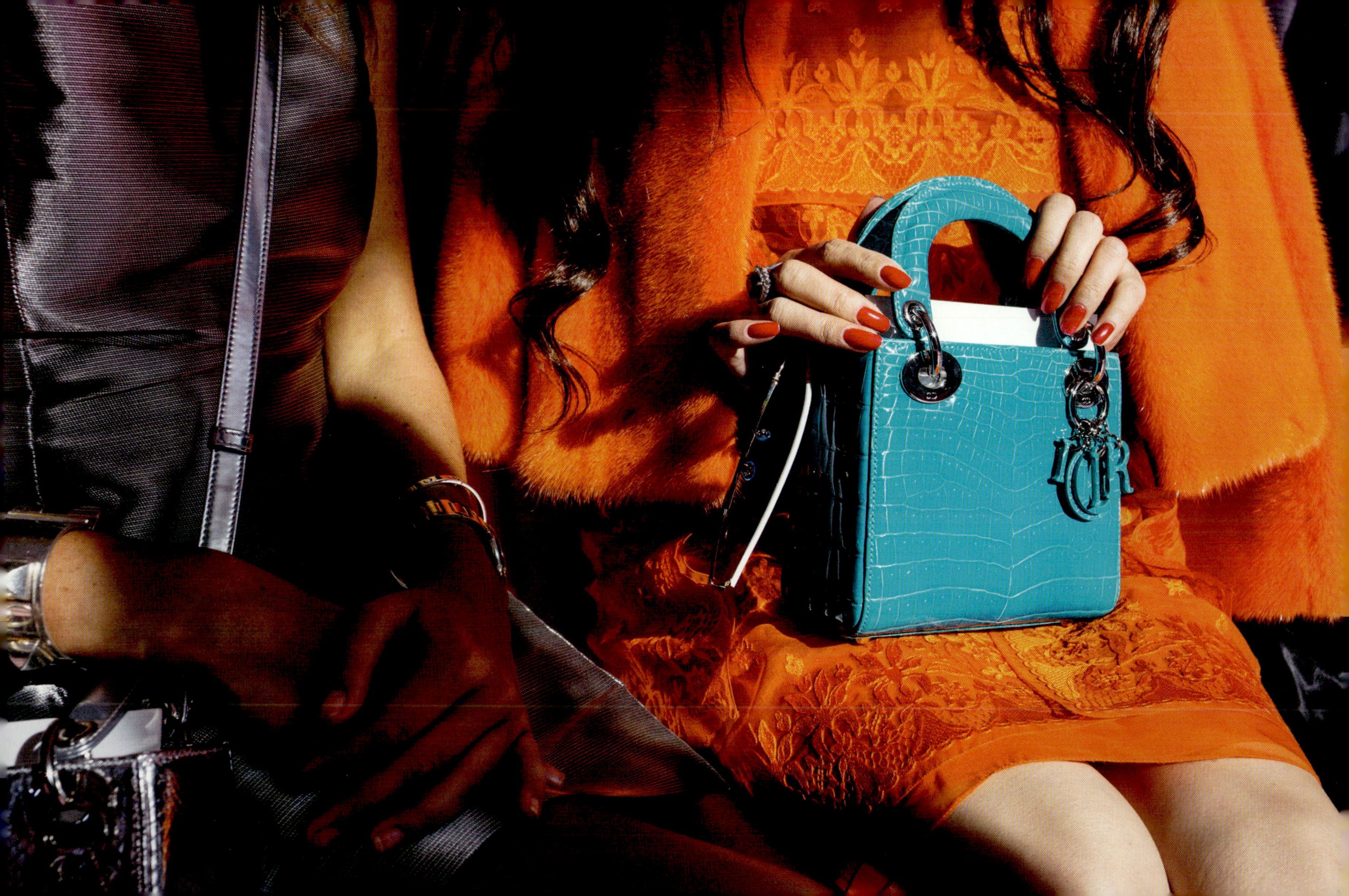

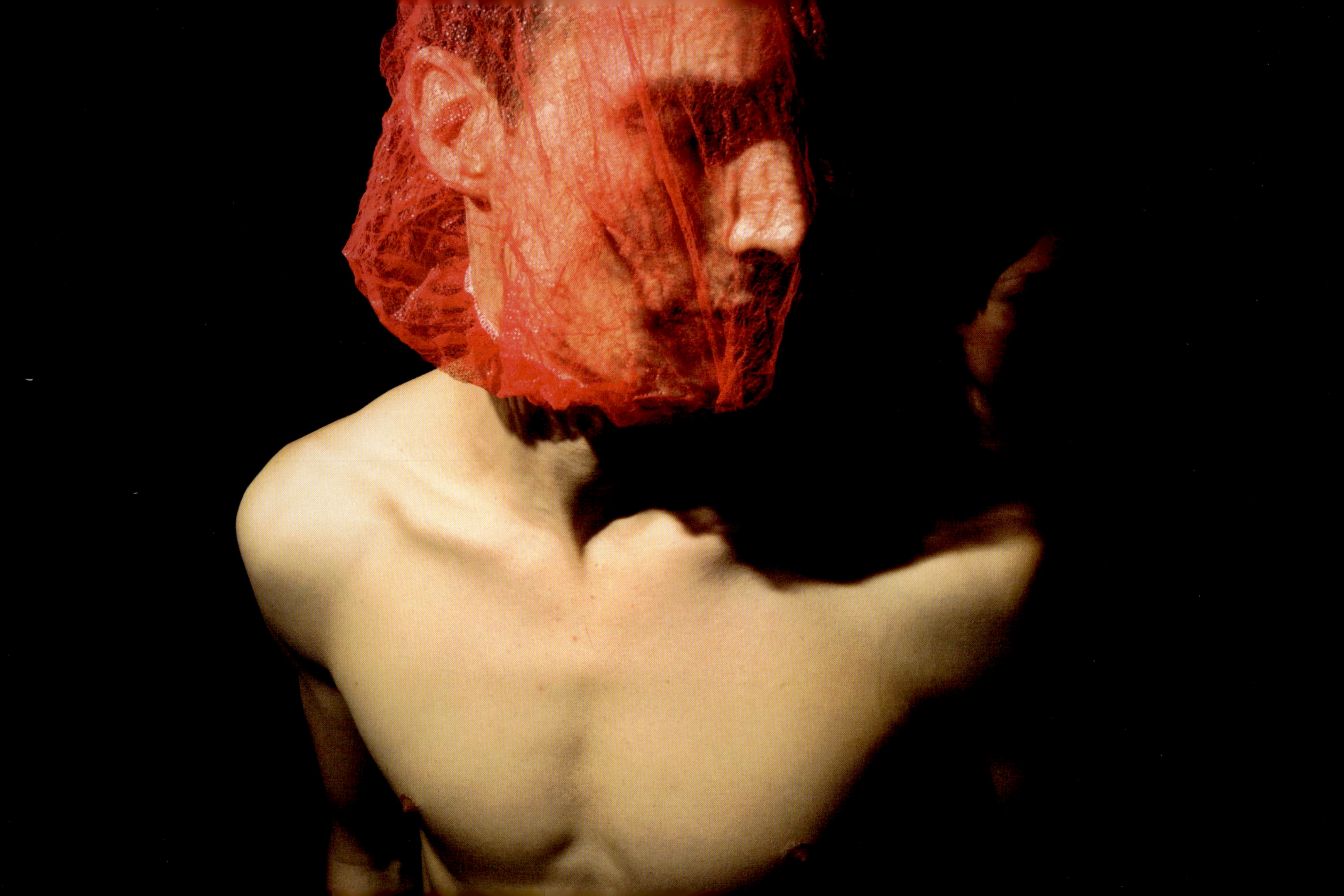

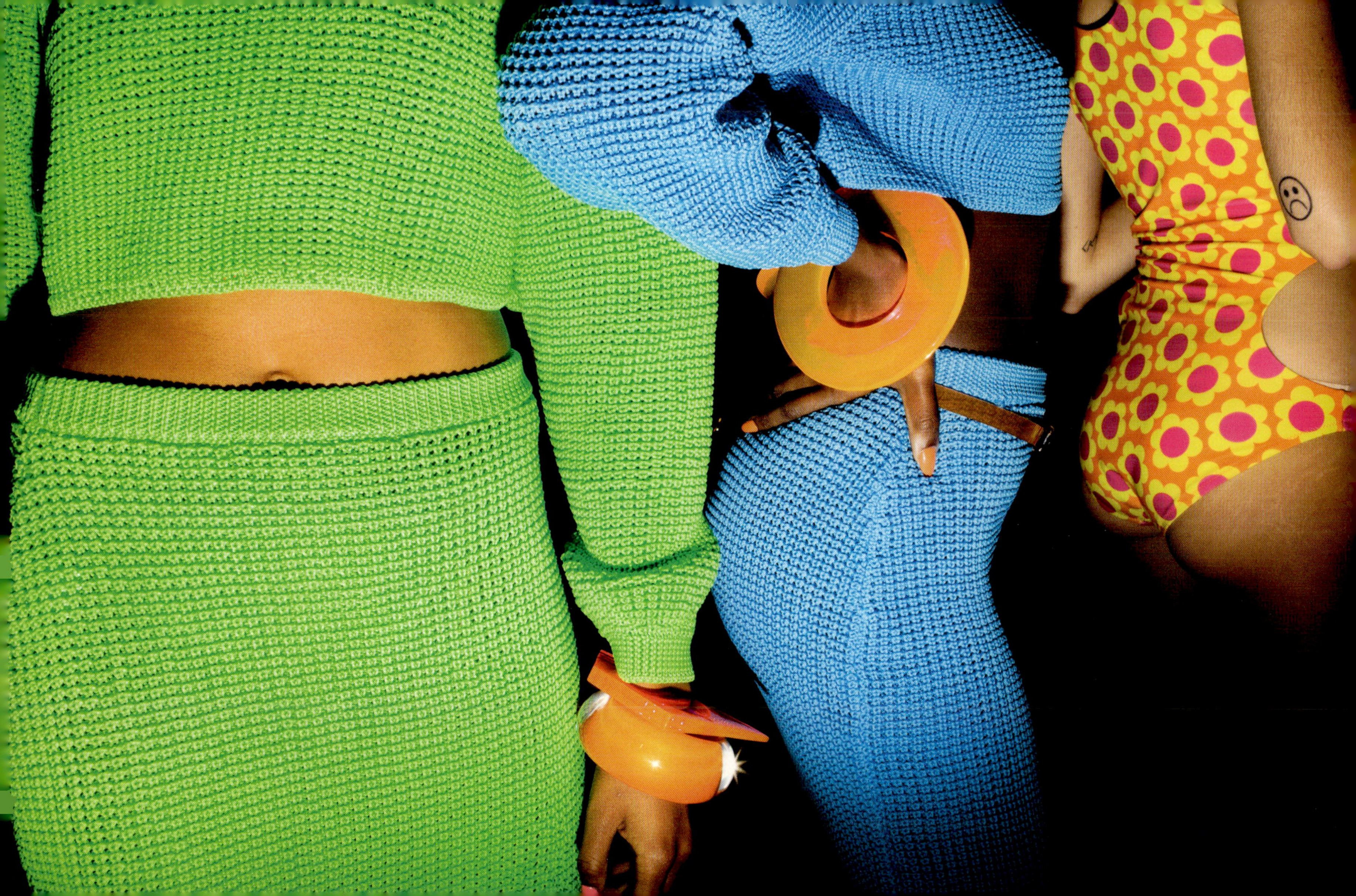

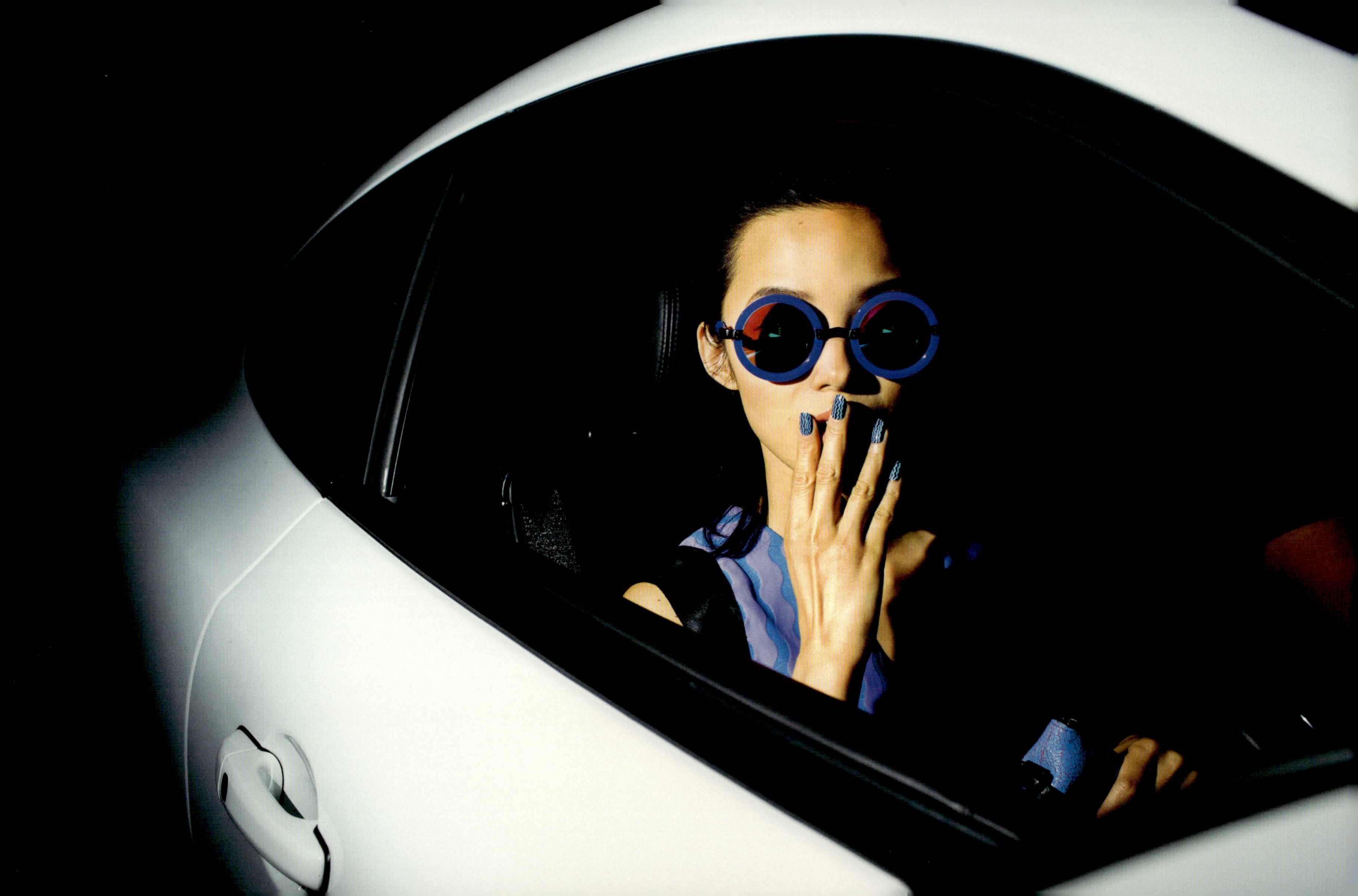

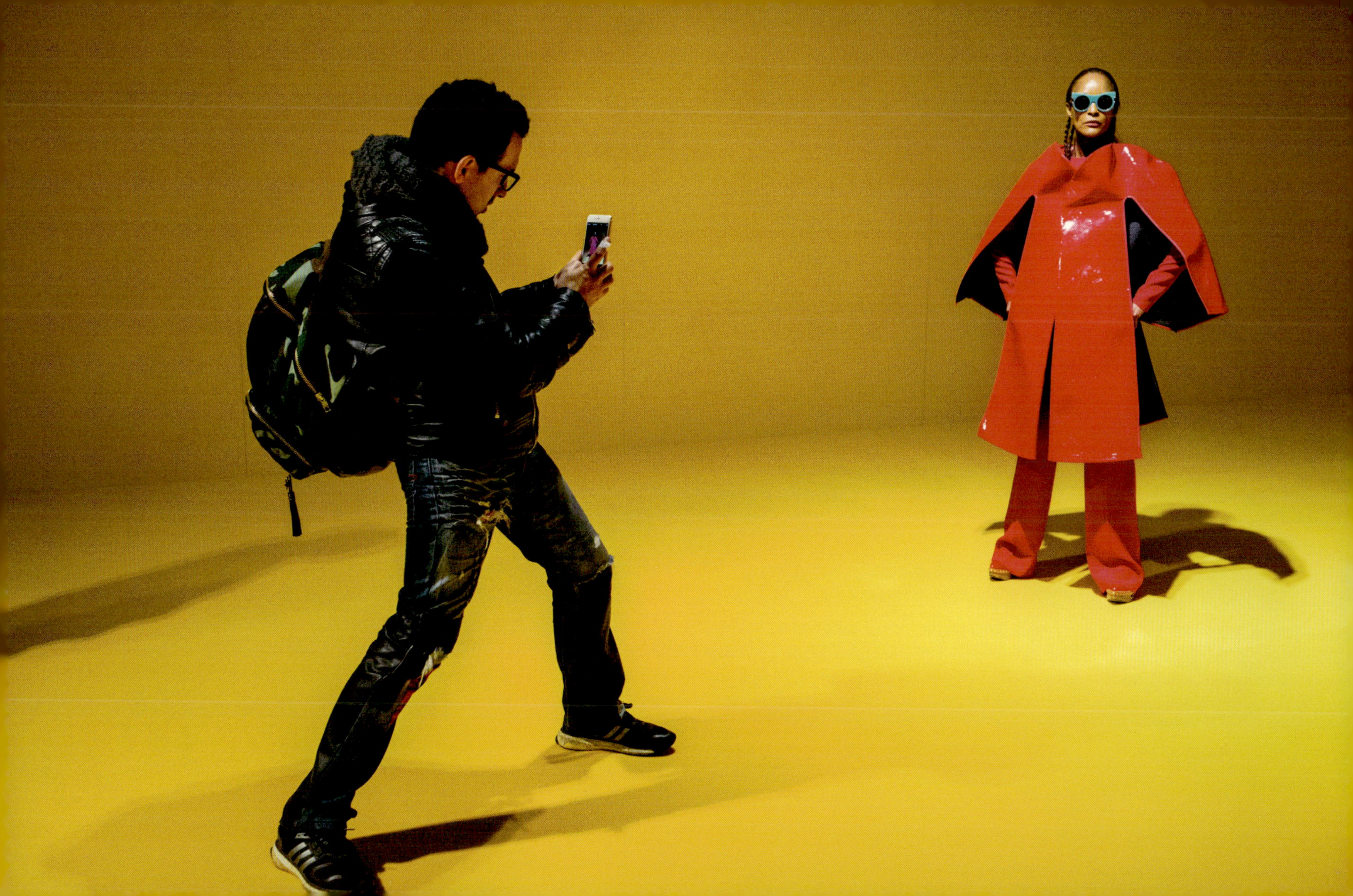

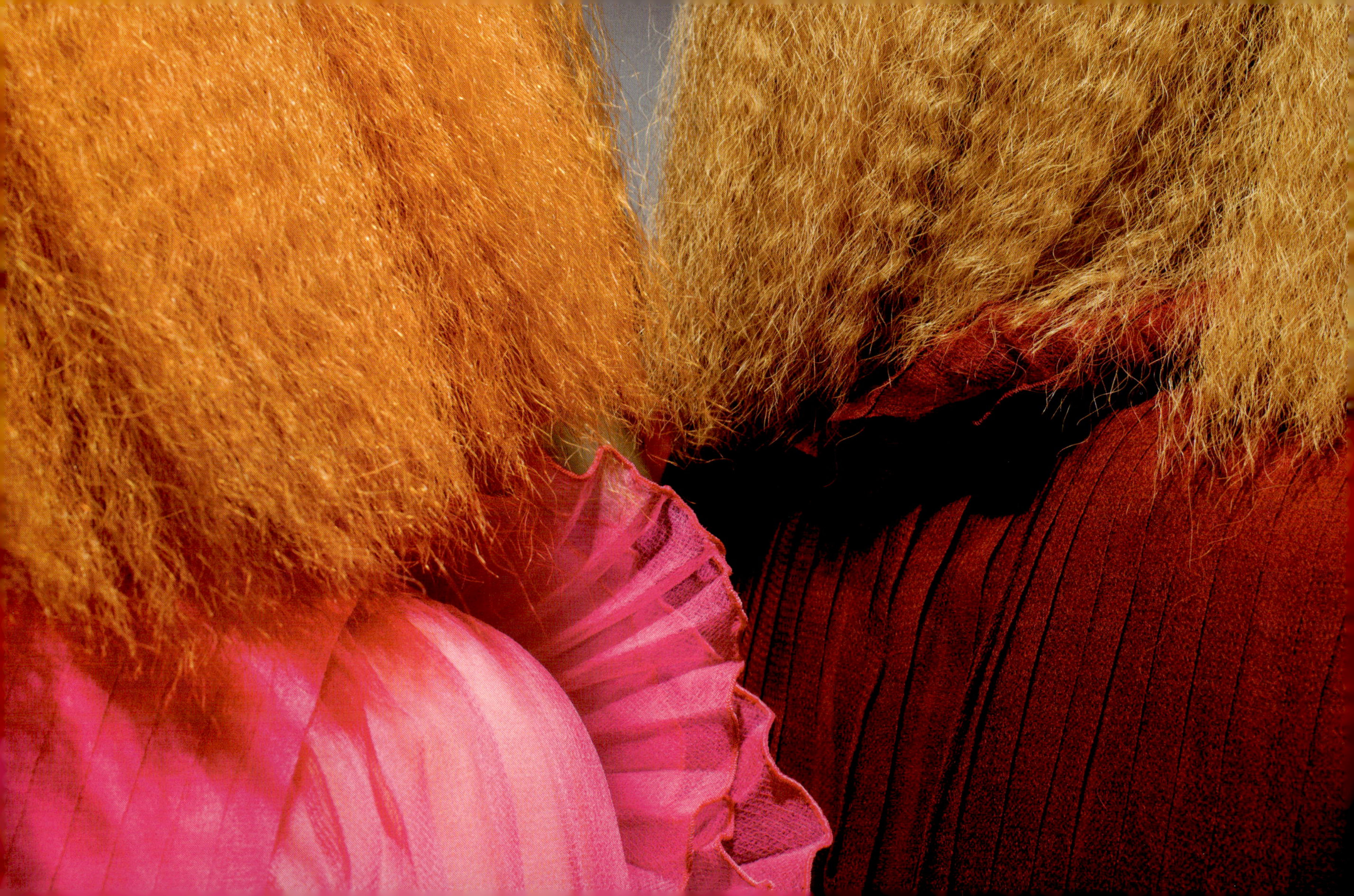

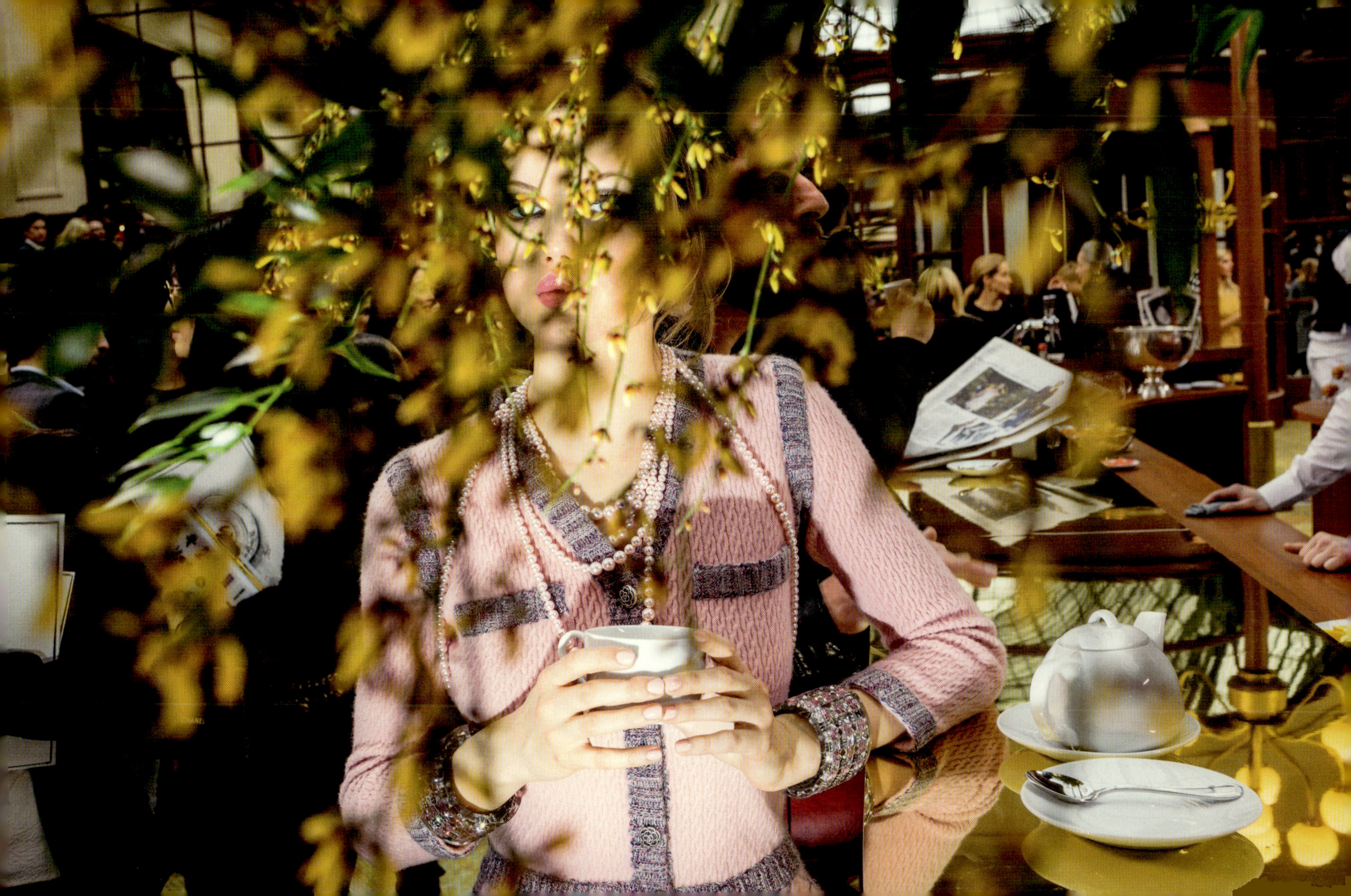

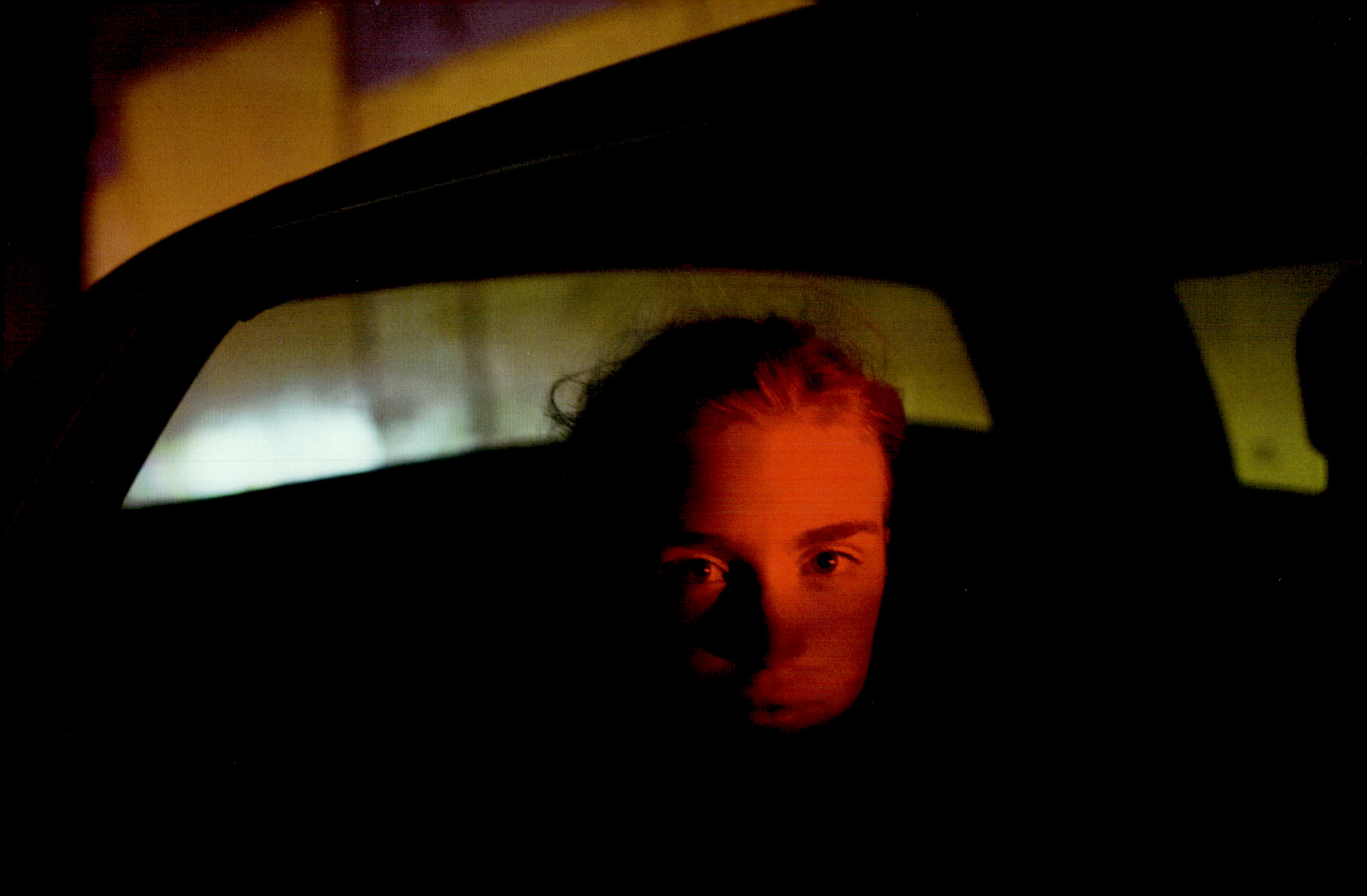

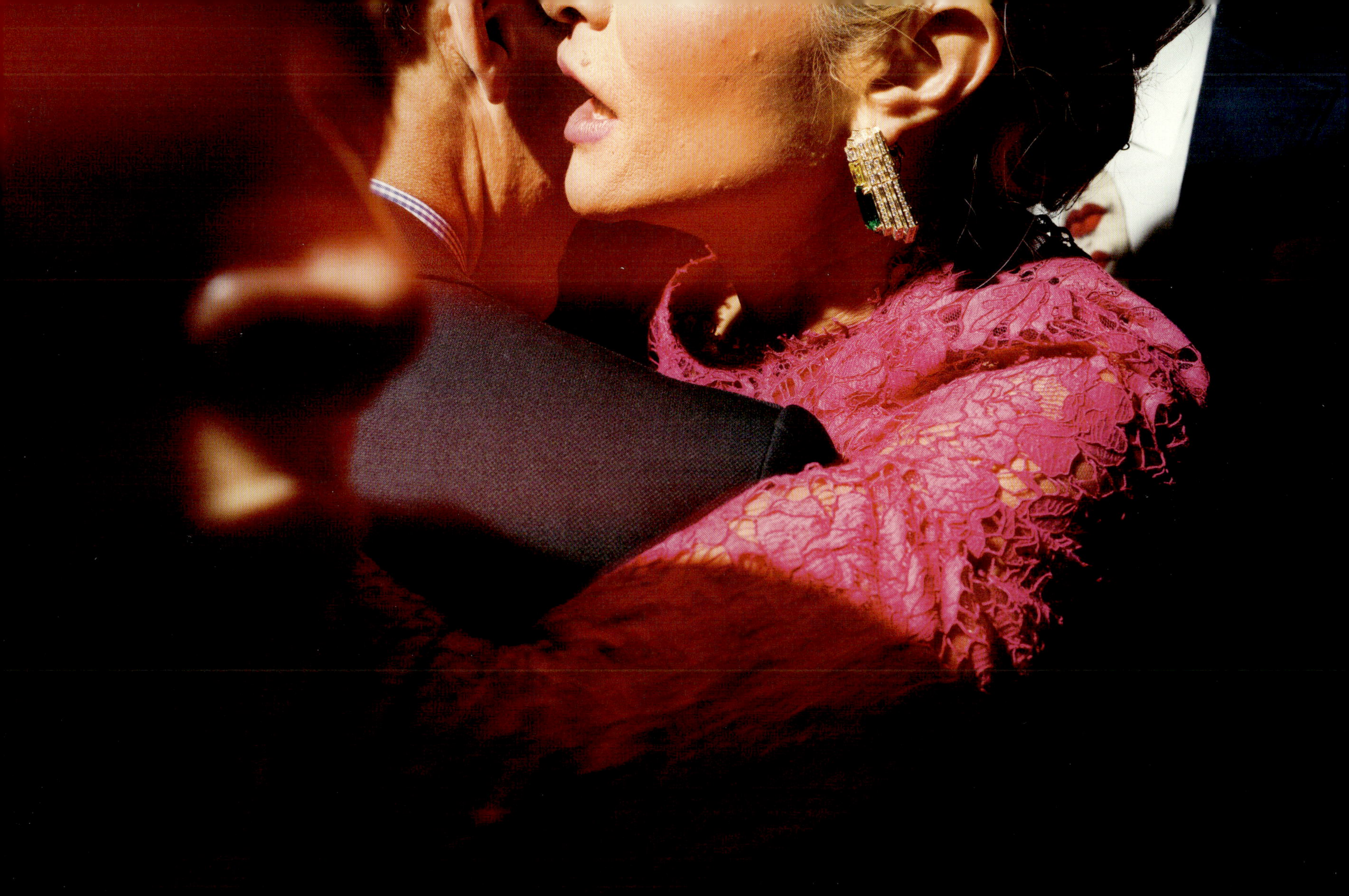

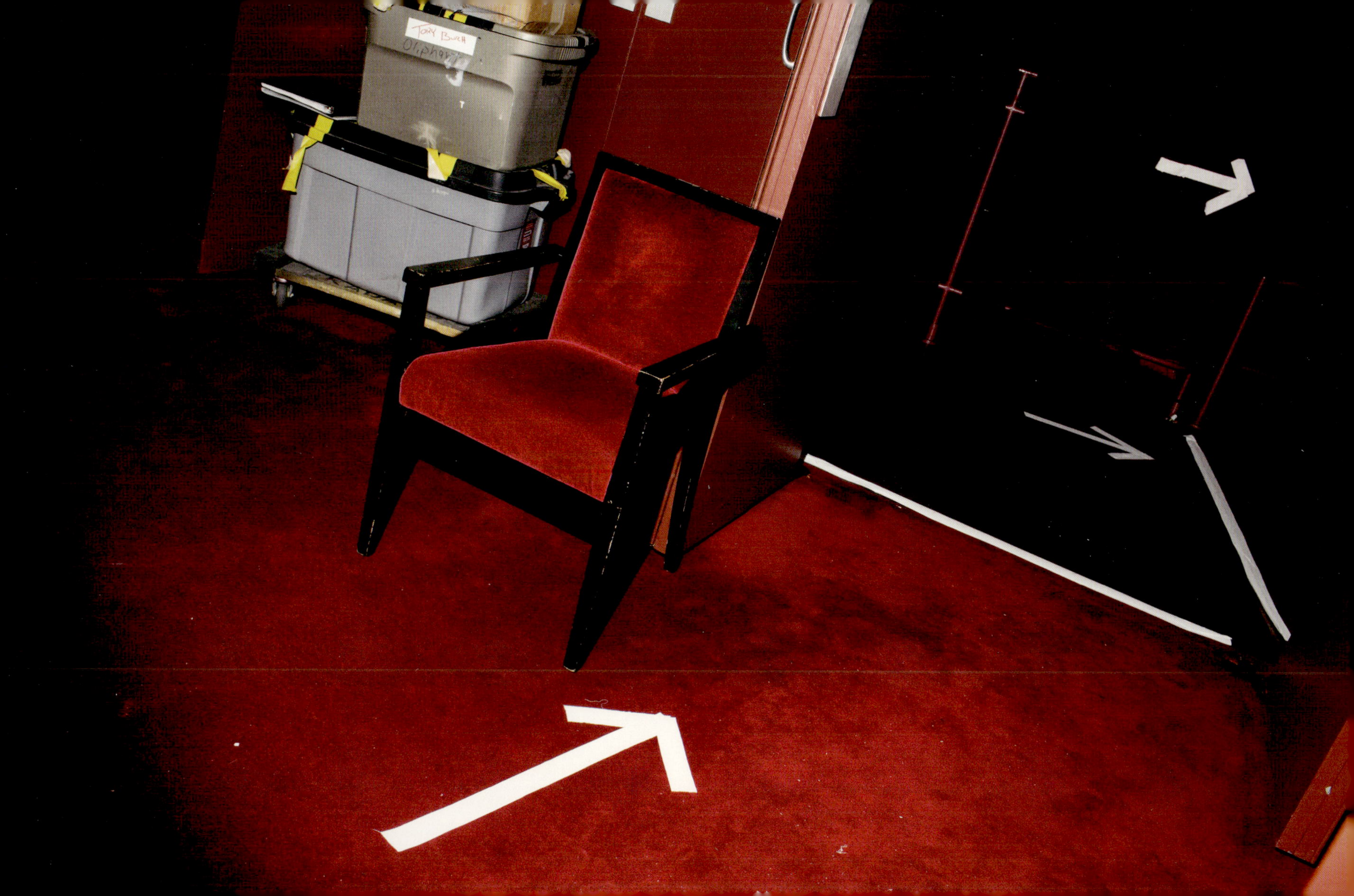
TORY BURCH
Oliphant

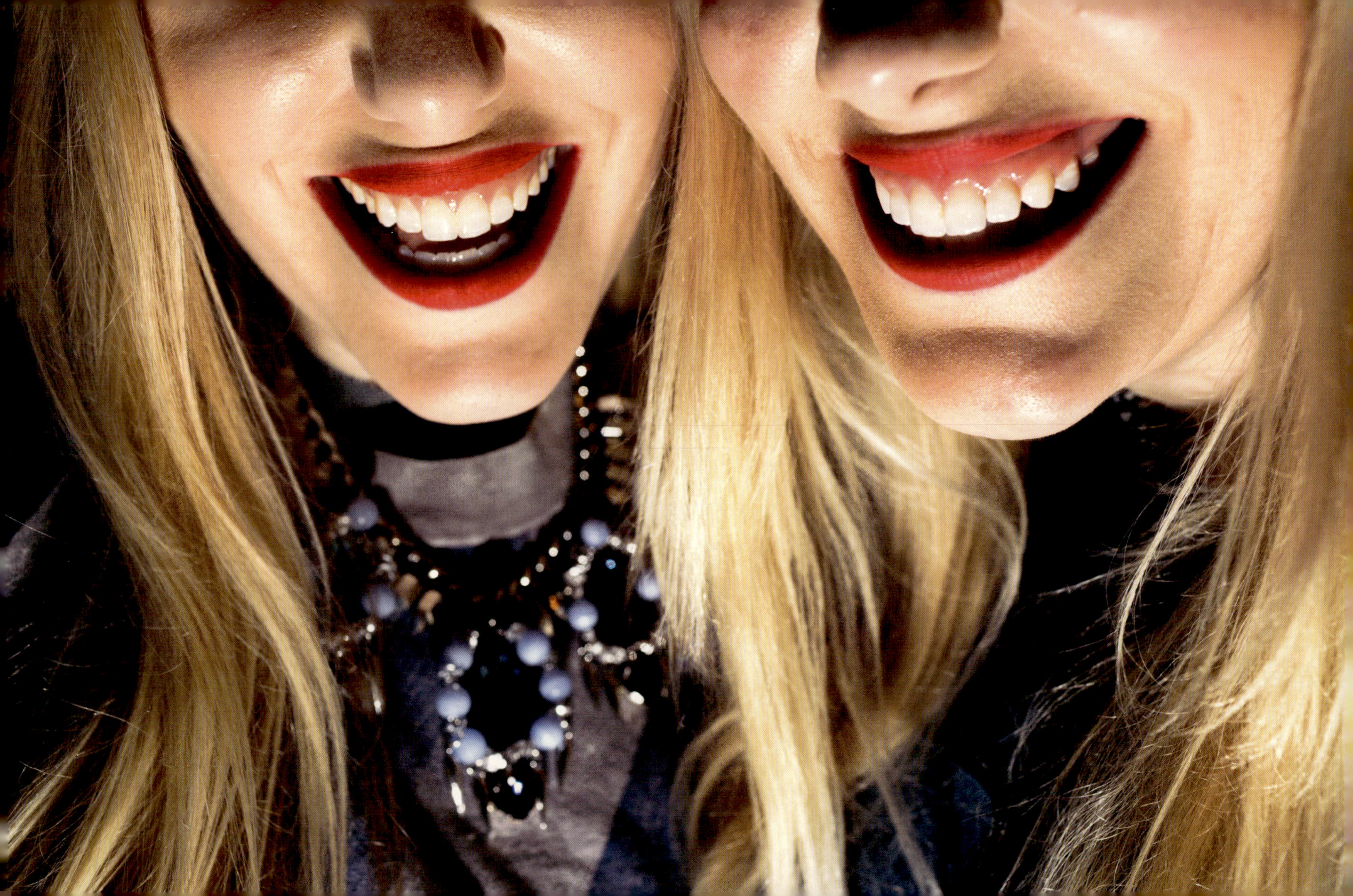

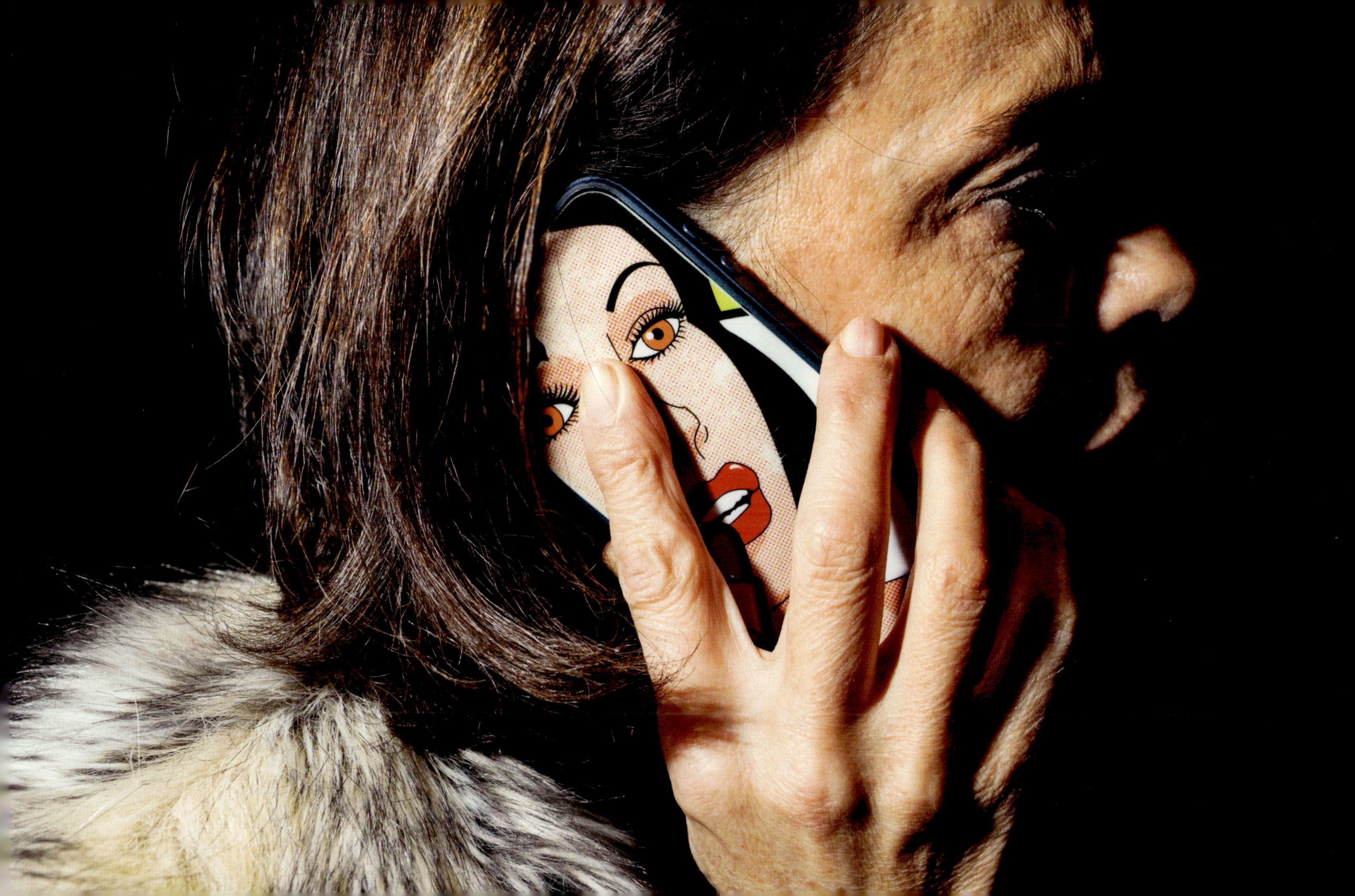

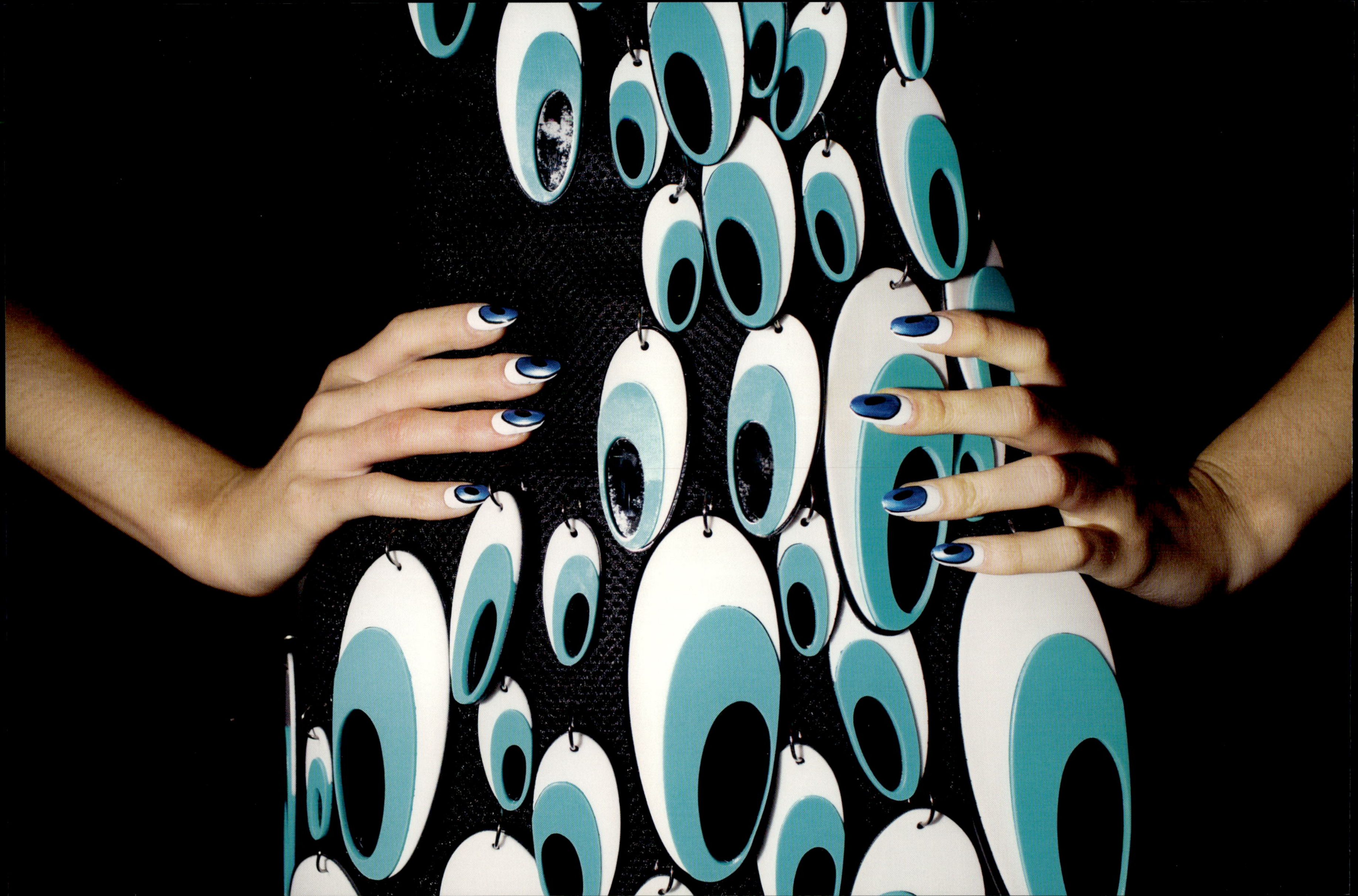

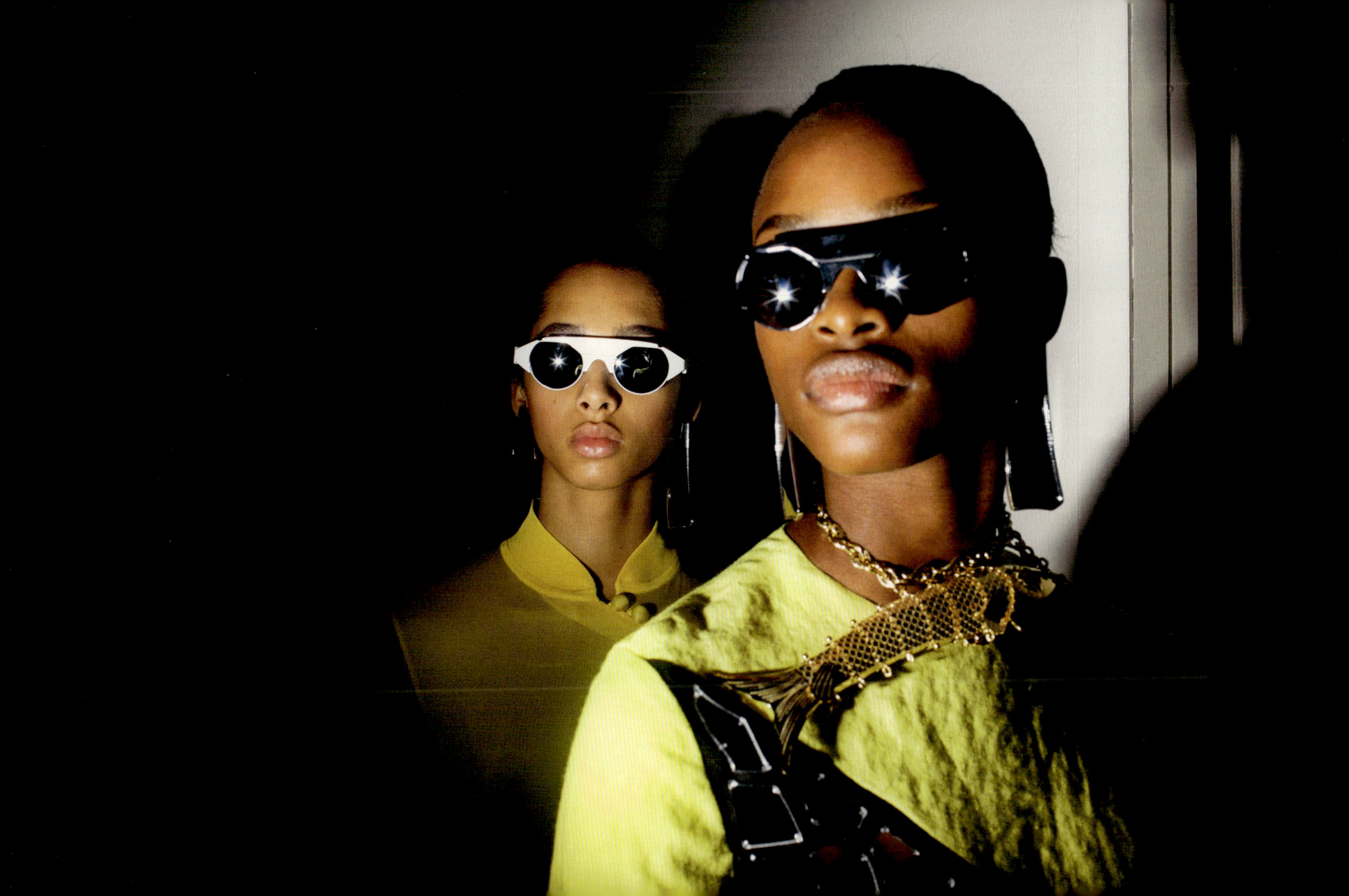

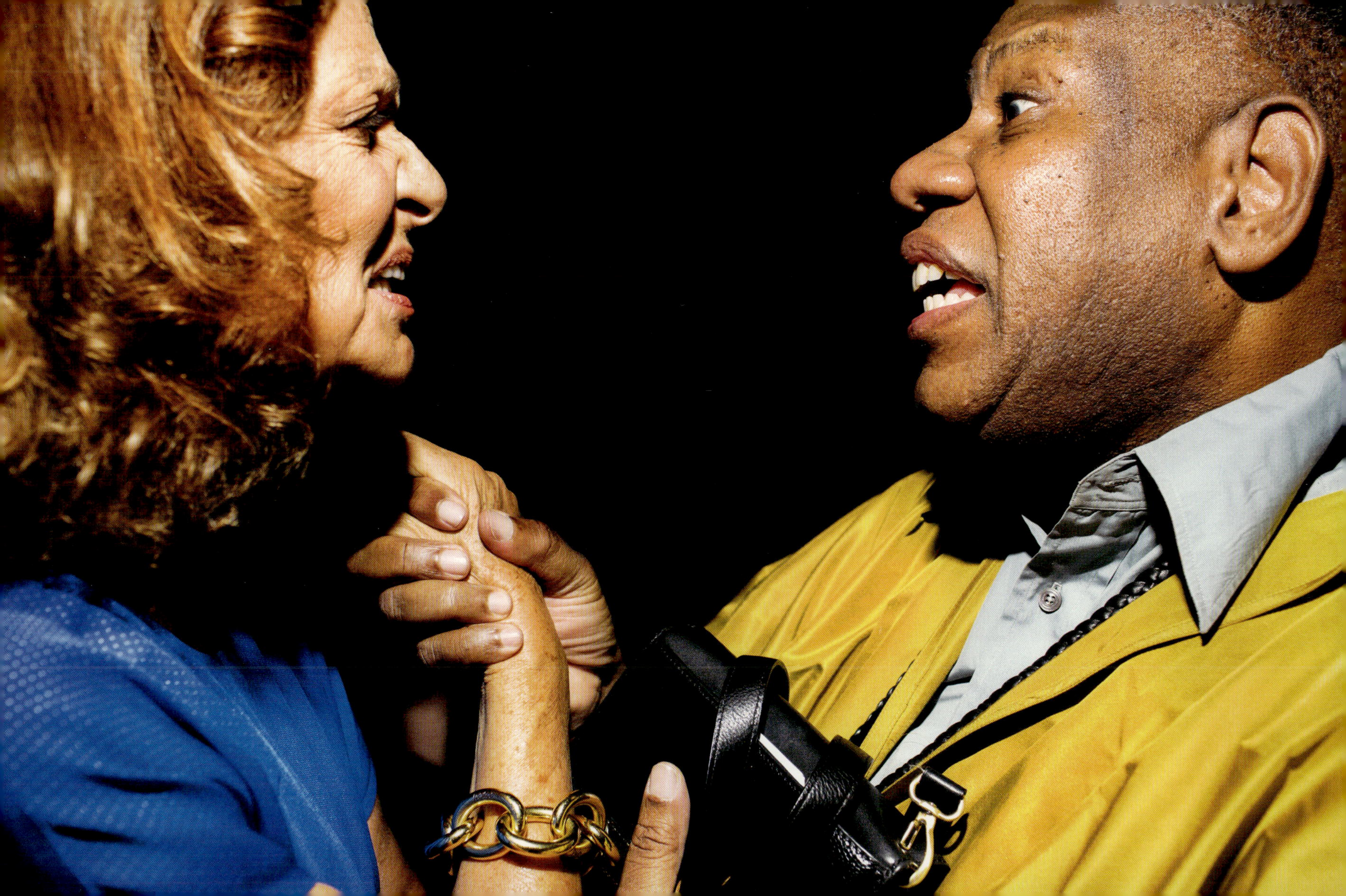

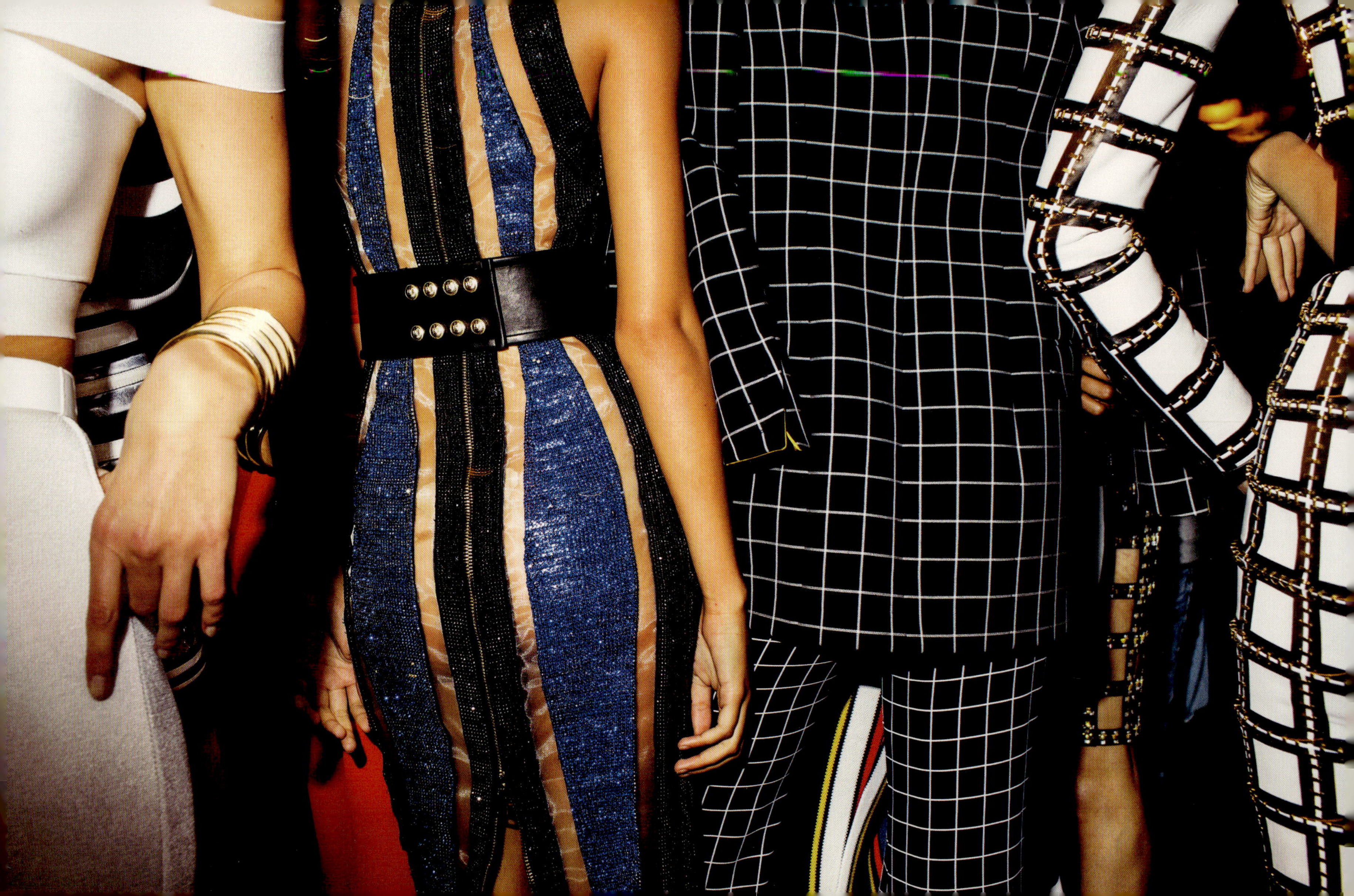

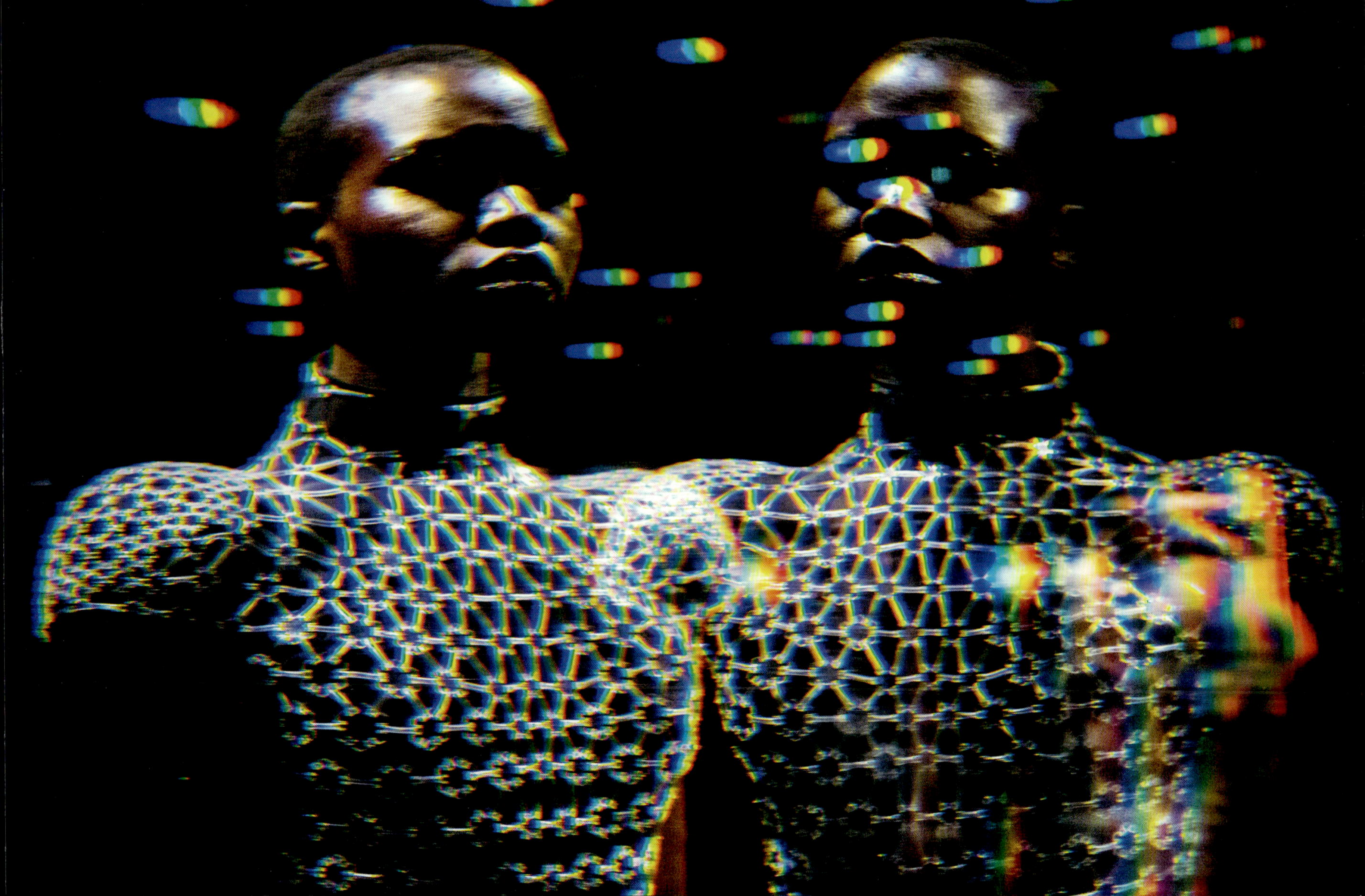

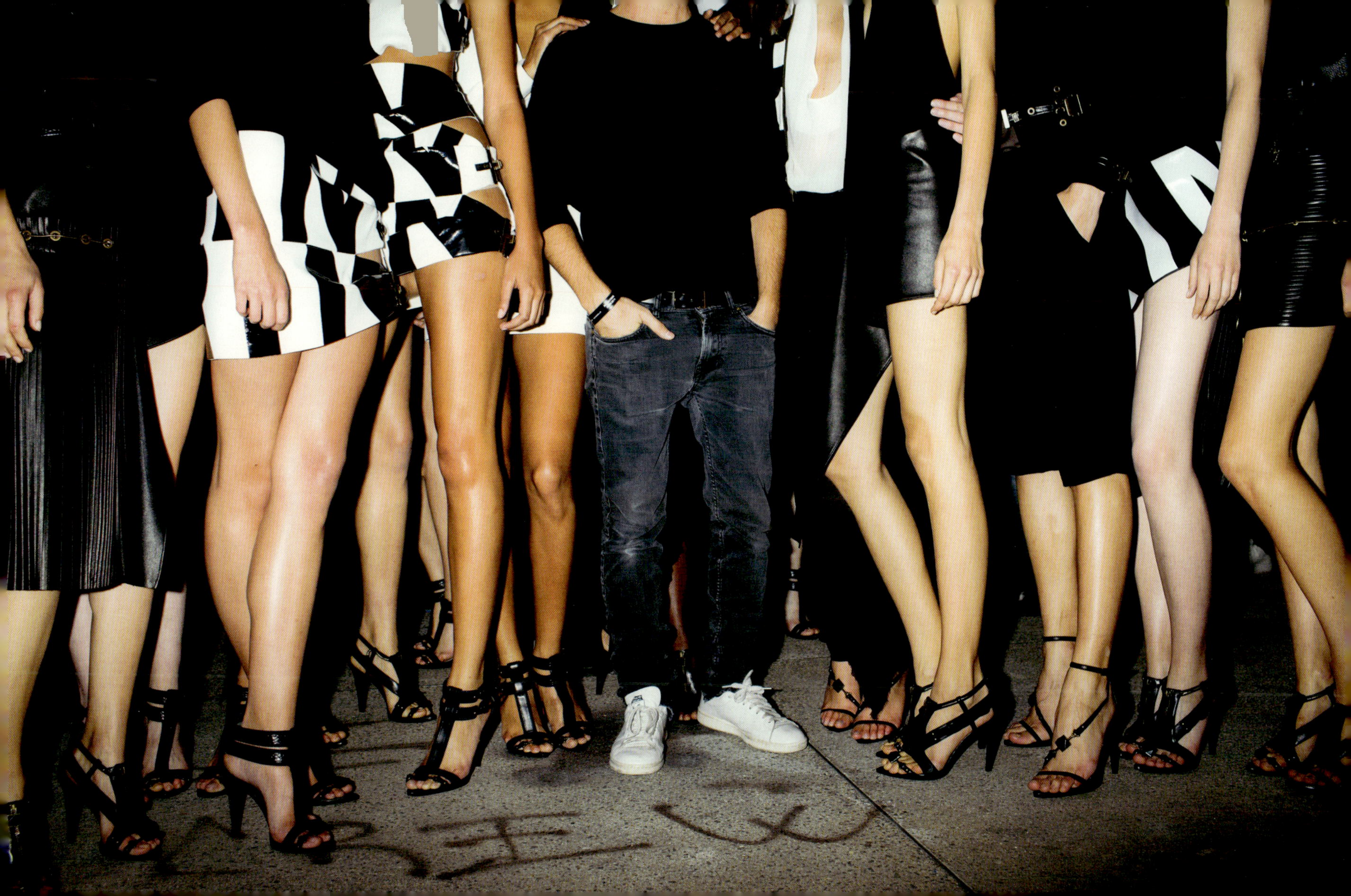

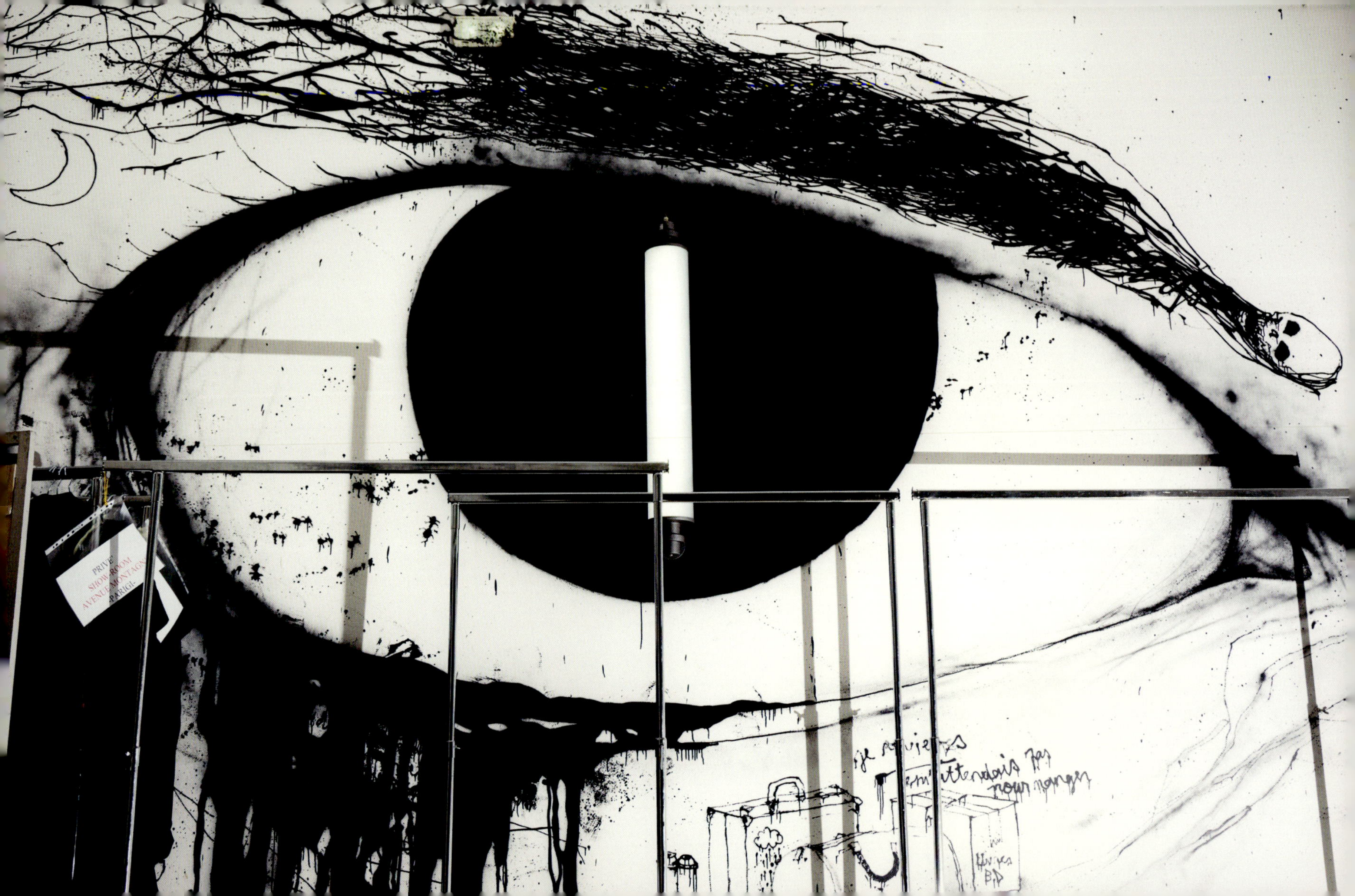
PRIVE'
SHOW-ROOM
AVENUE MONTAGN
-PARIGI-
m'attendais pas
pour manger

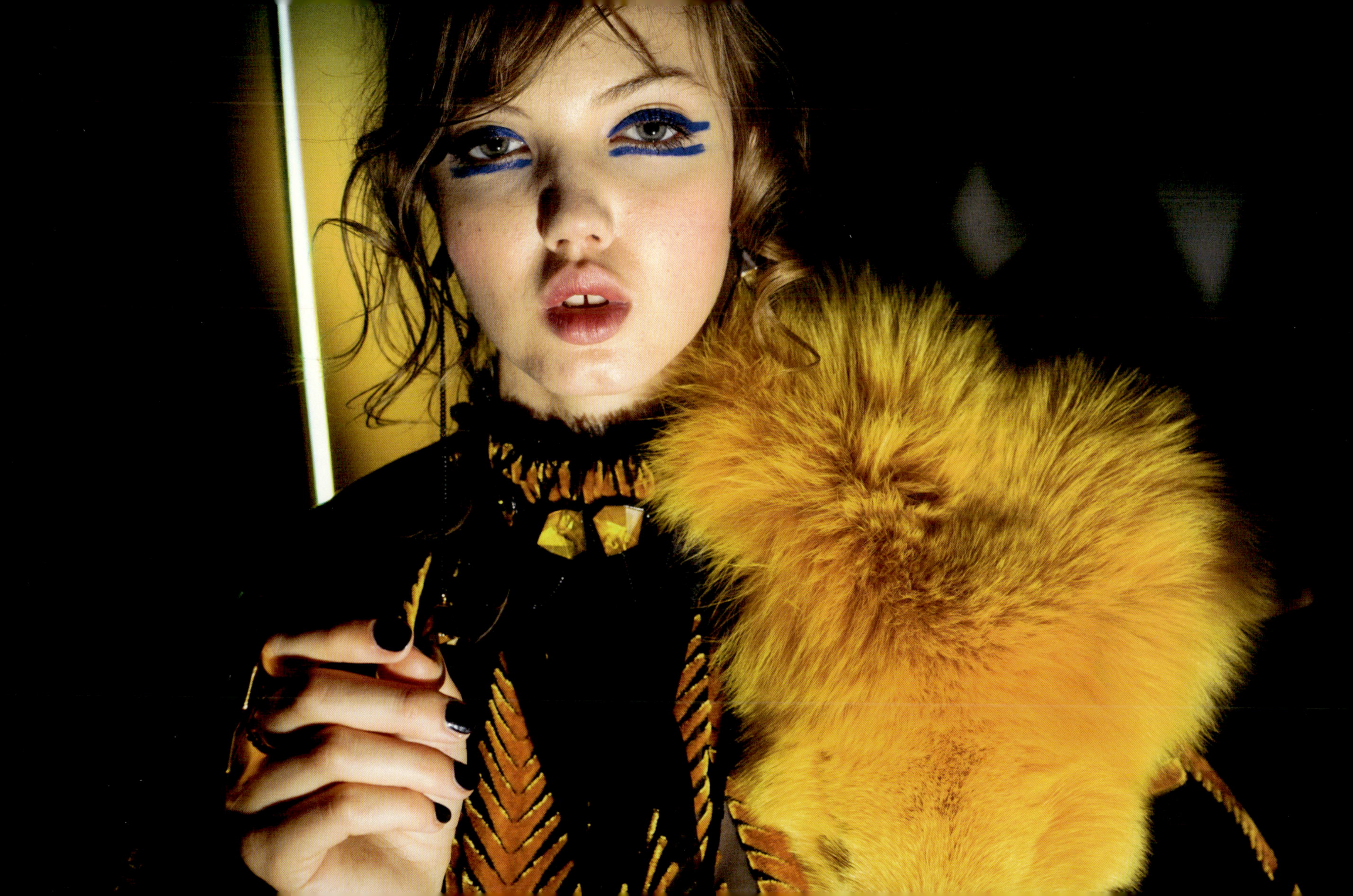

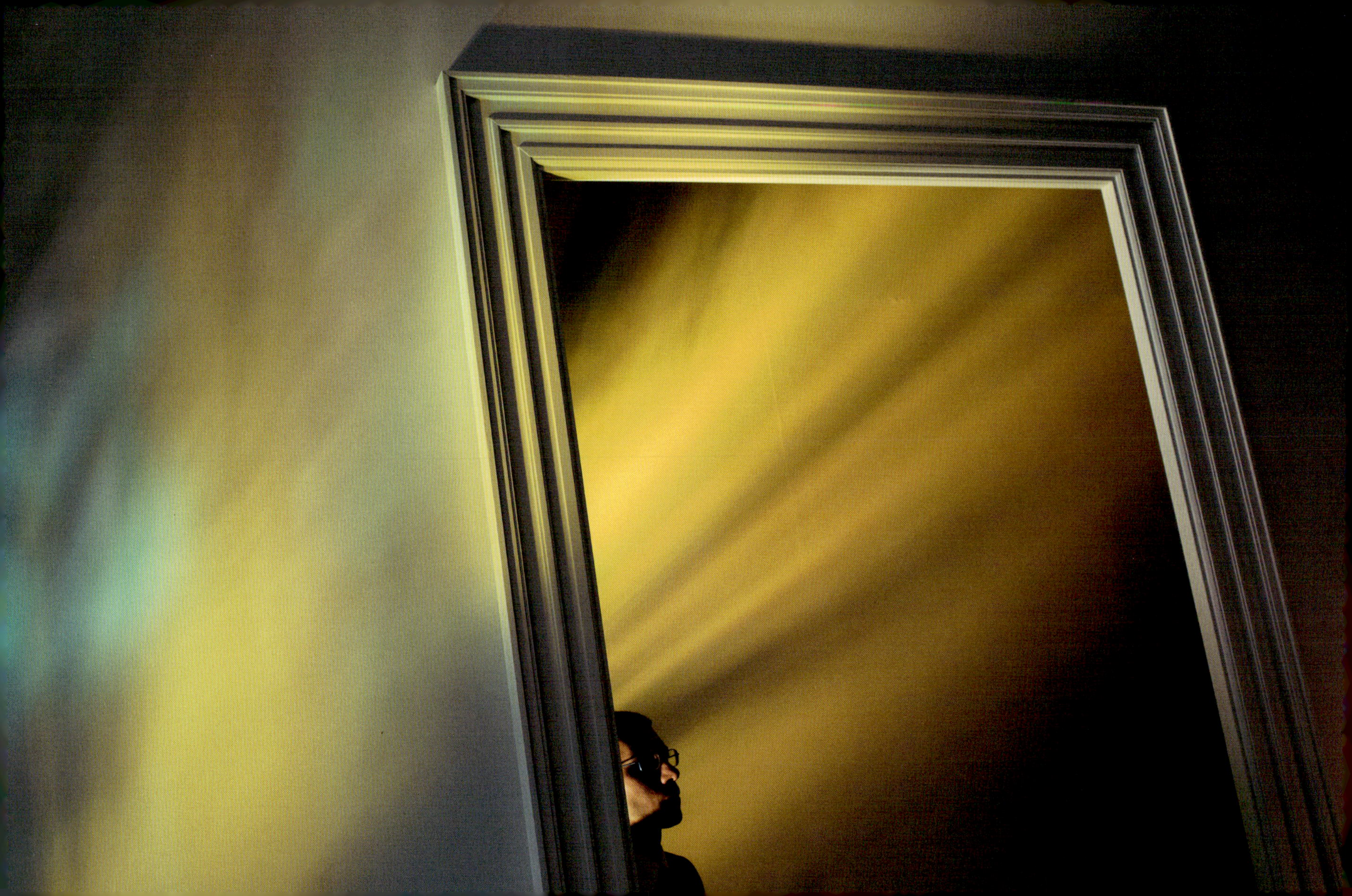

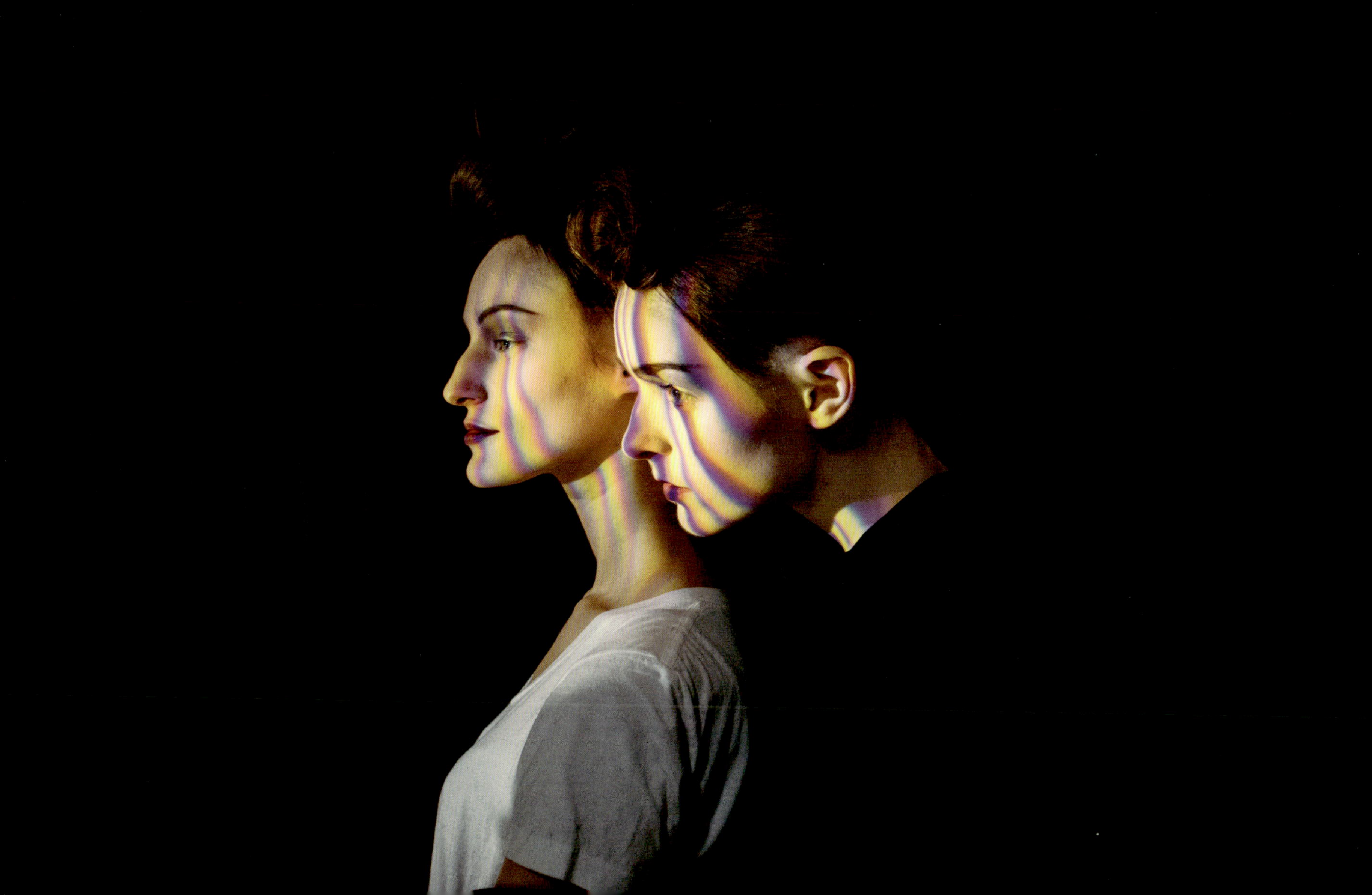

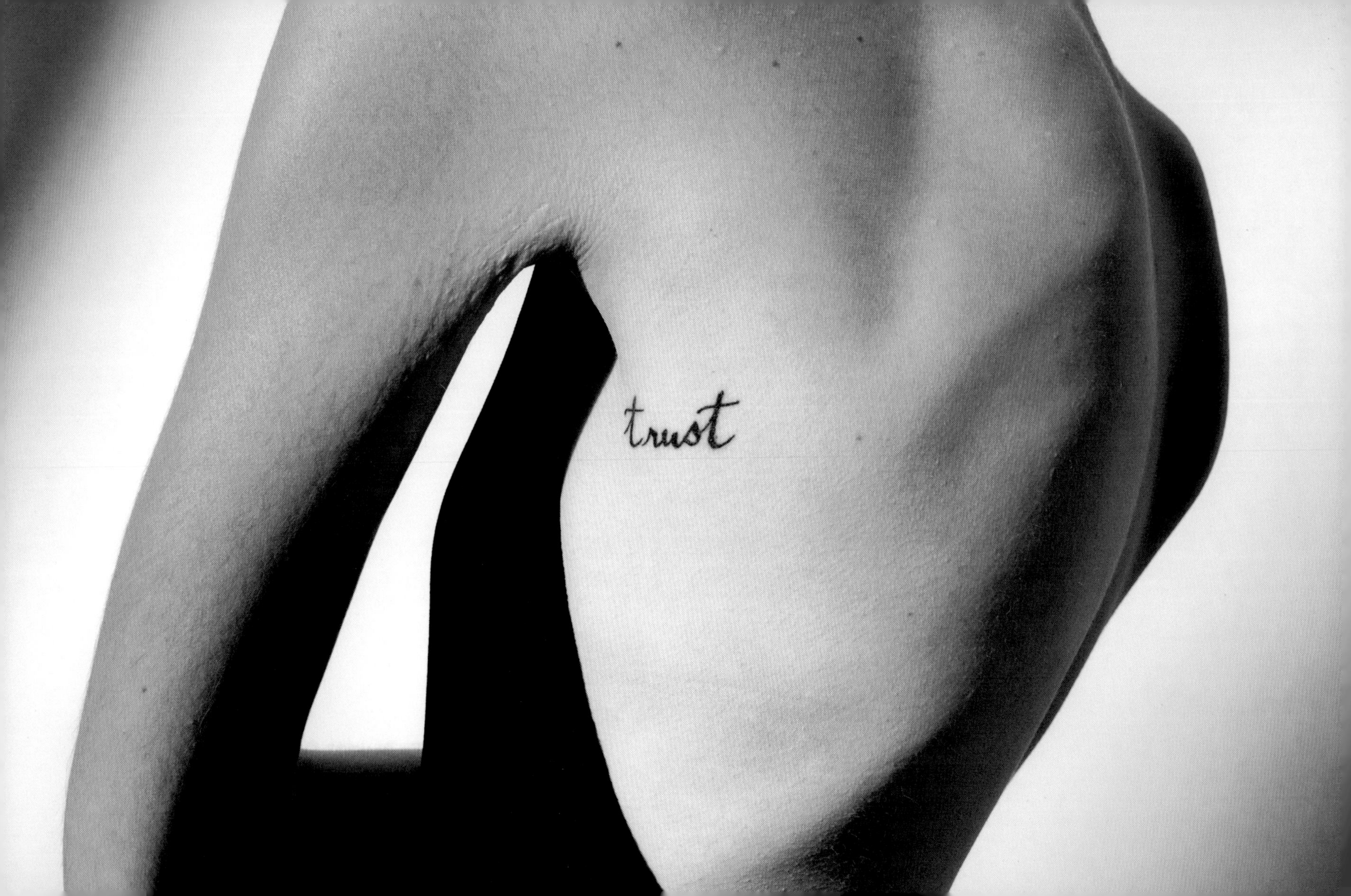
trust

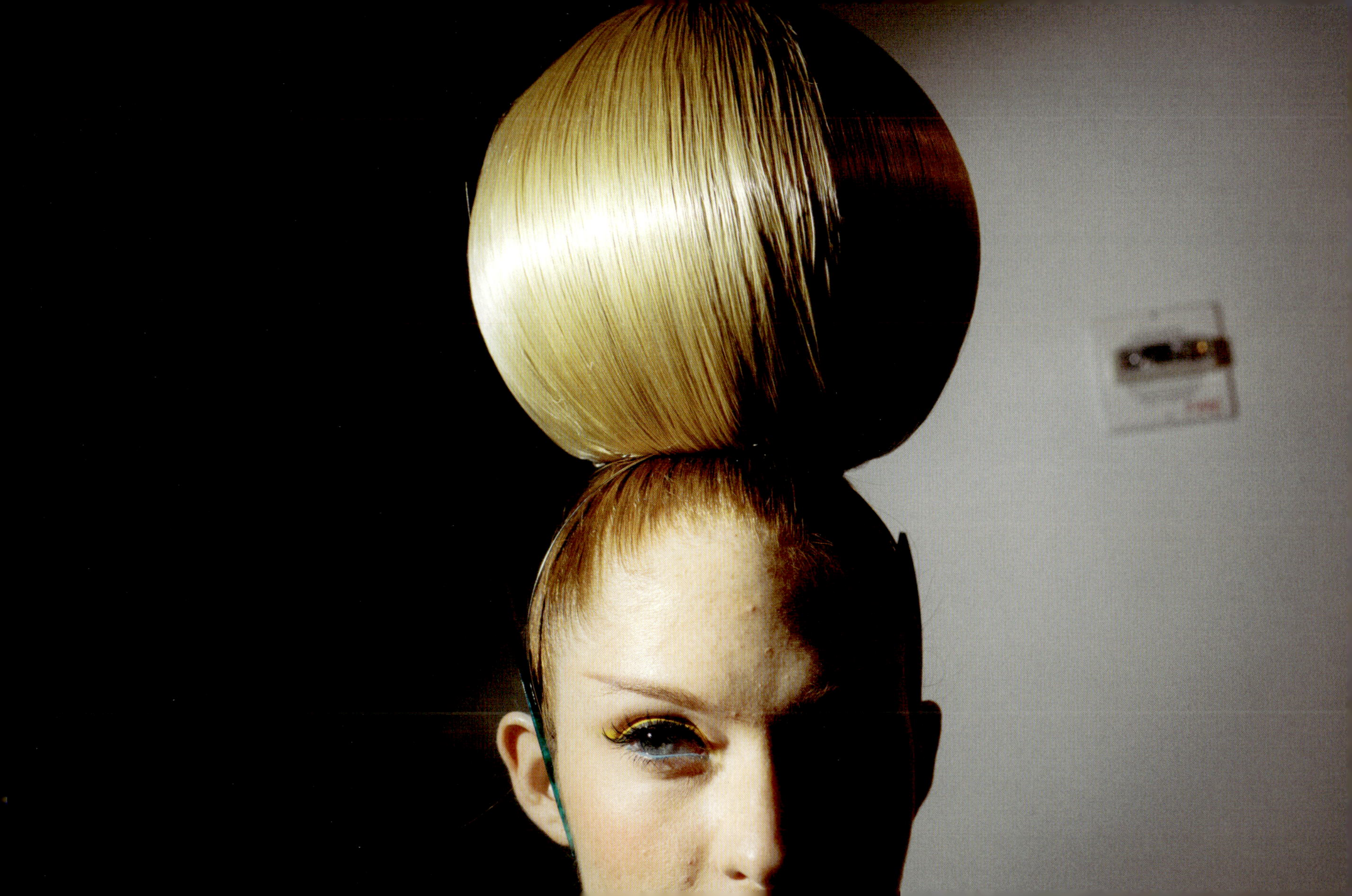

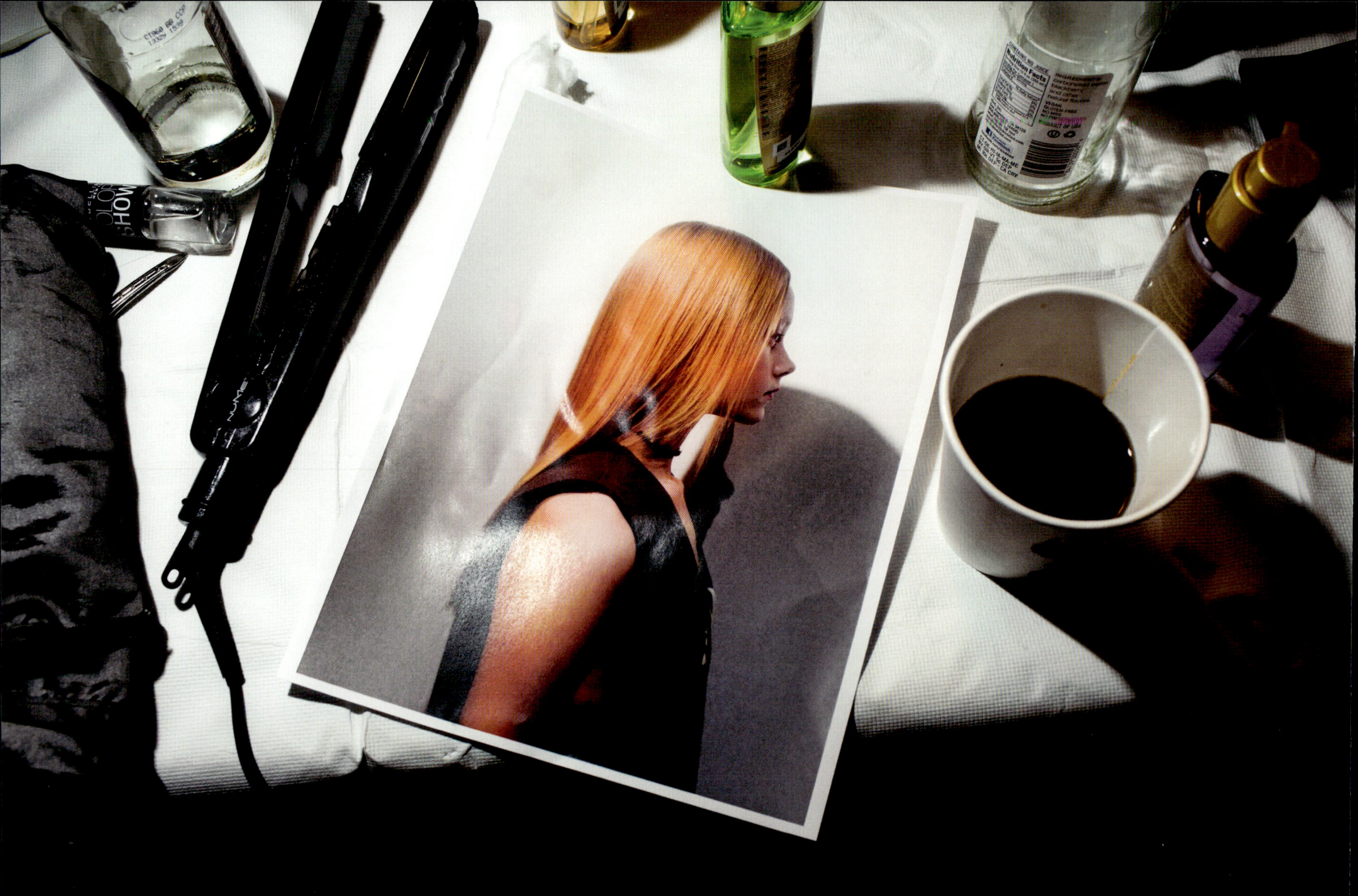
SHOW
Nutrition Facts
INGREDIENTS
VEGAN
GLUTEN-FREE
PRODUCT OF USA

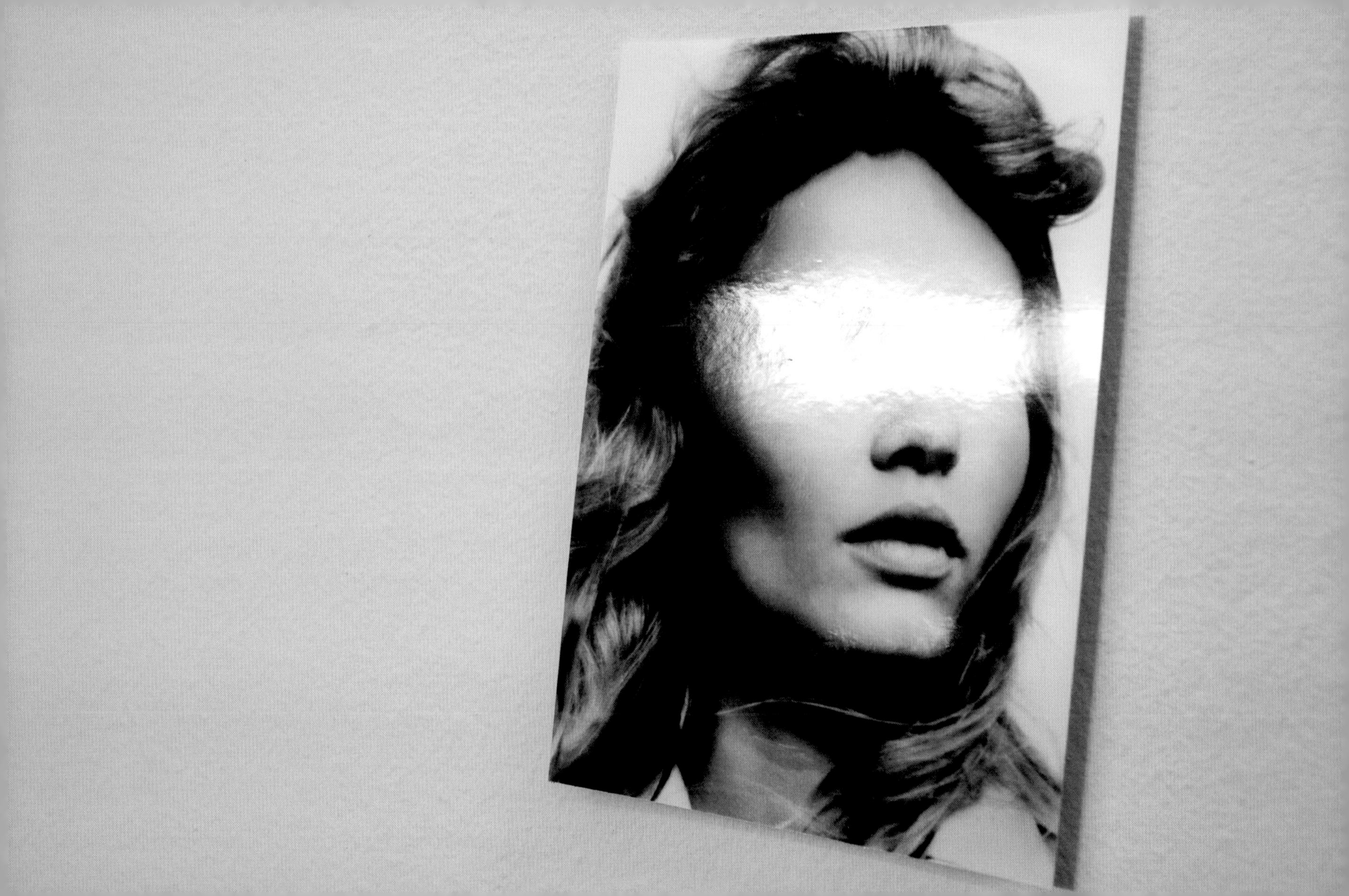

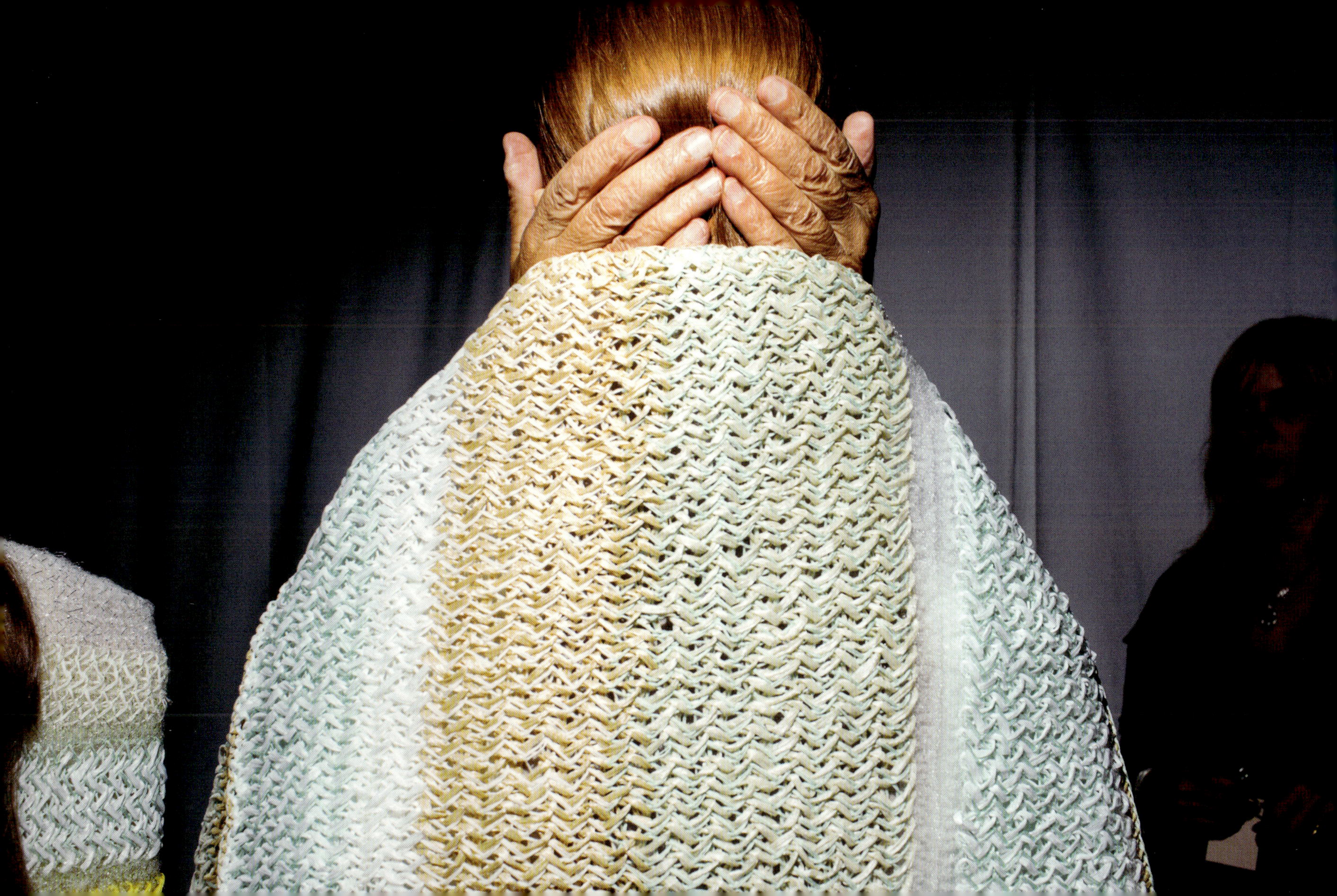

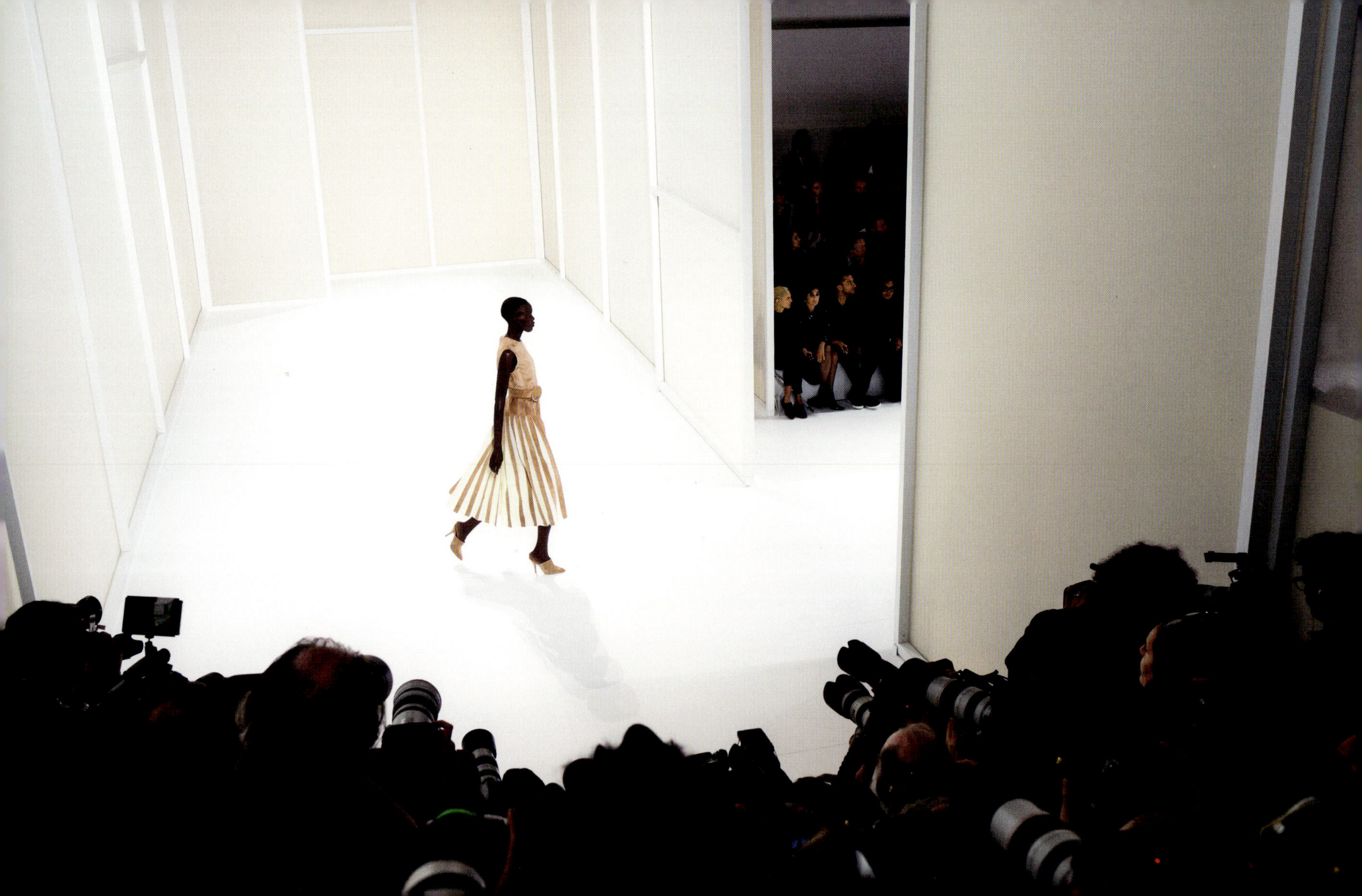

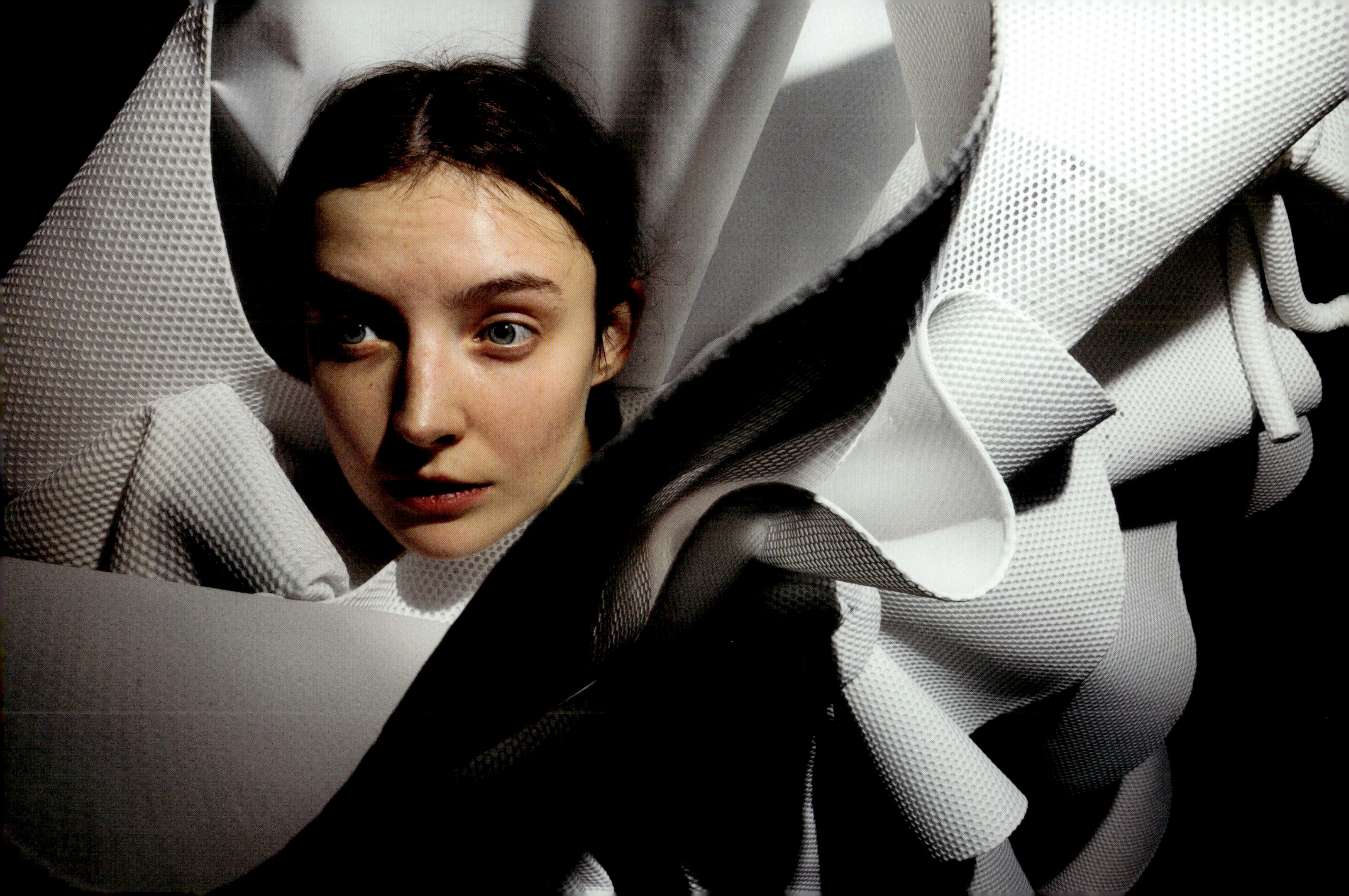

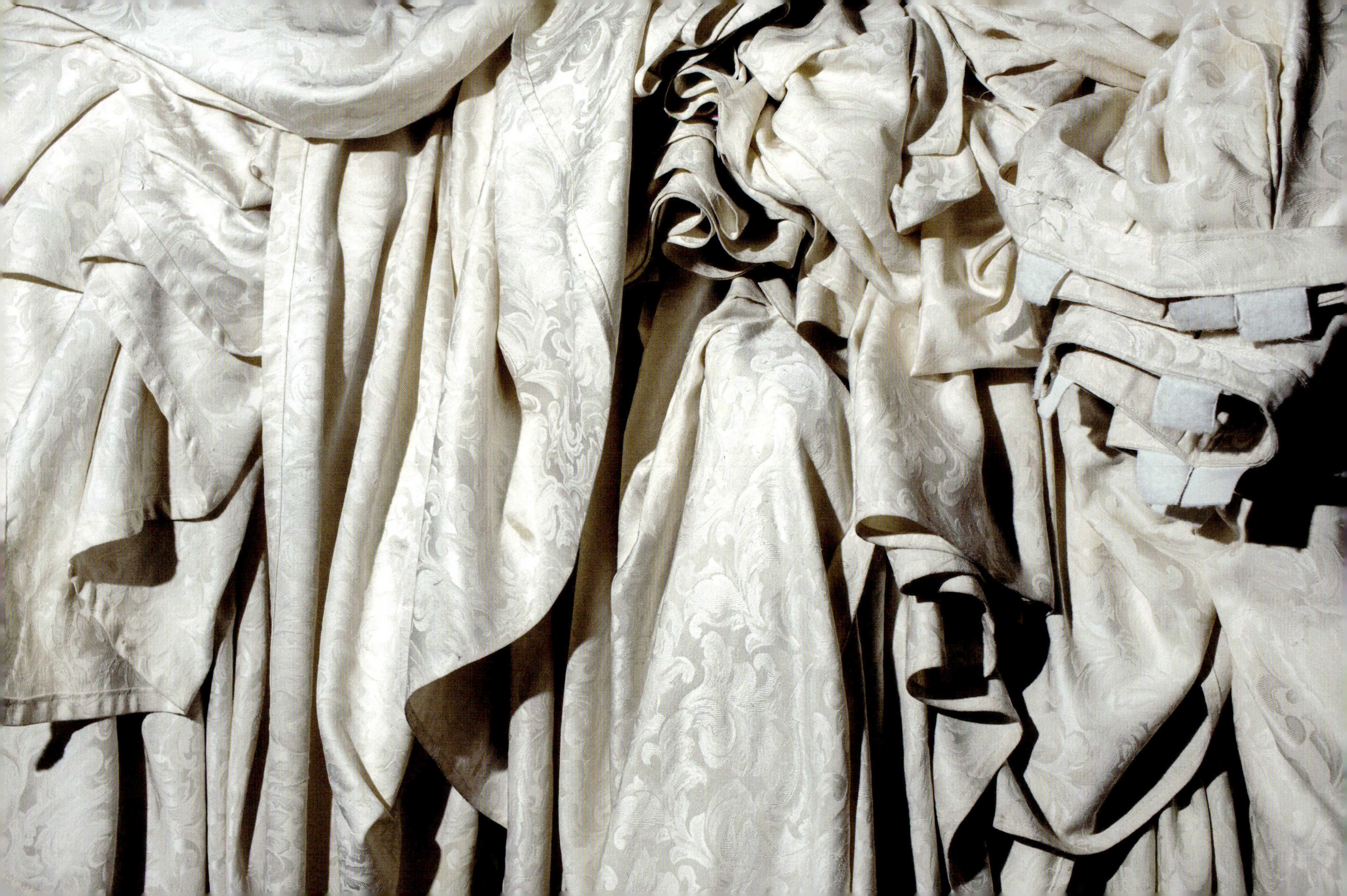

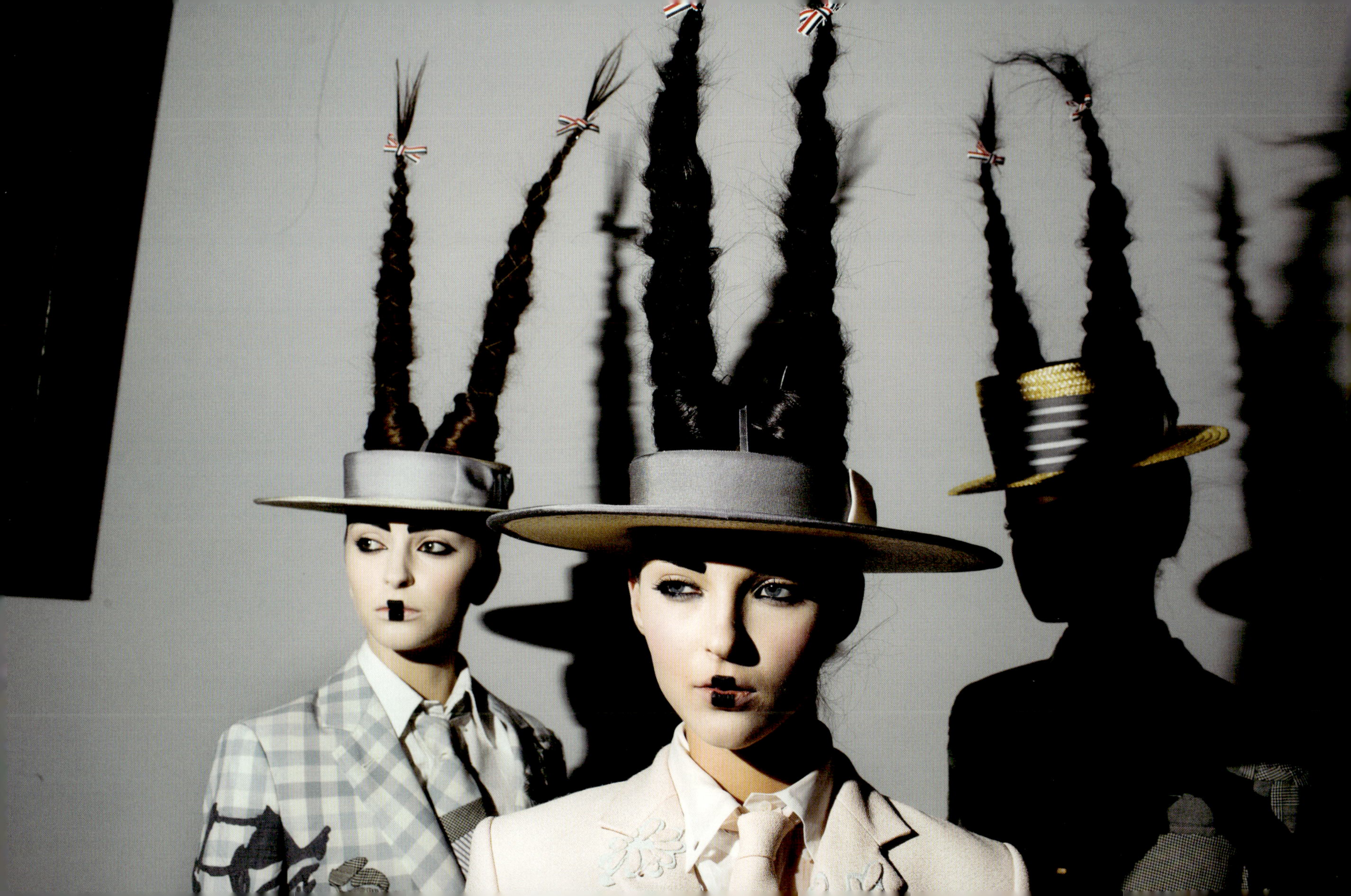

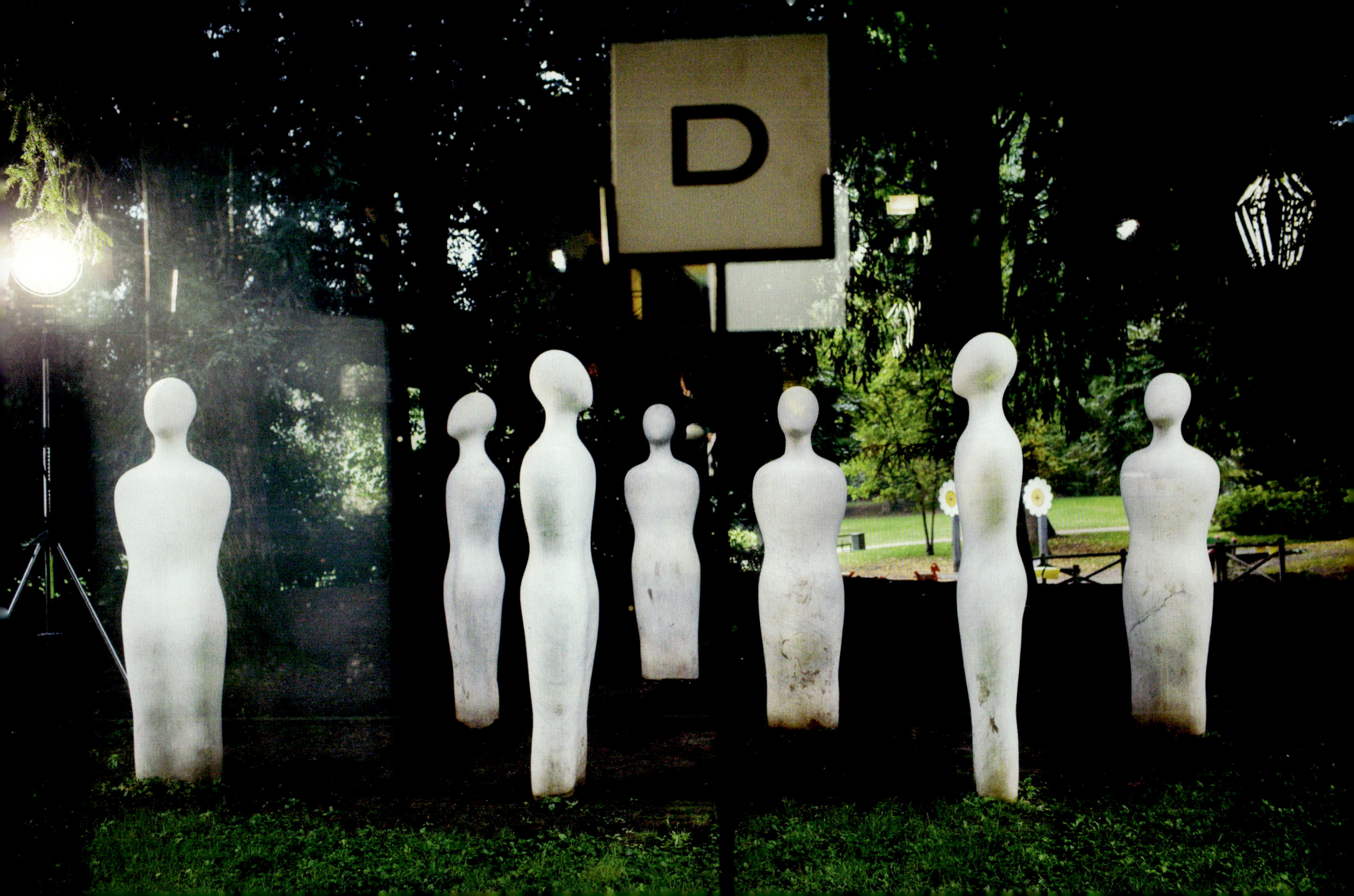
D

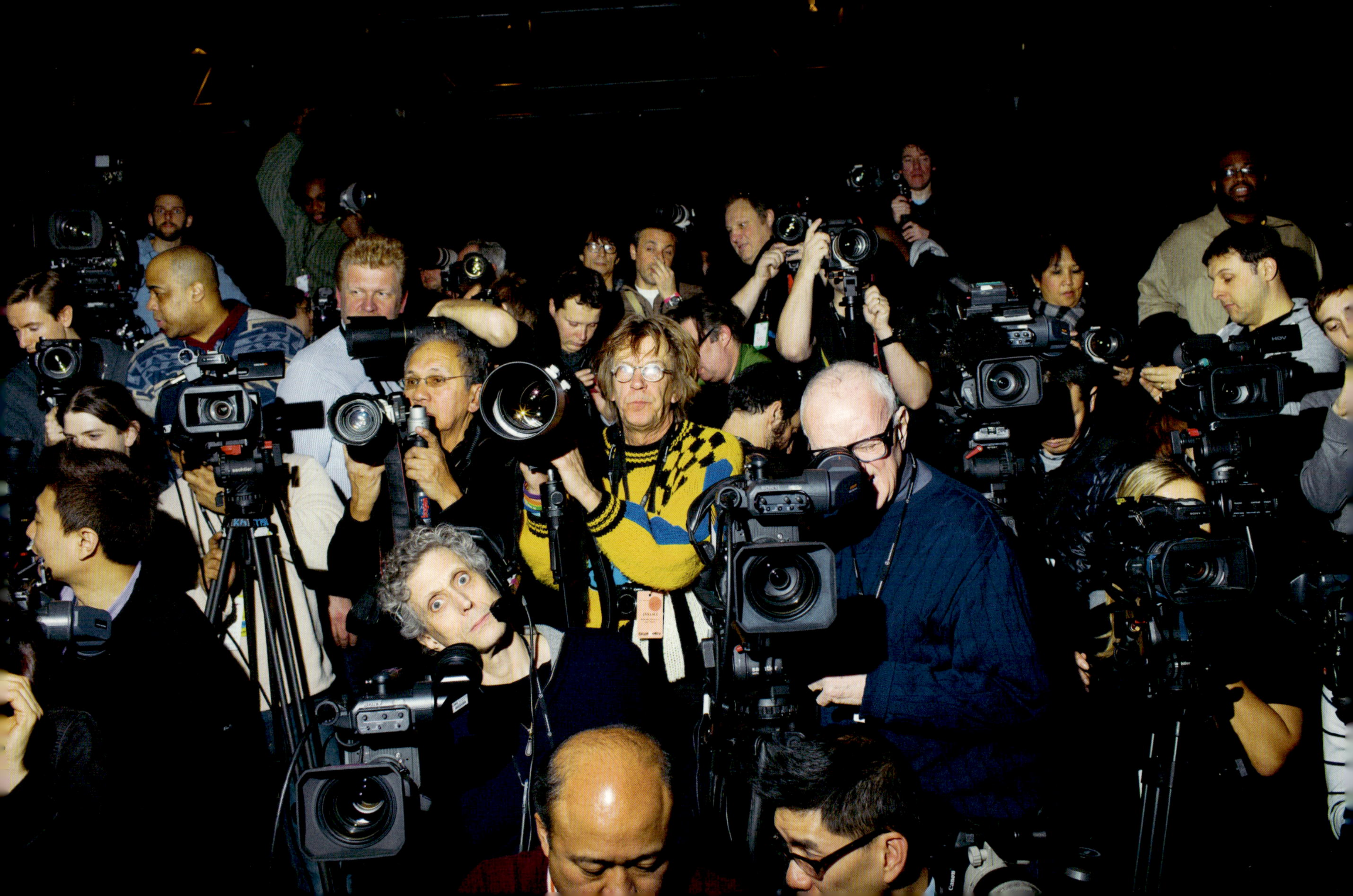

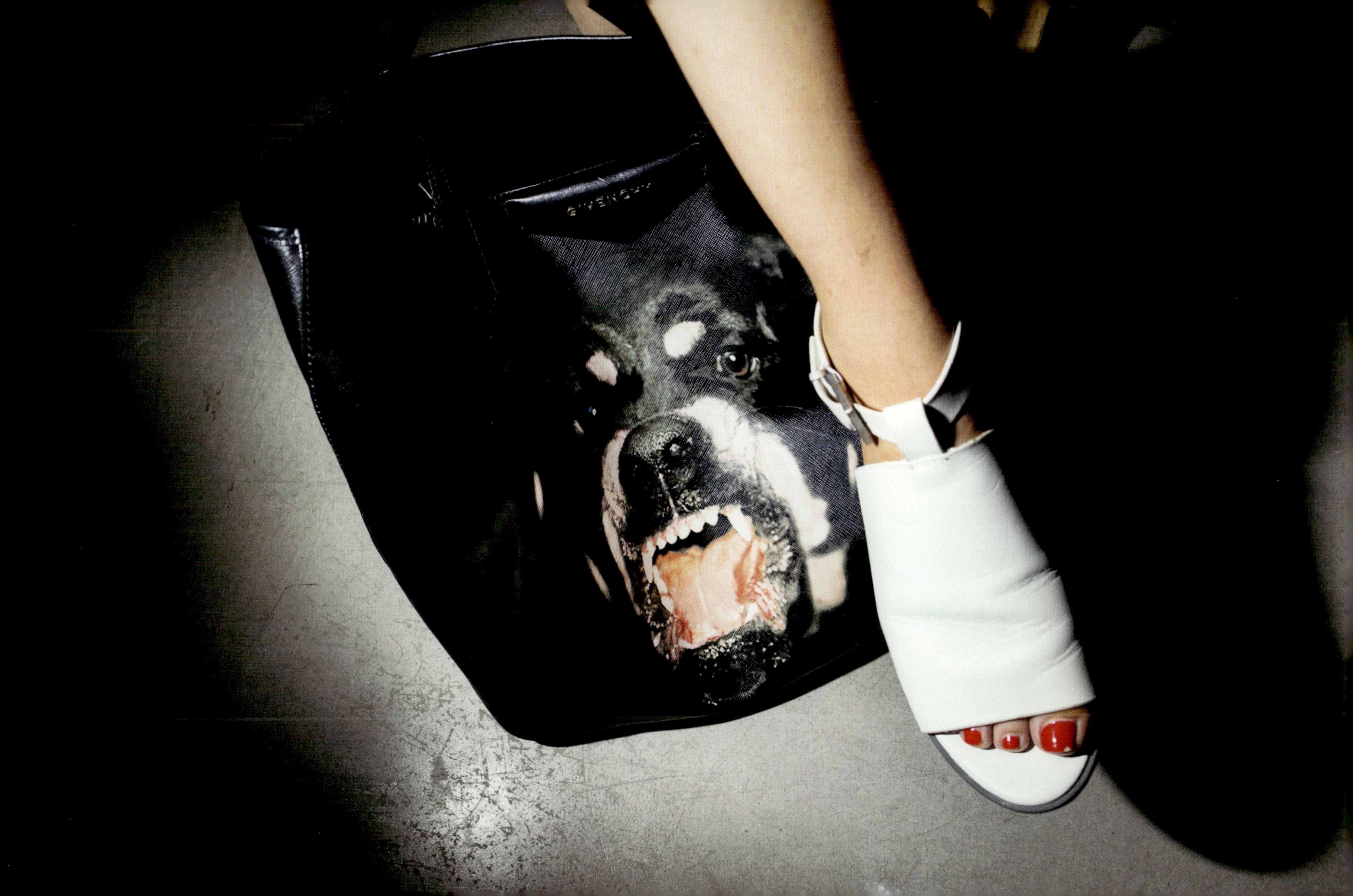
GIVENCHY

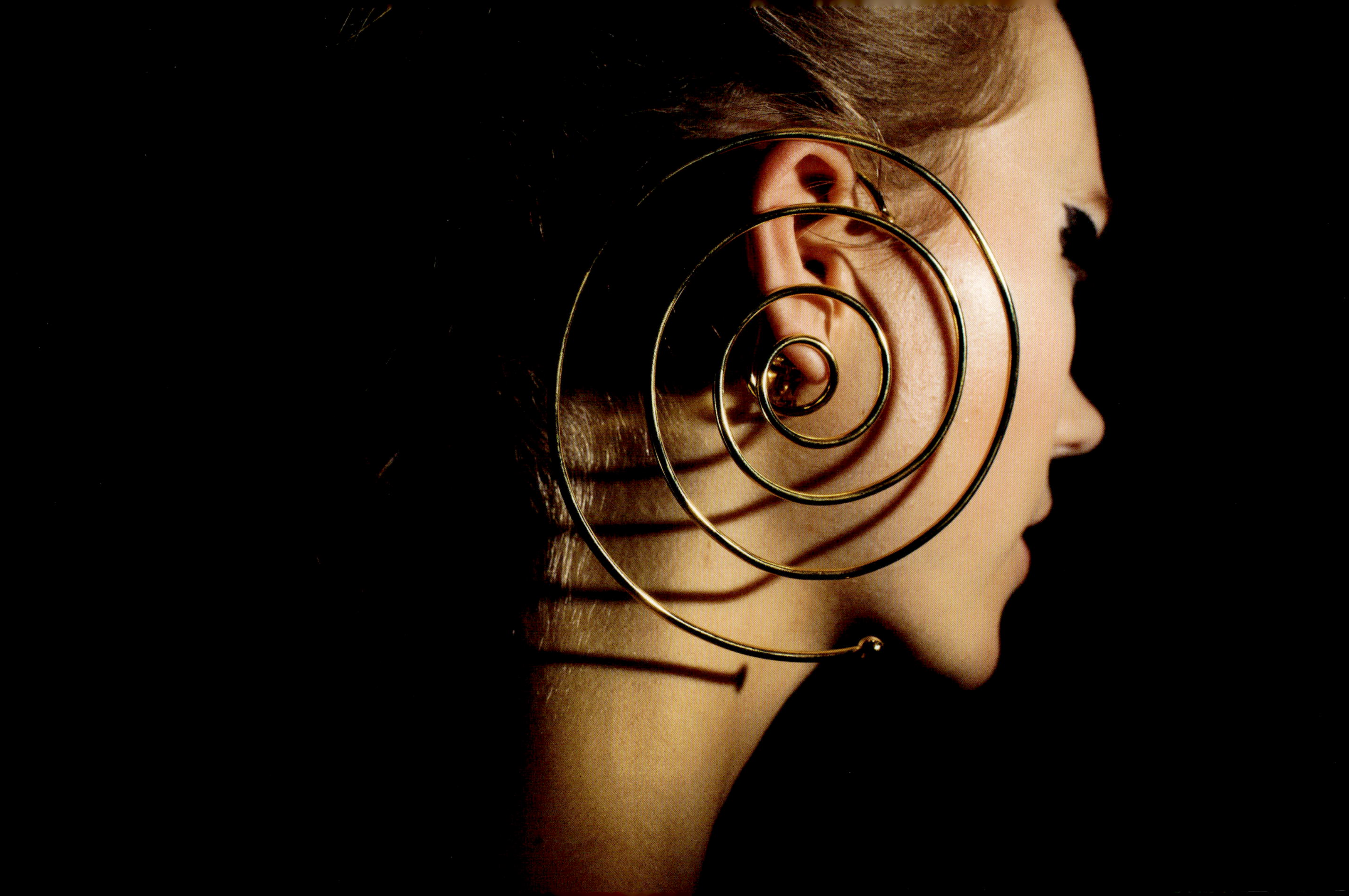

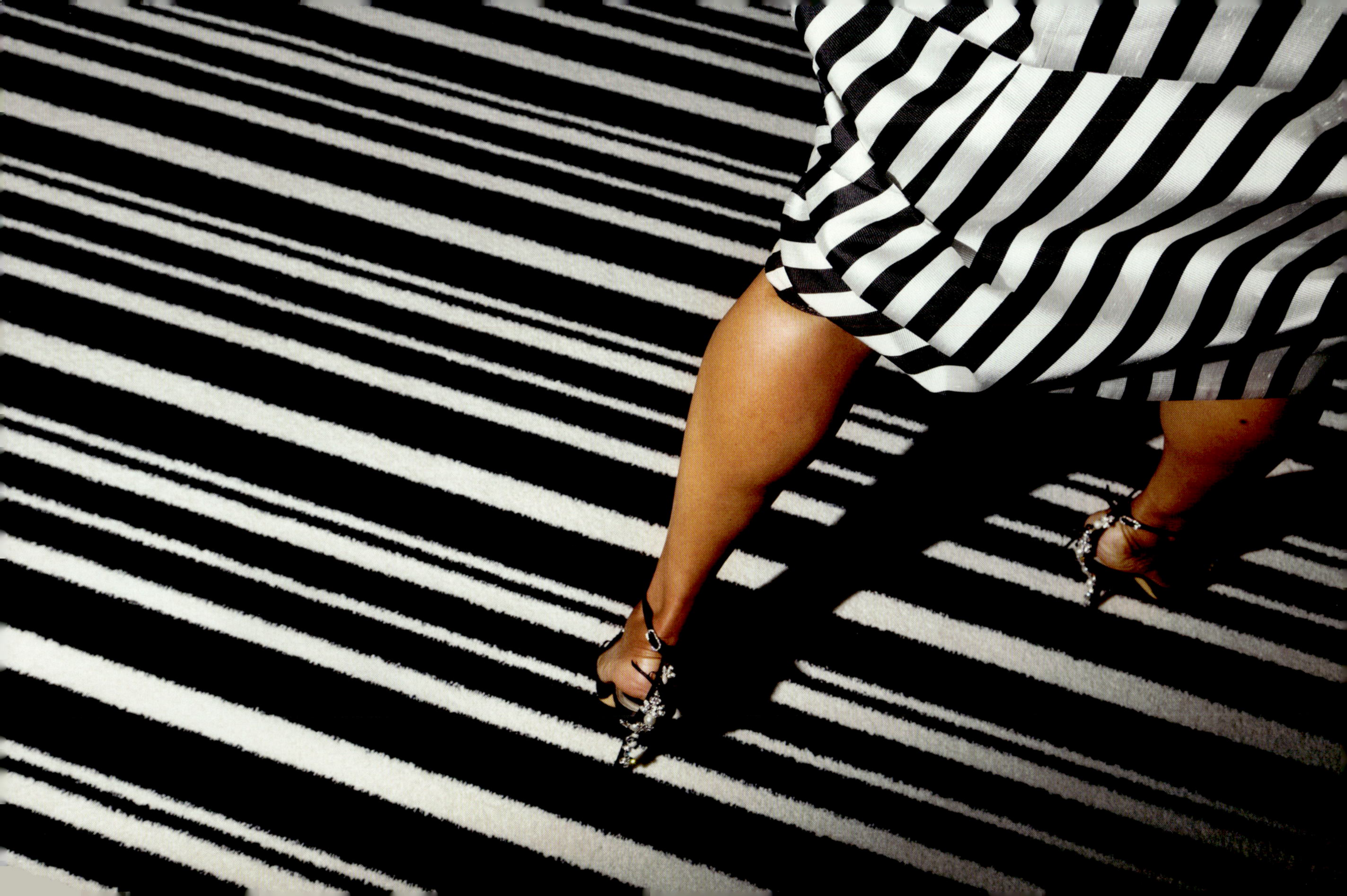

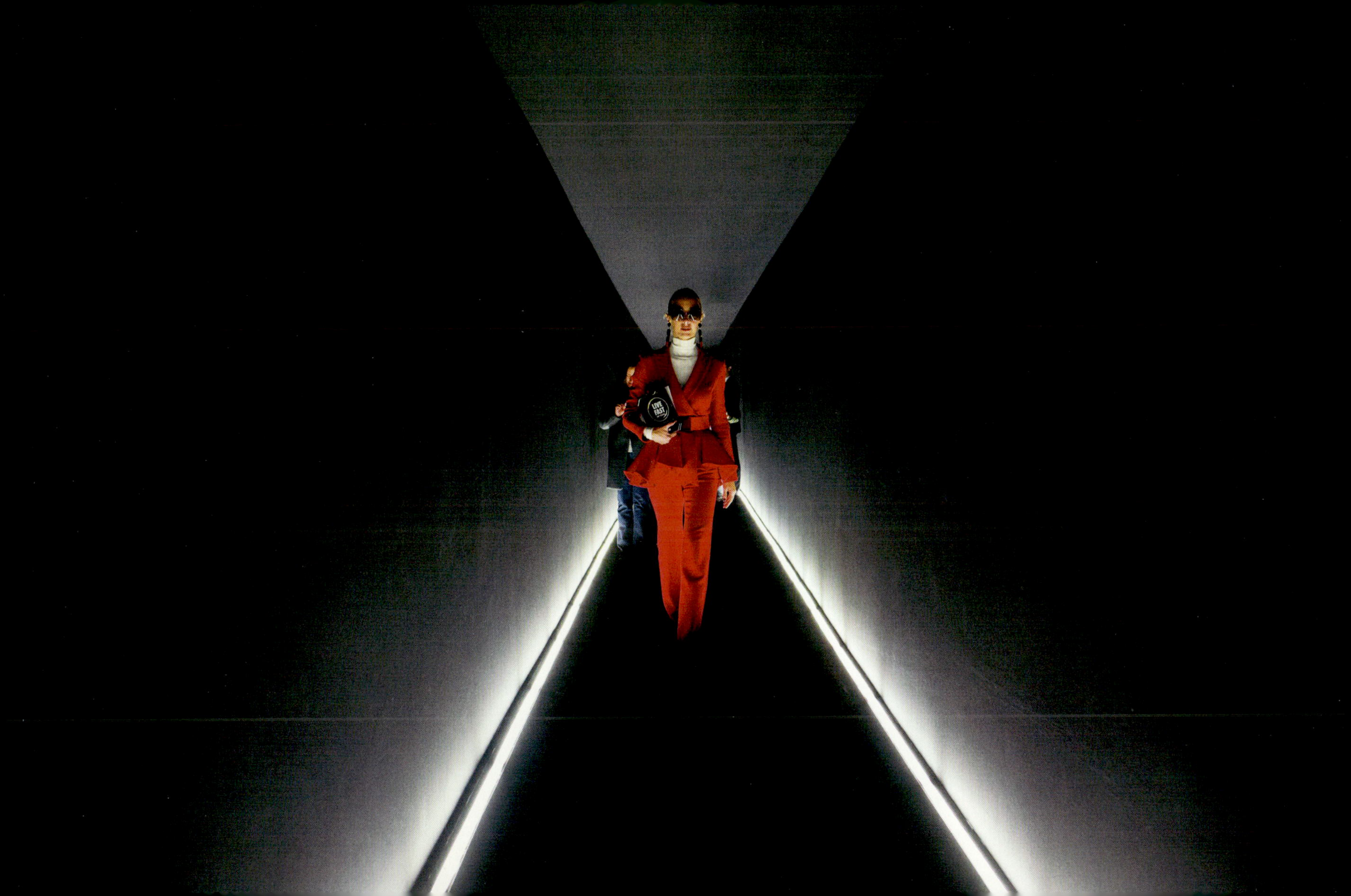
LIVE
FAST

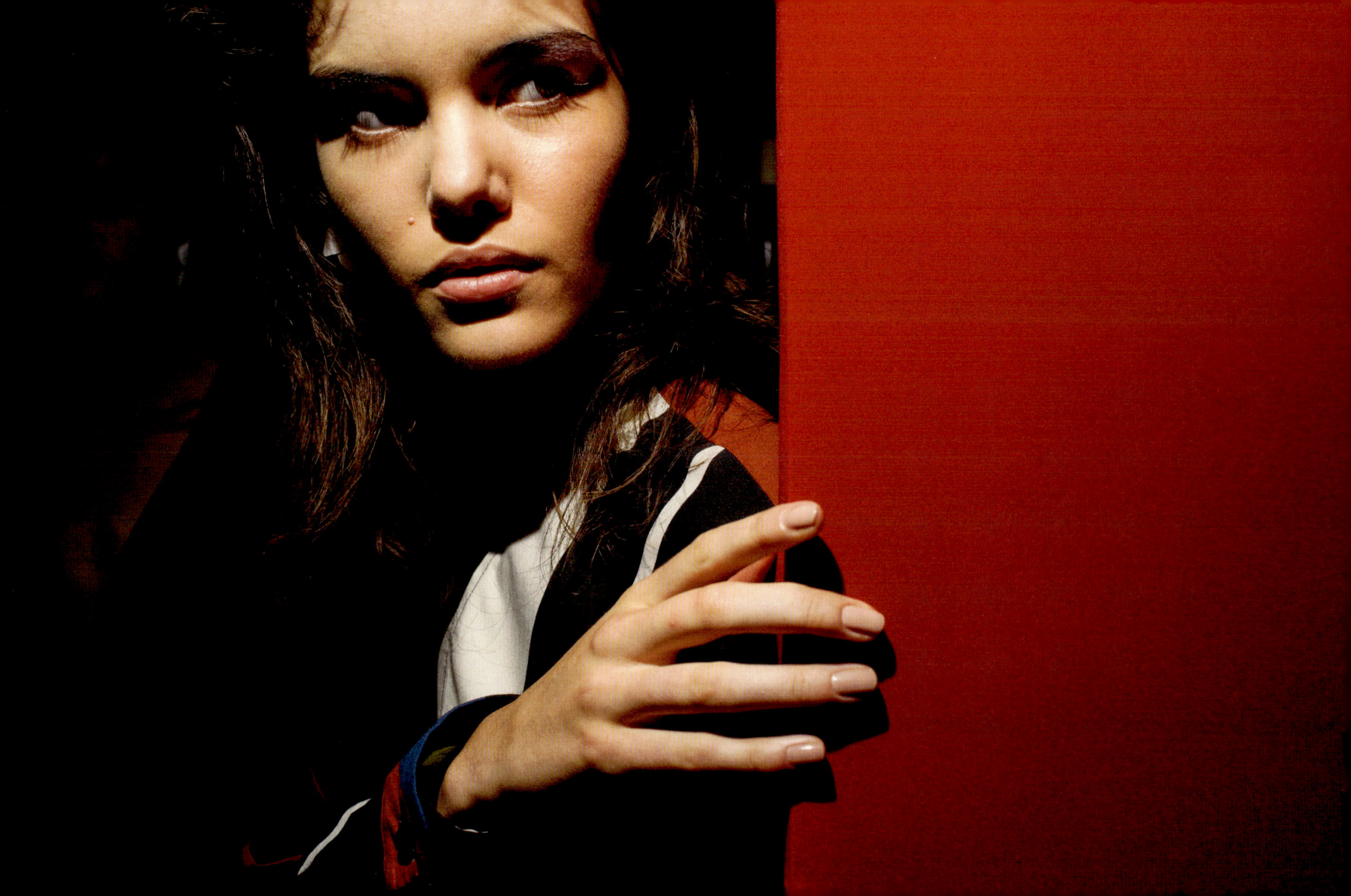

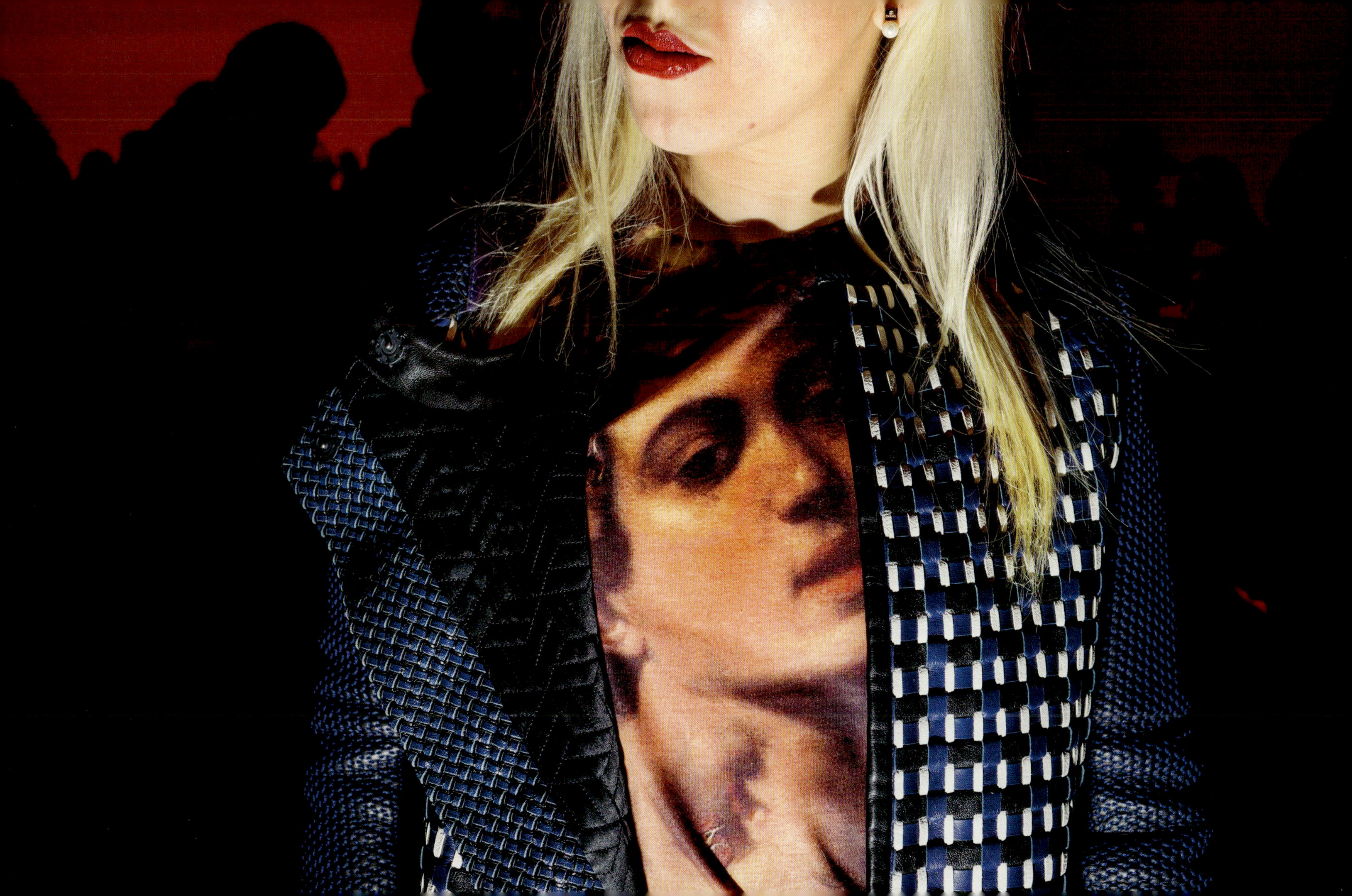

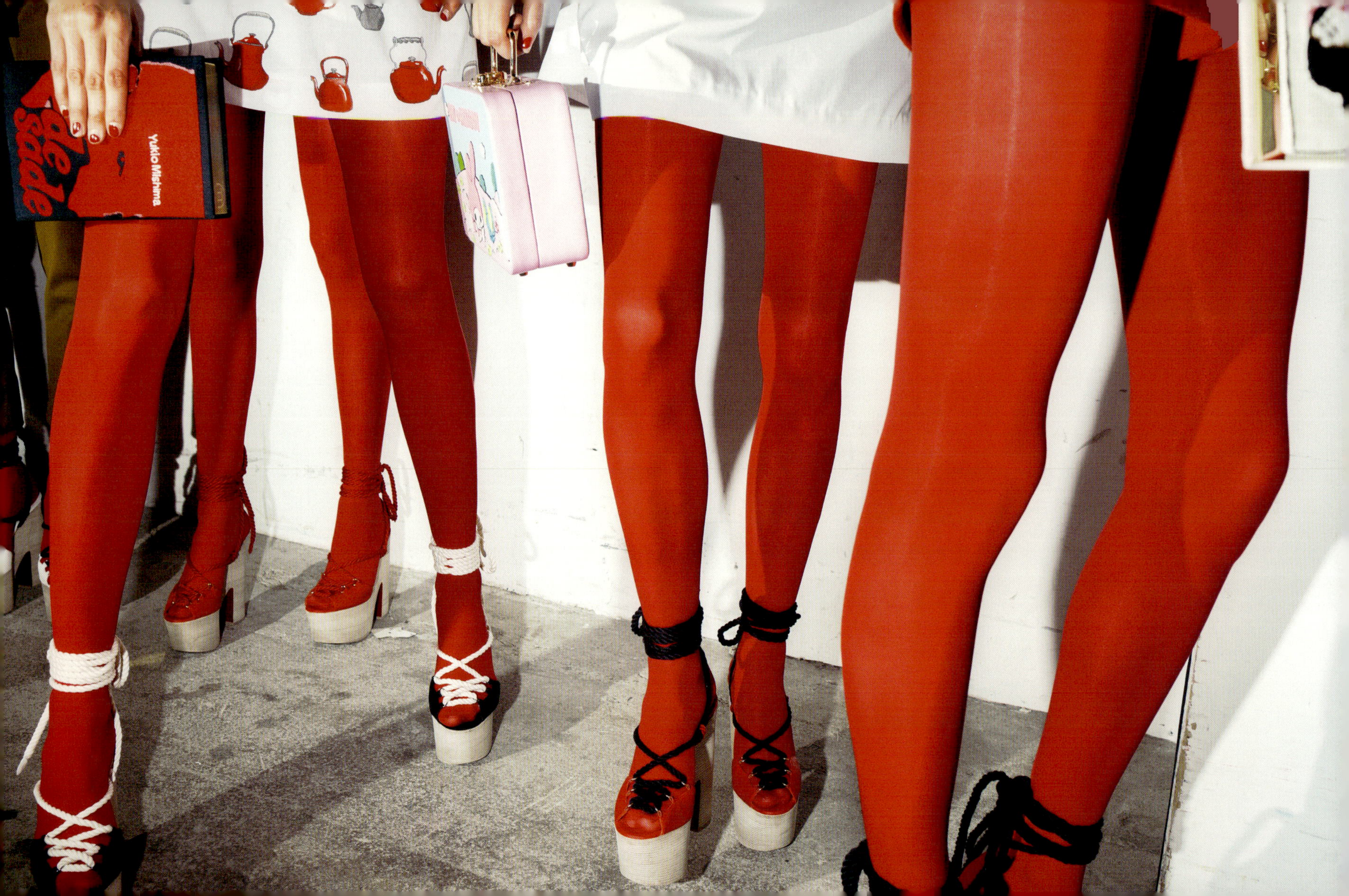
de sade
Yukio Mishima

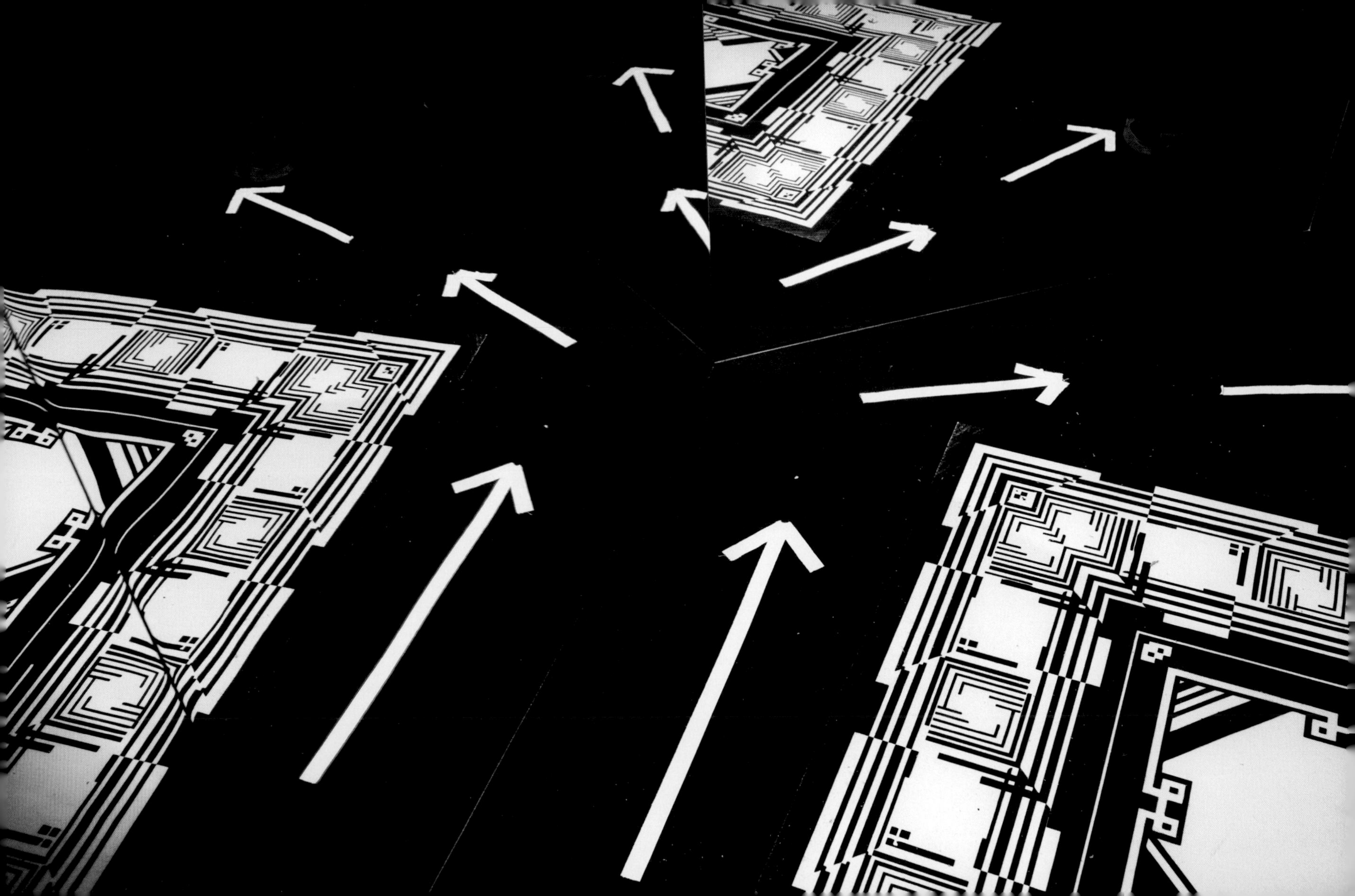

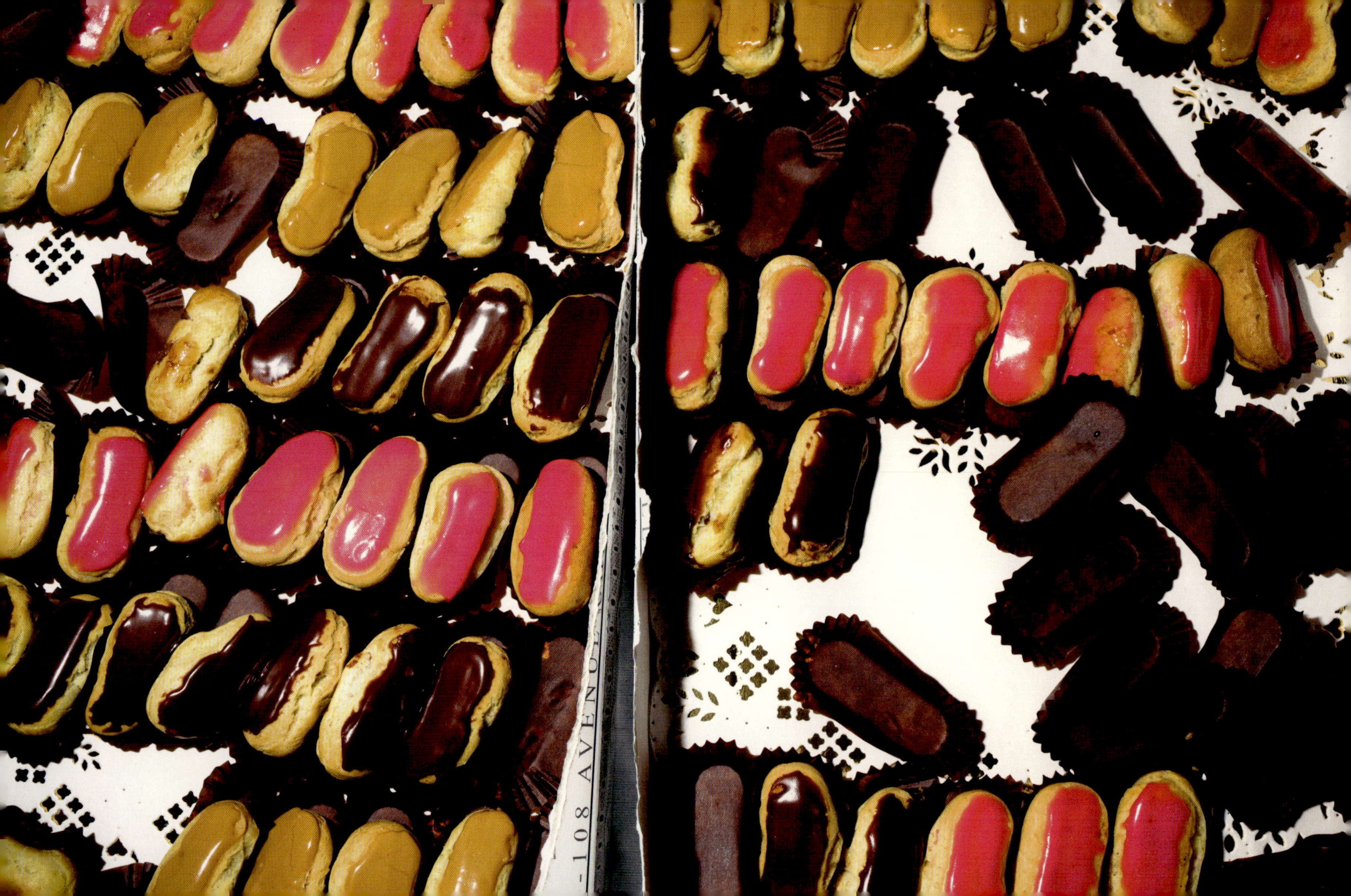
108 AVENUE

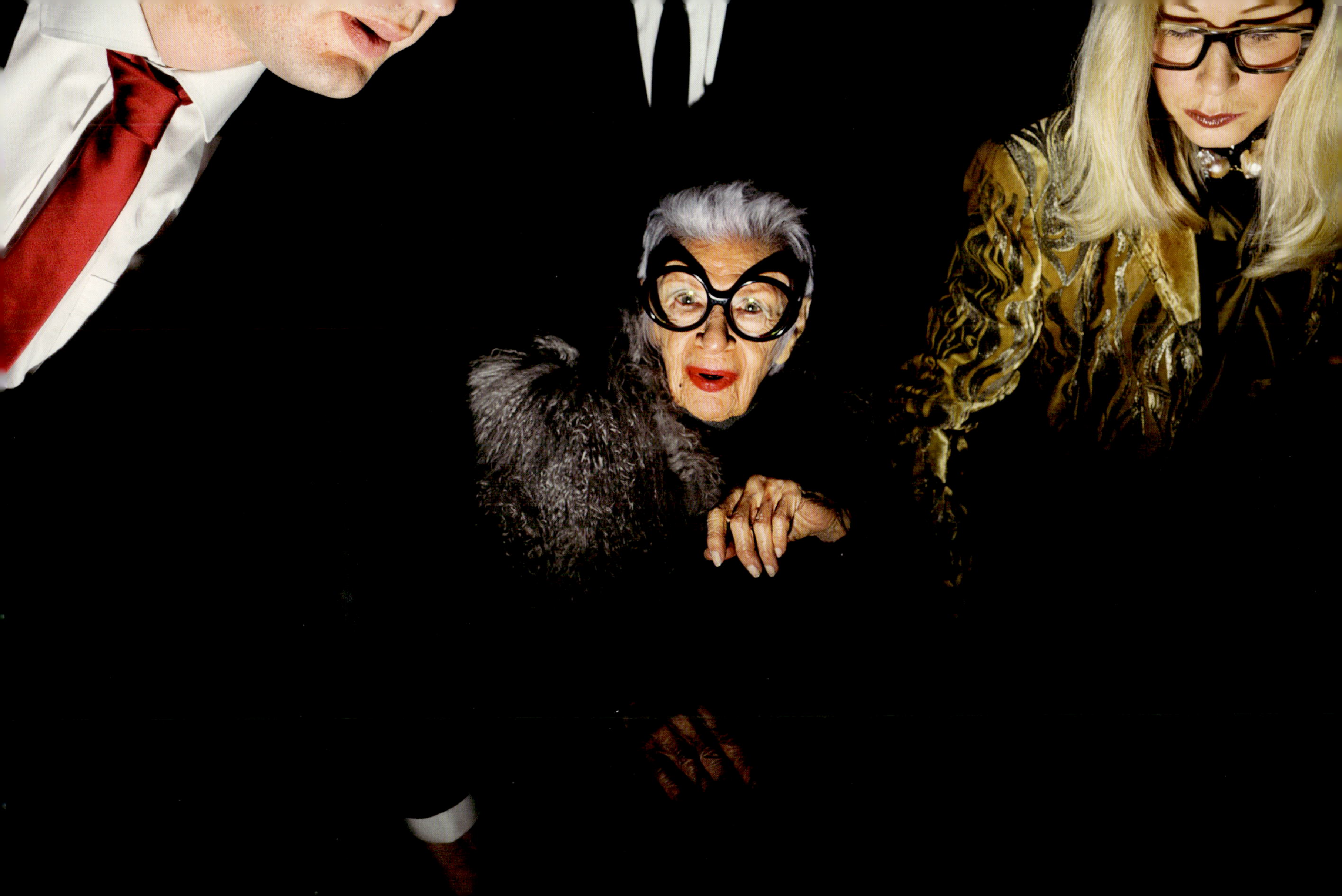

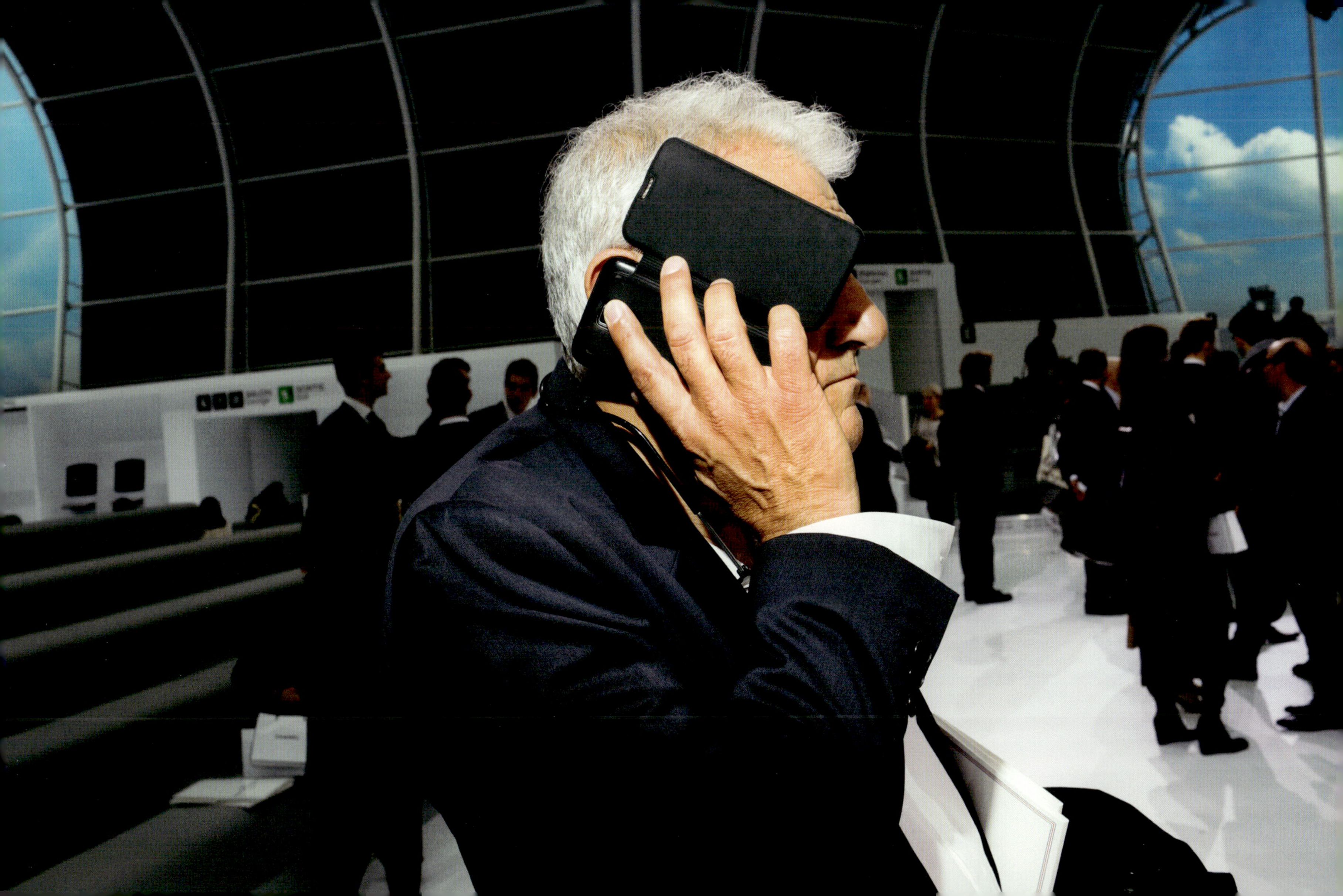

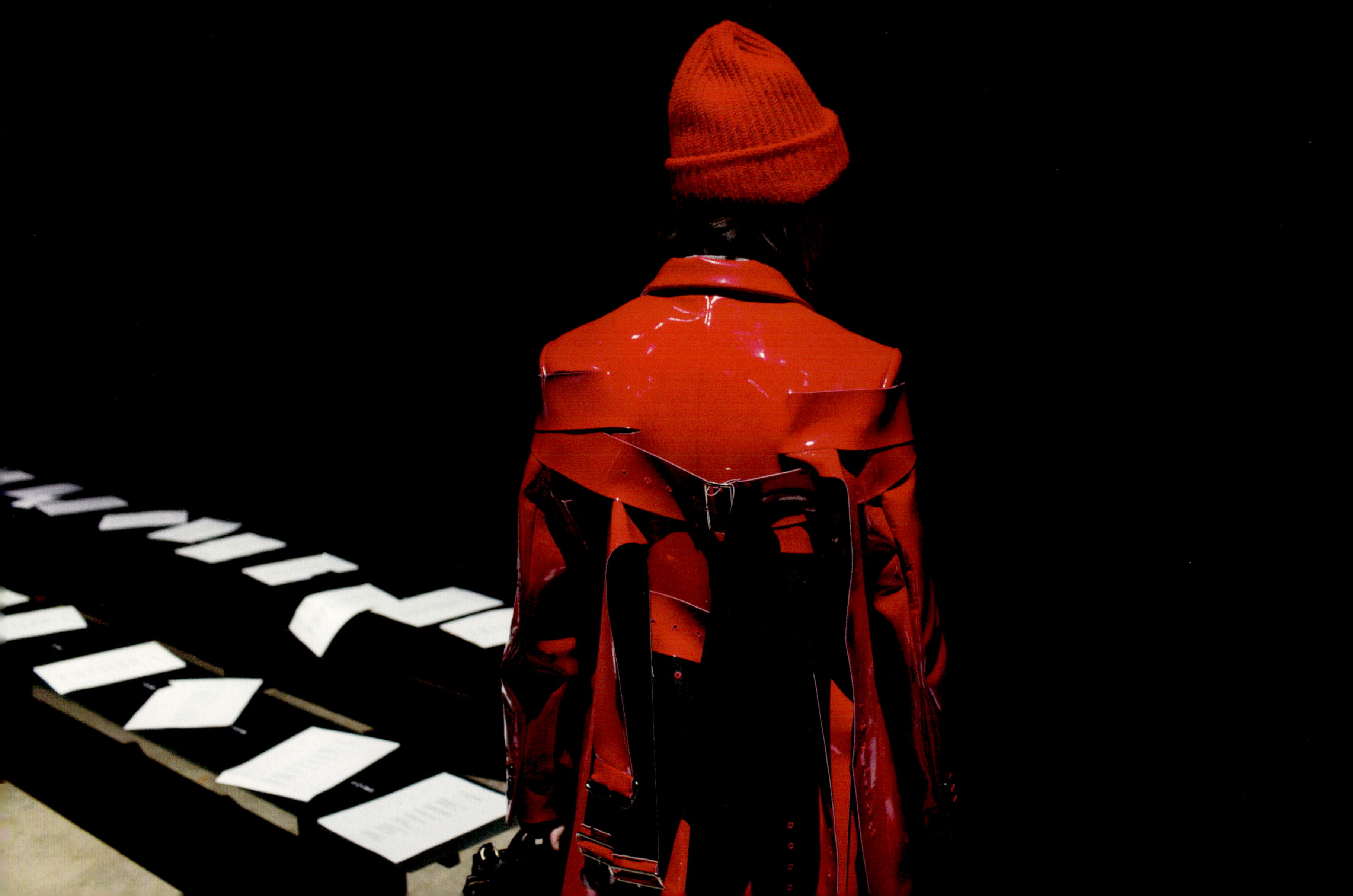

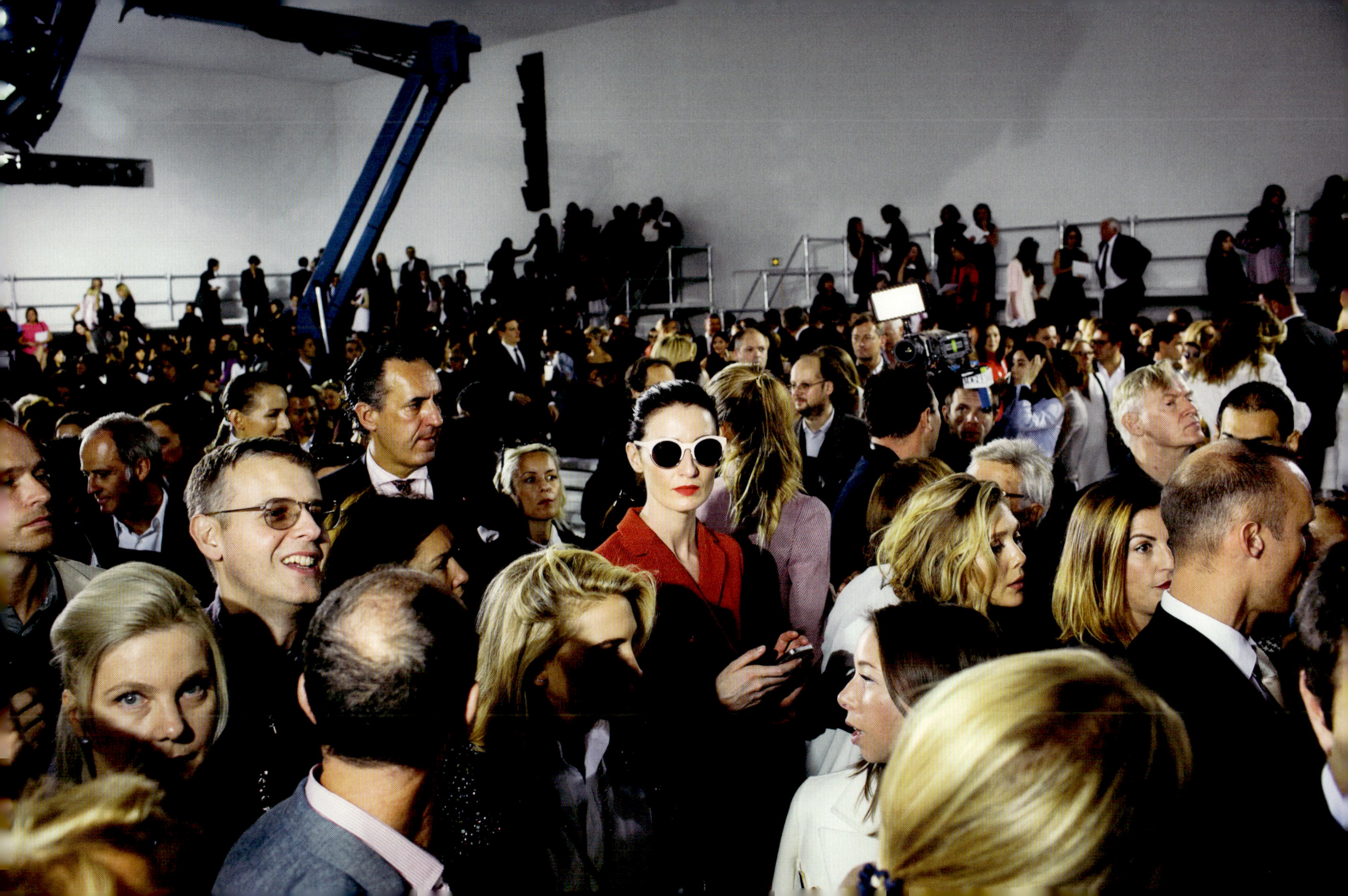

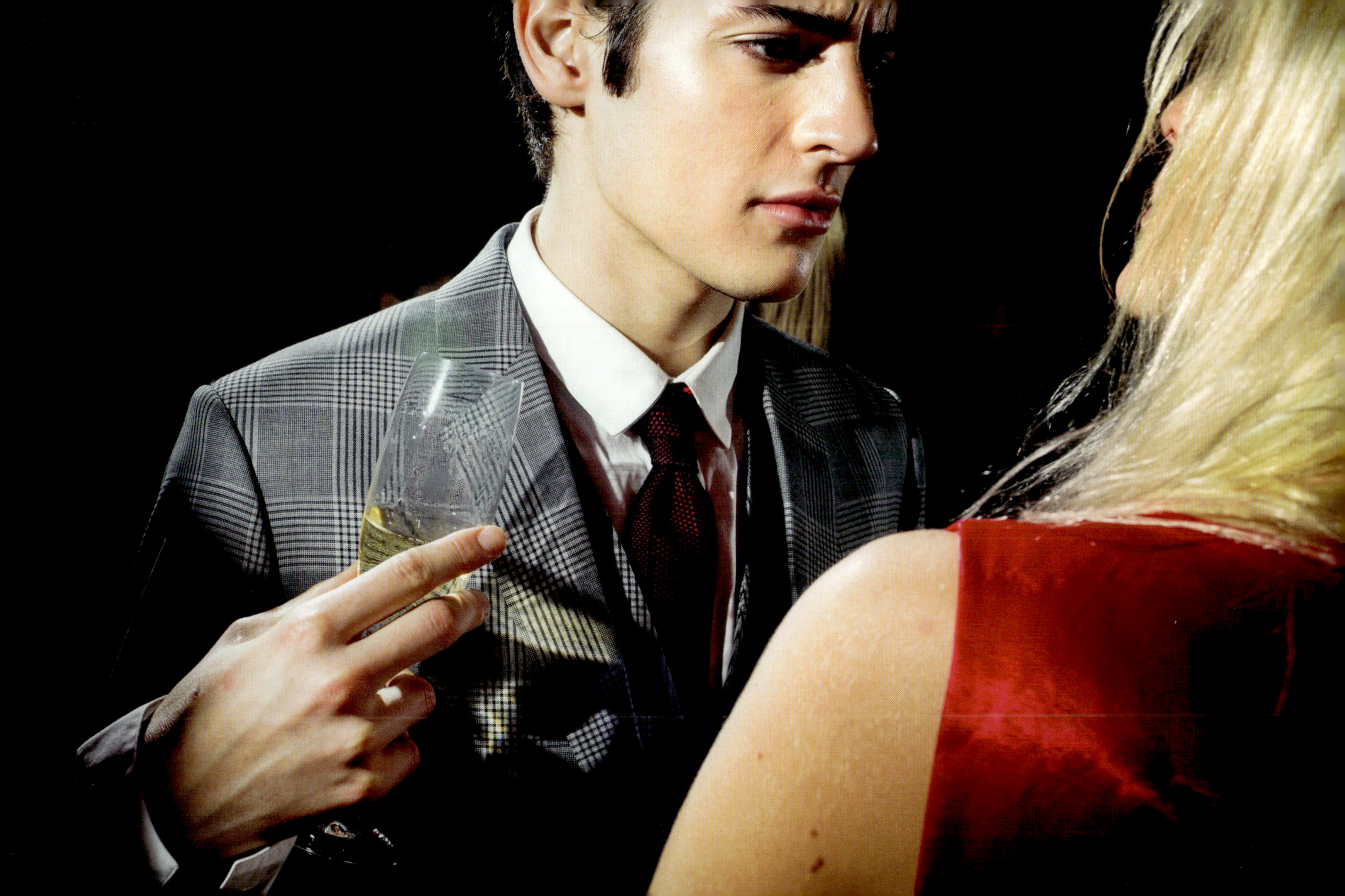

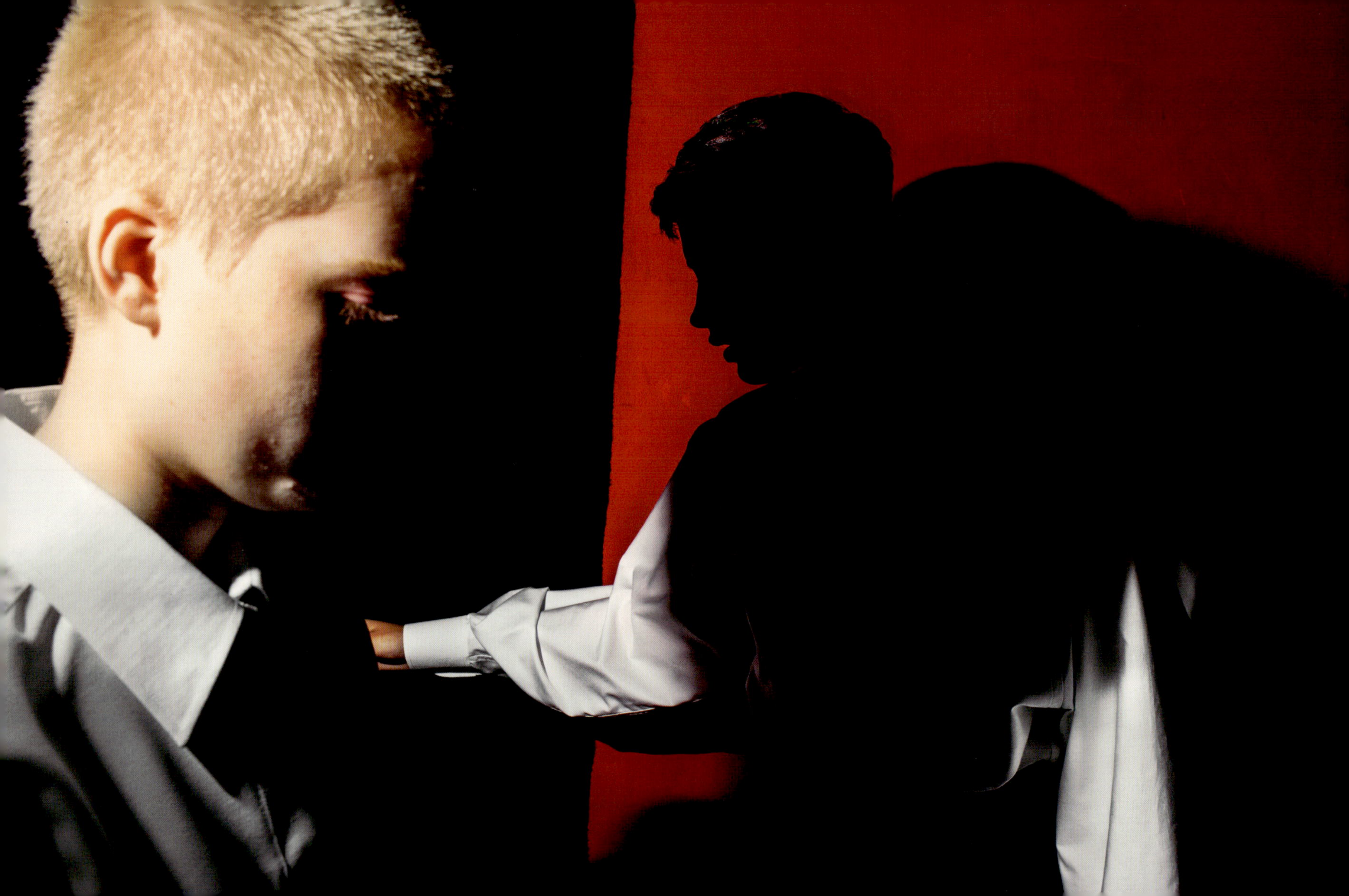

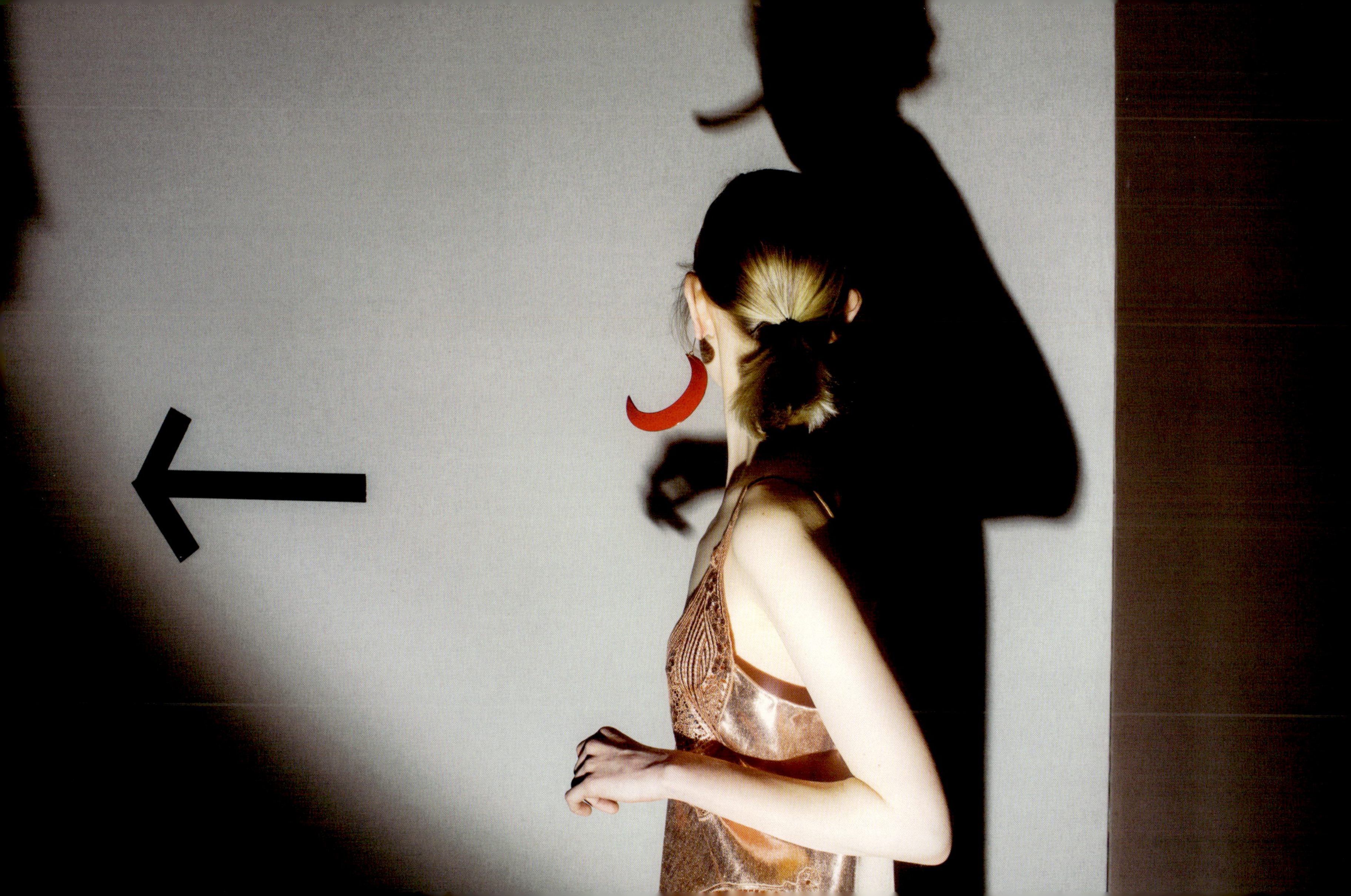

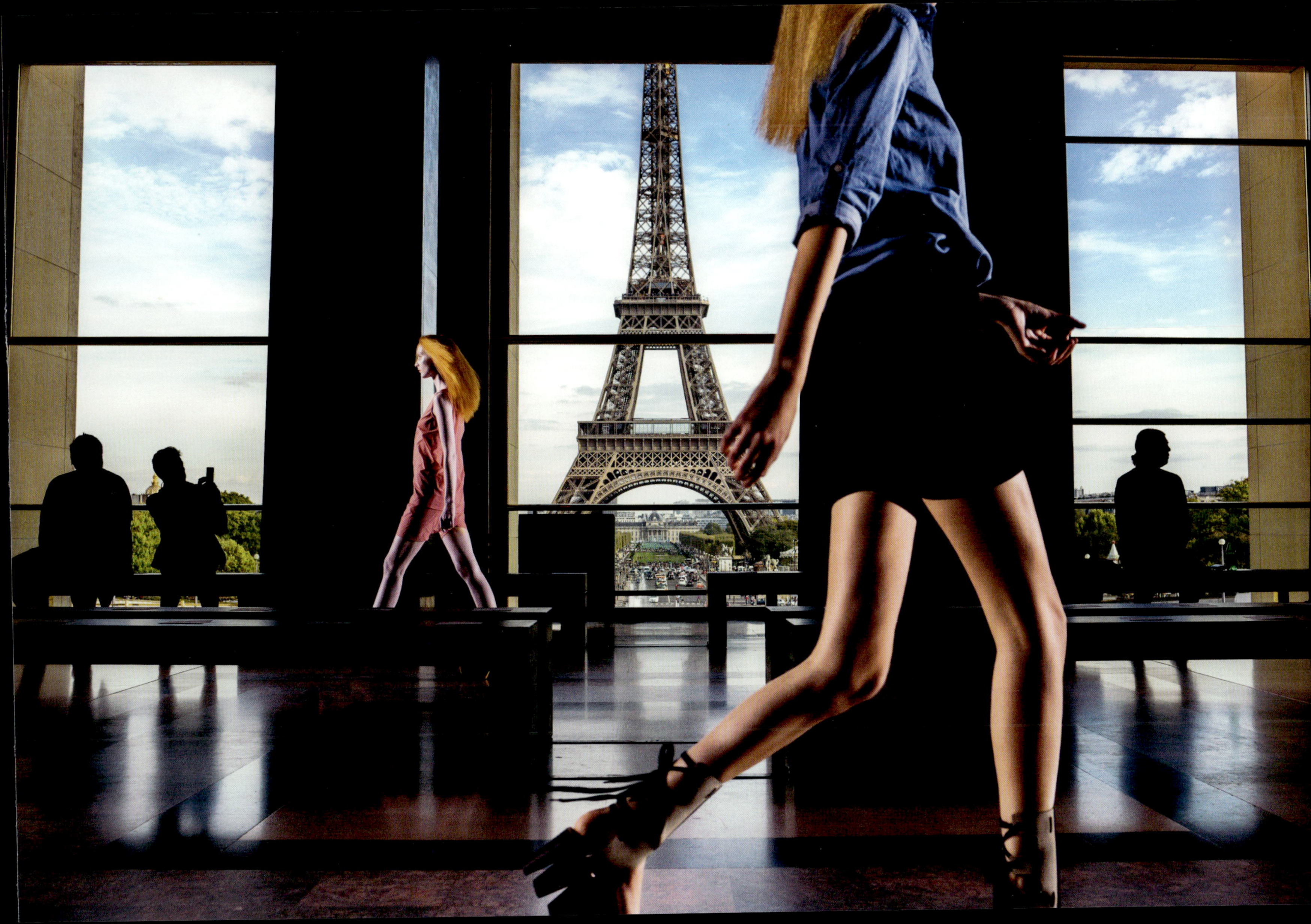

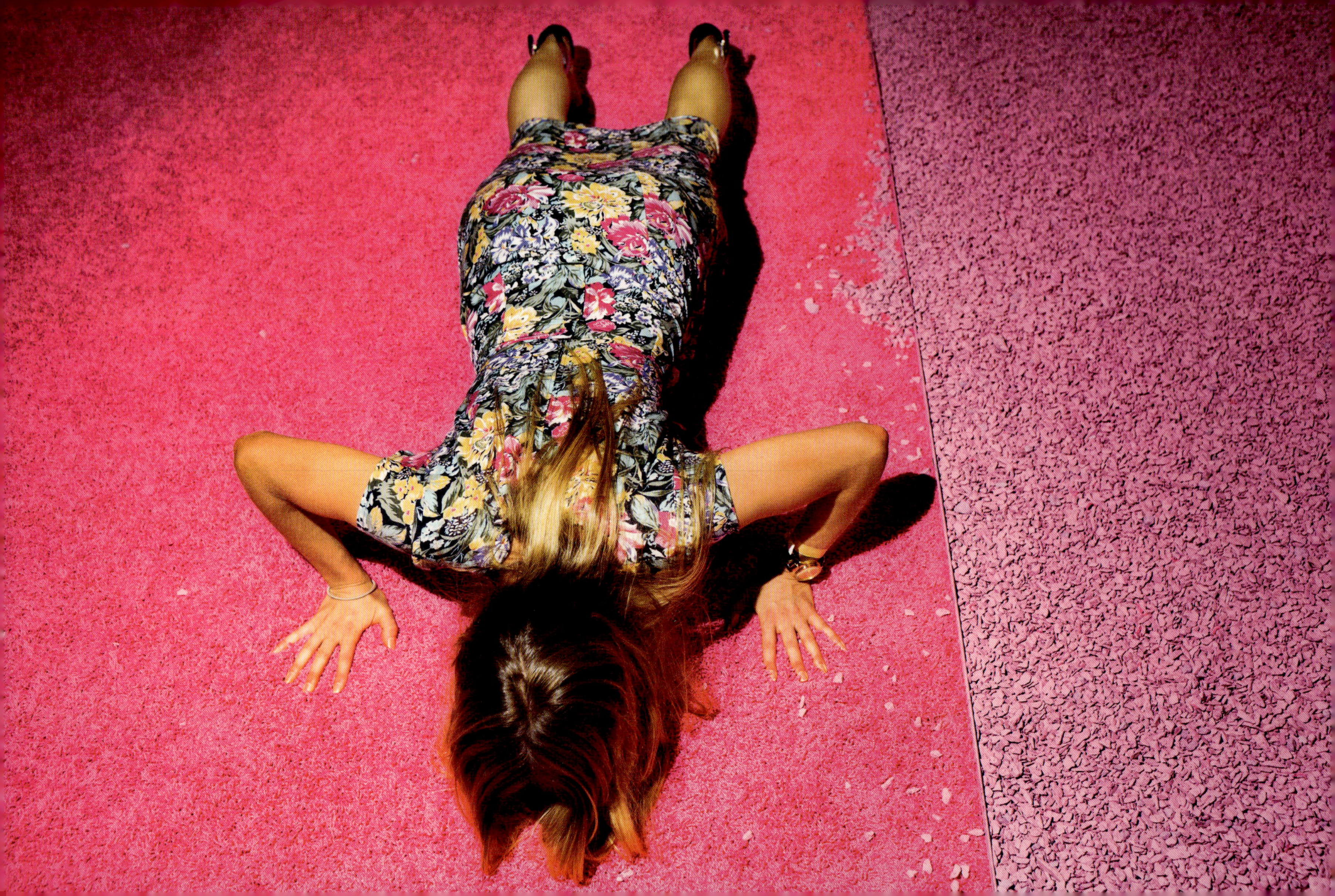

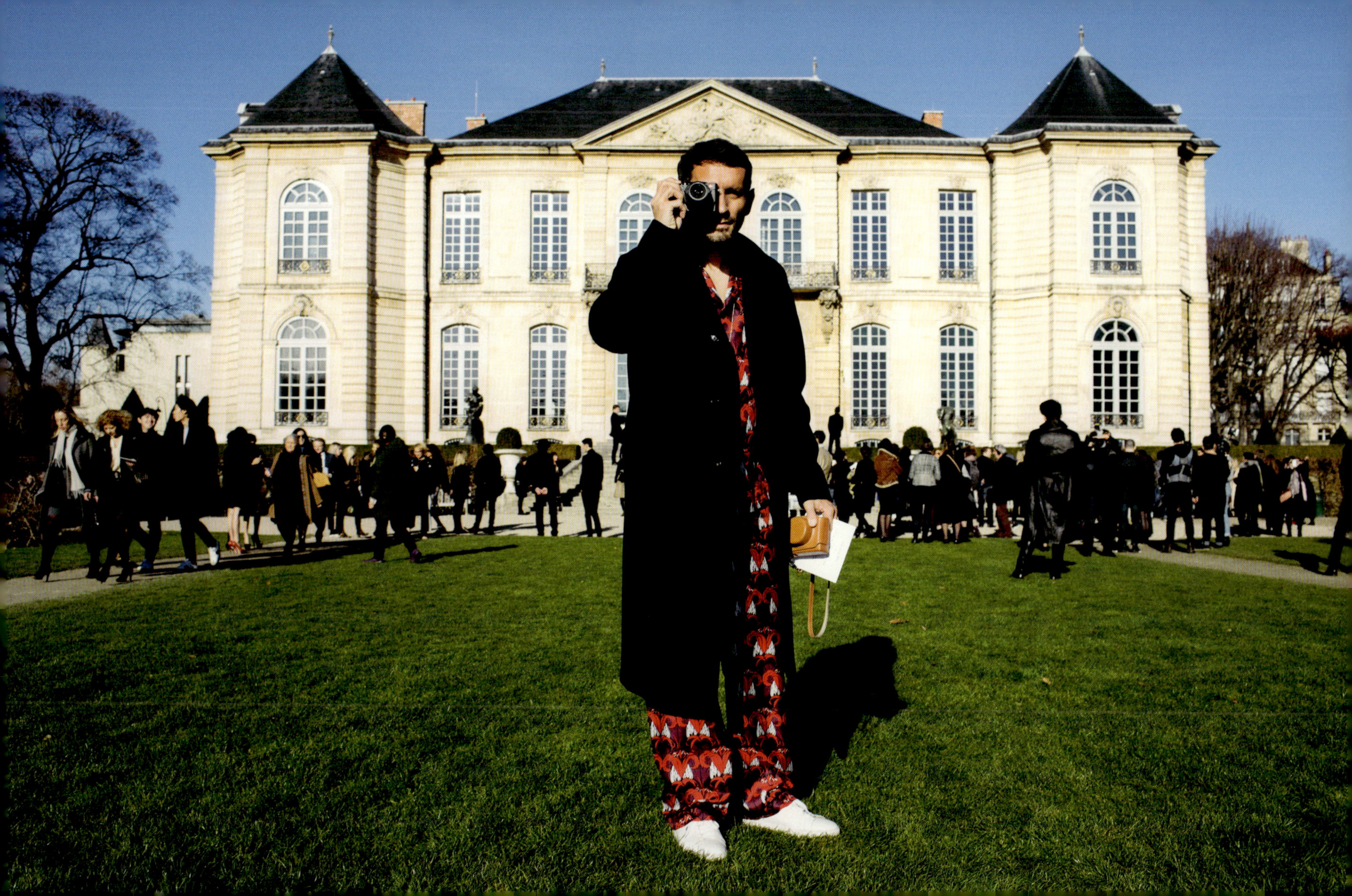

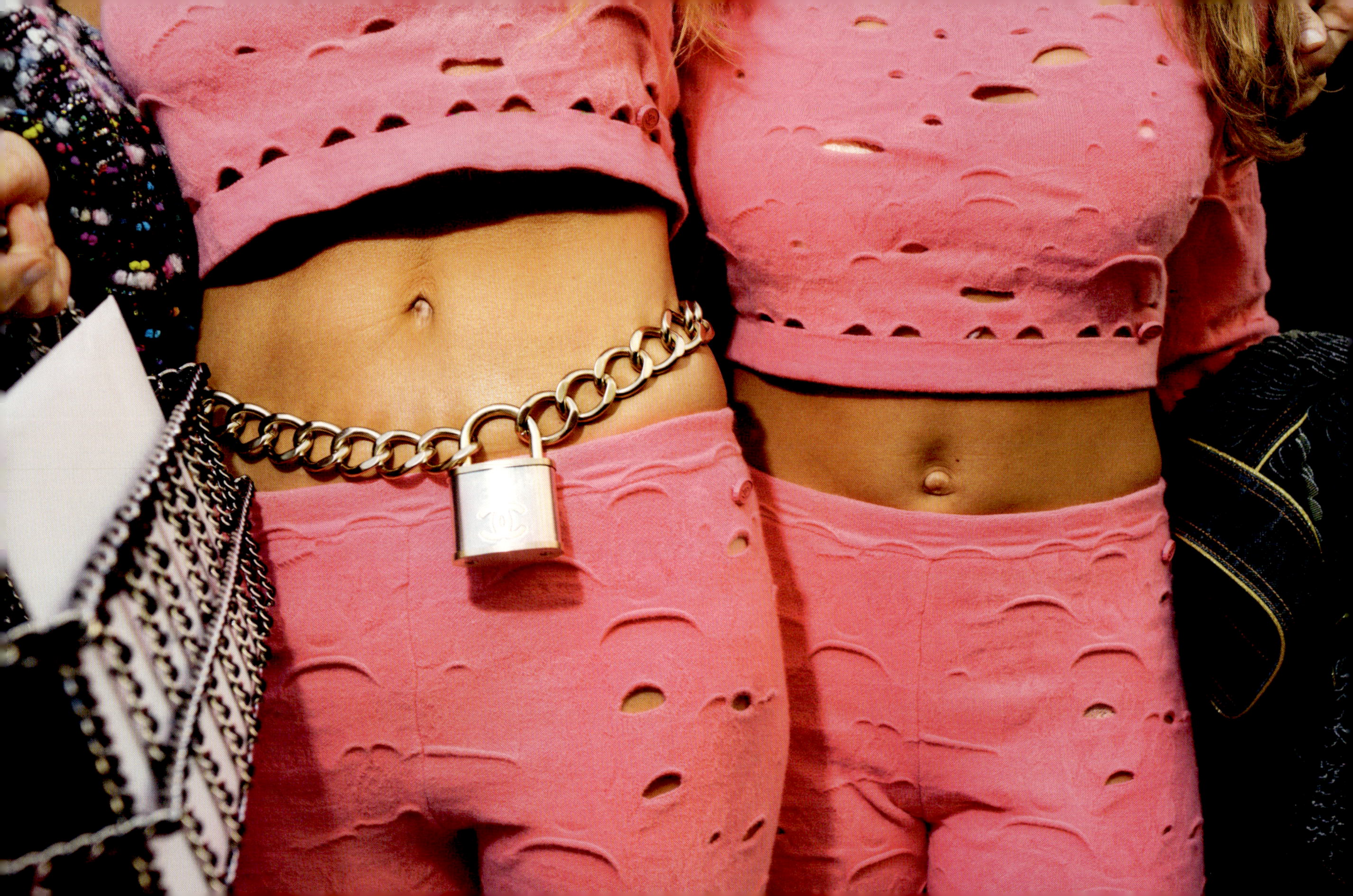

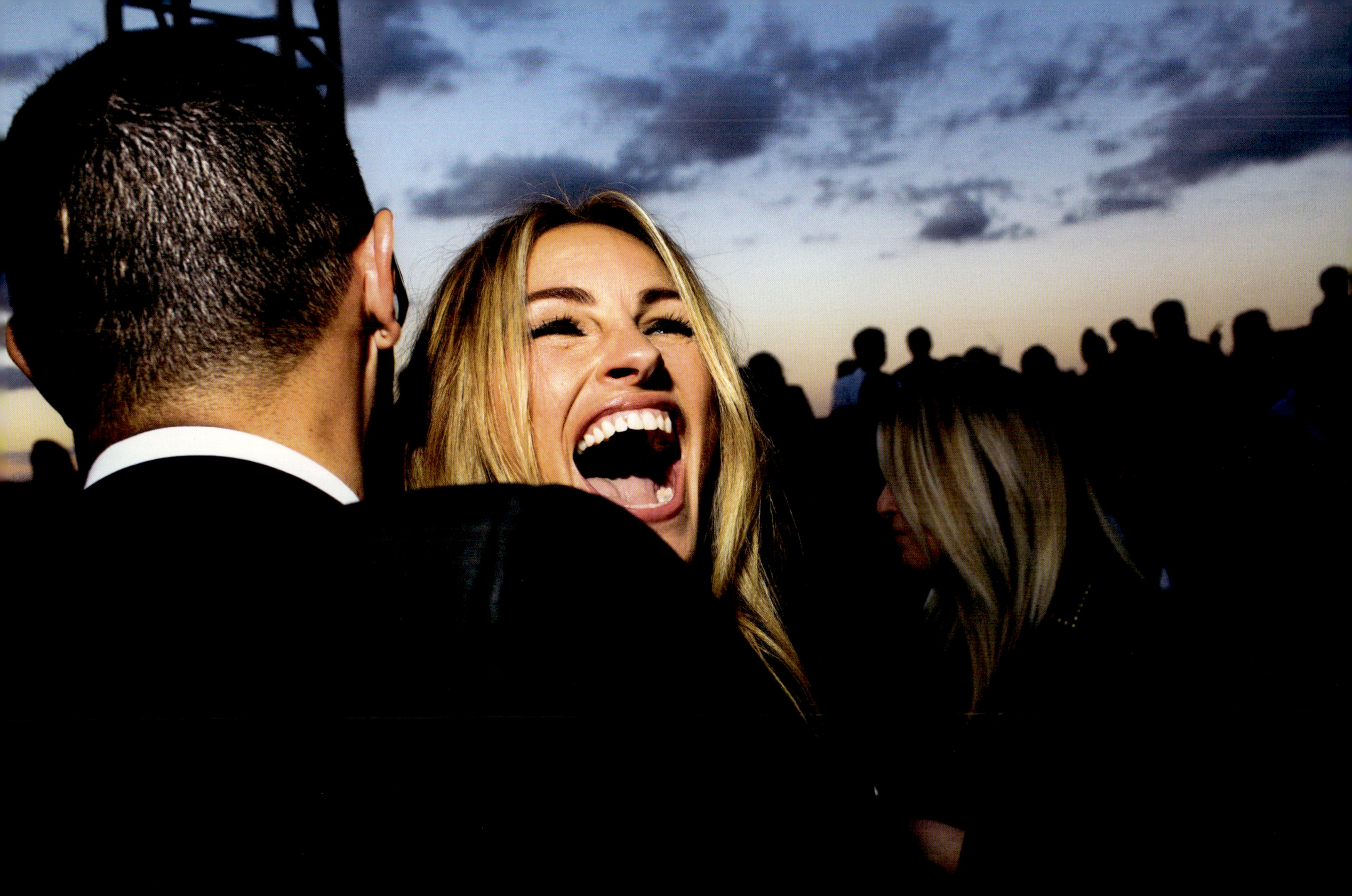

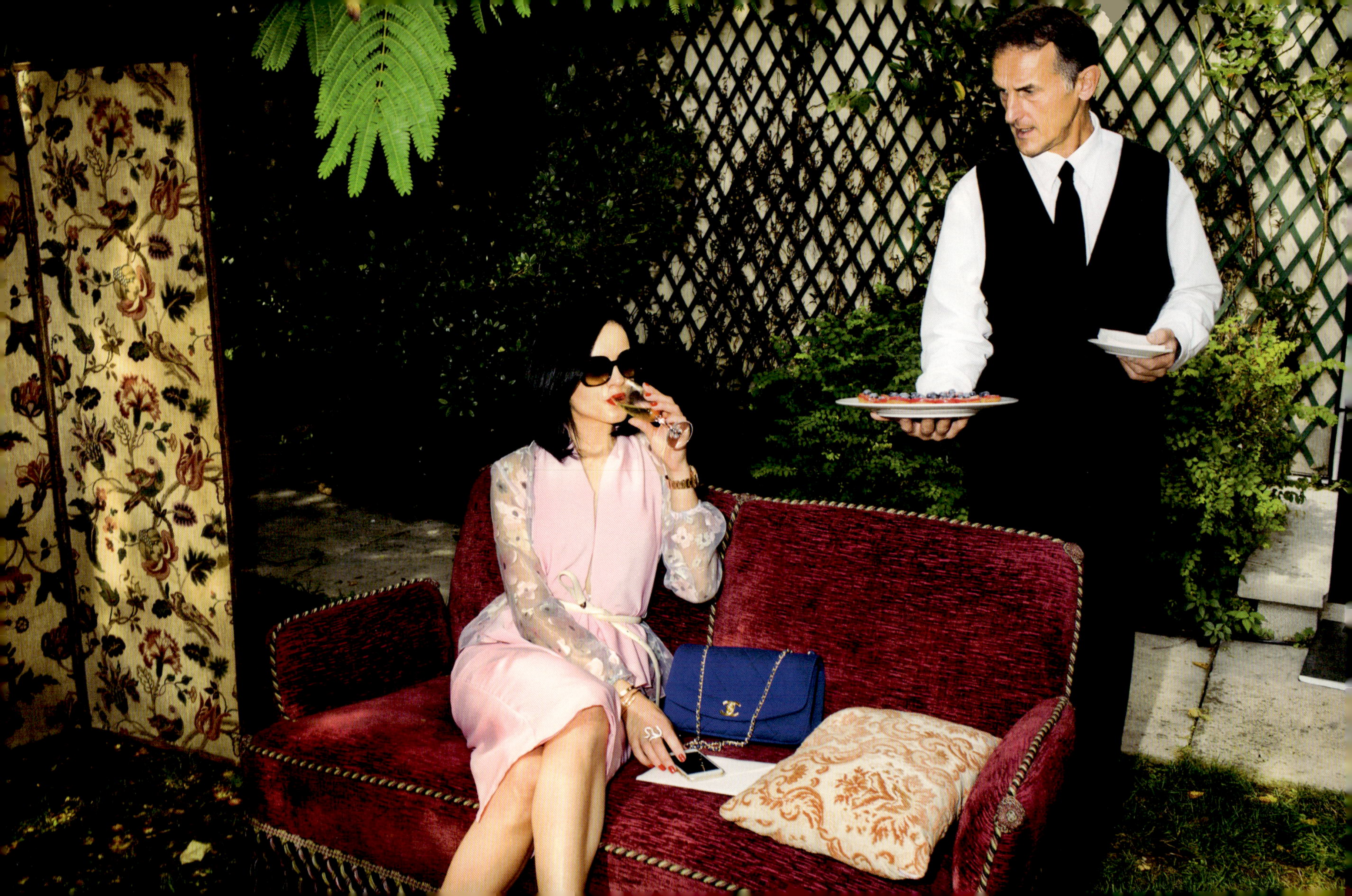

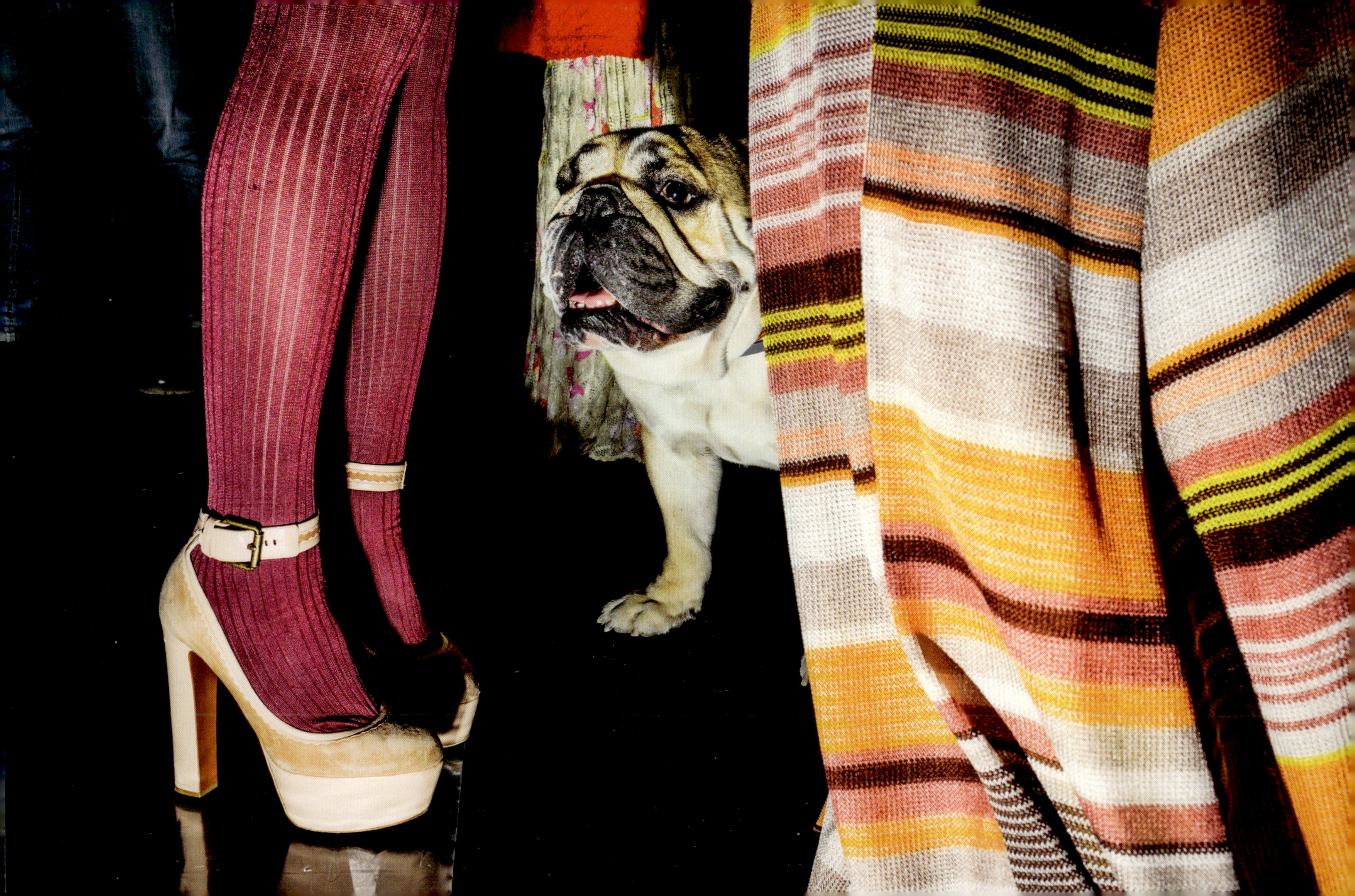

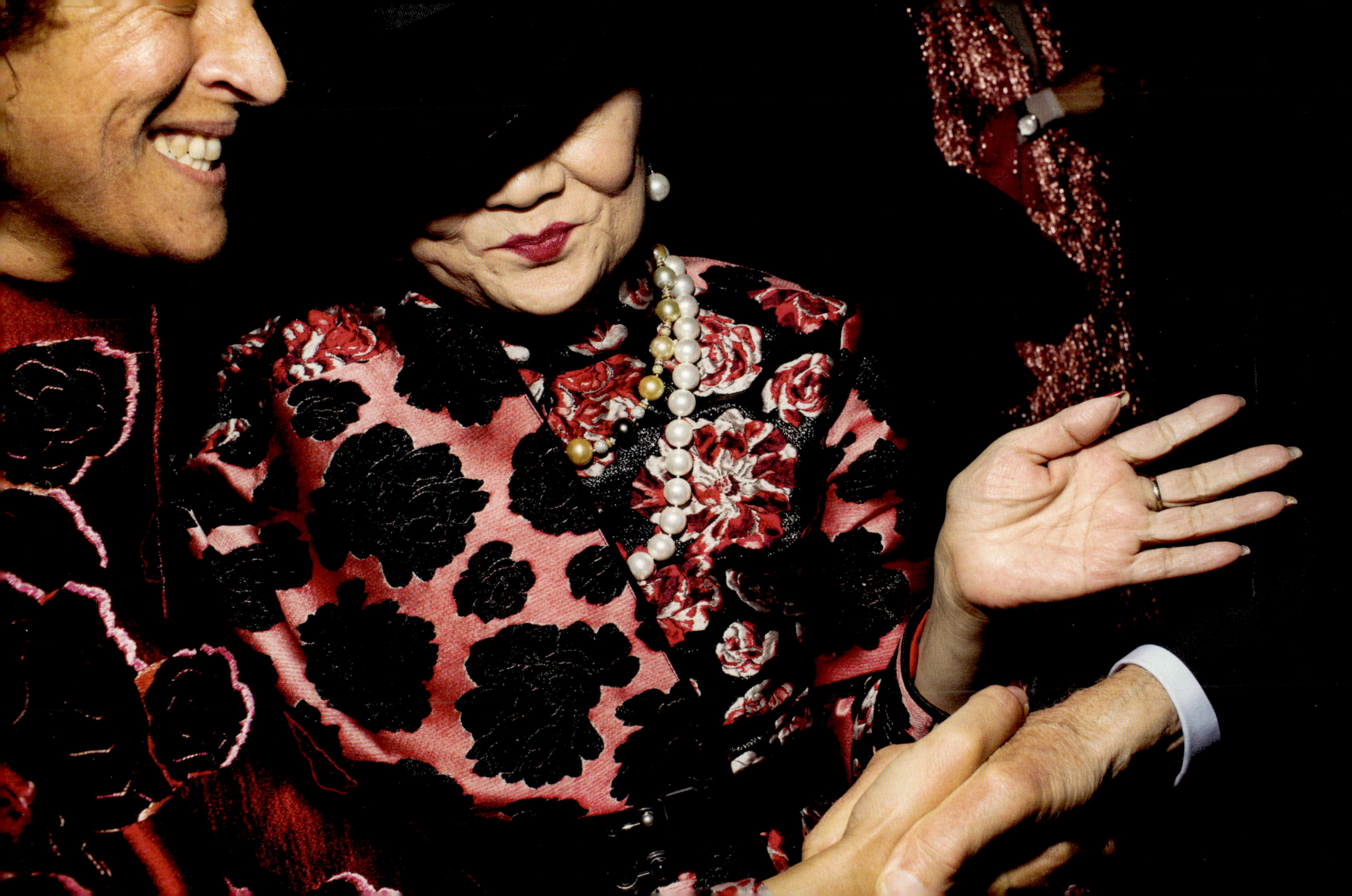

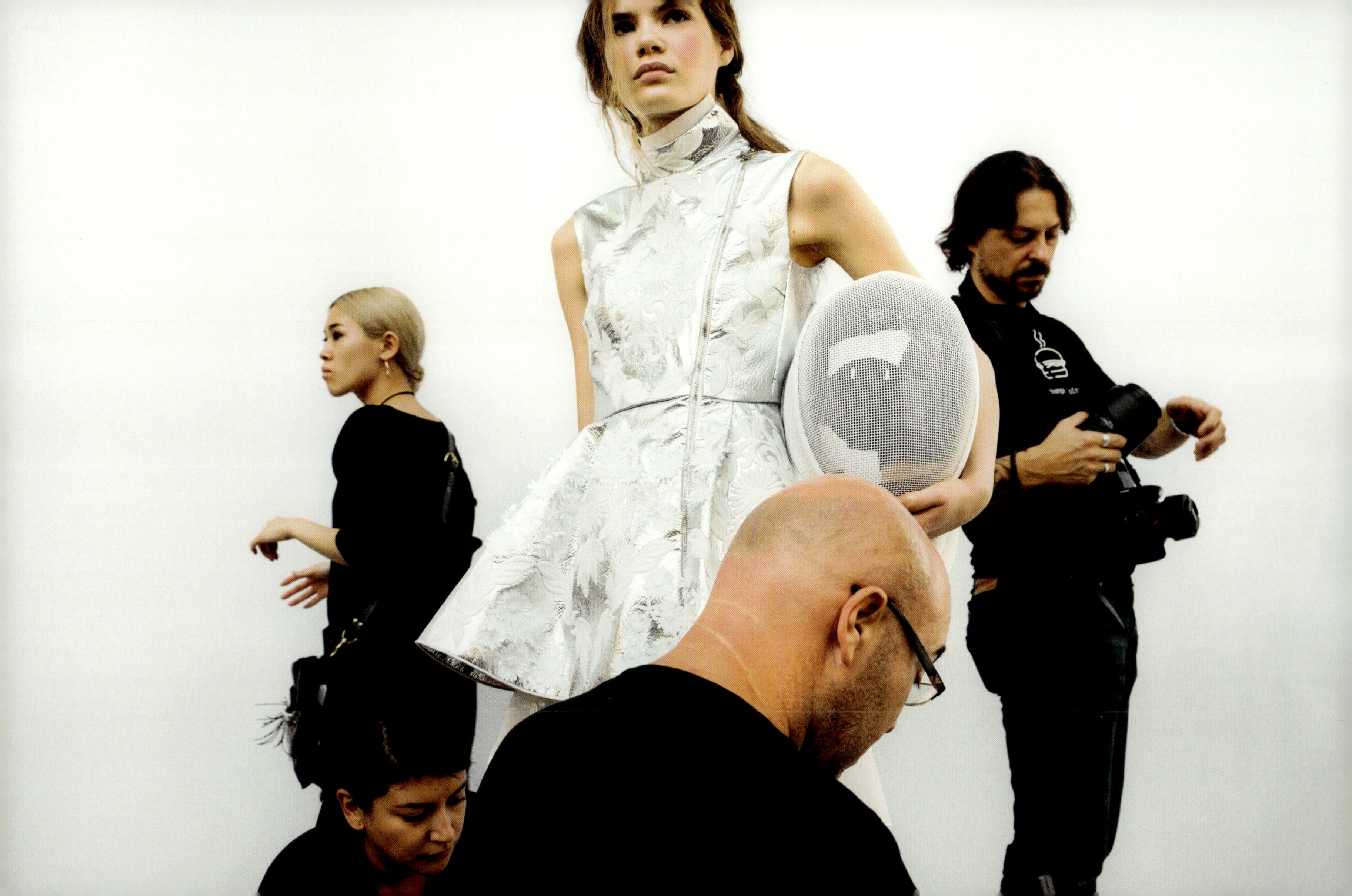

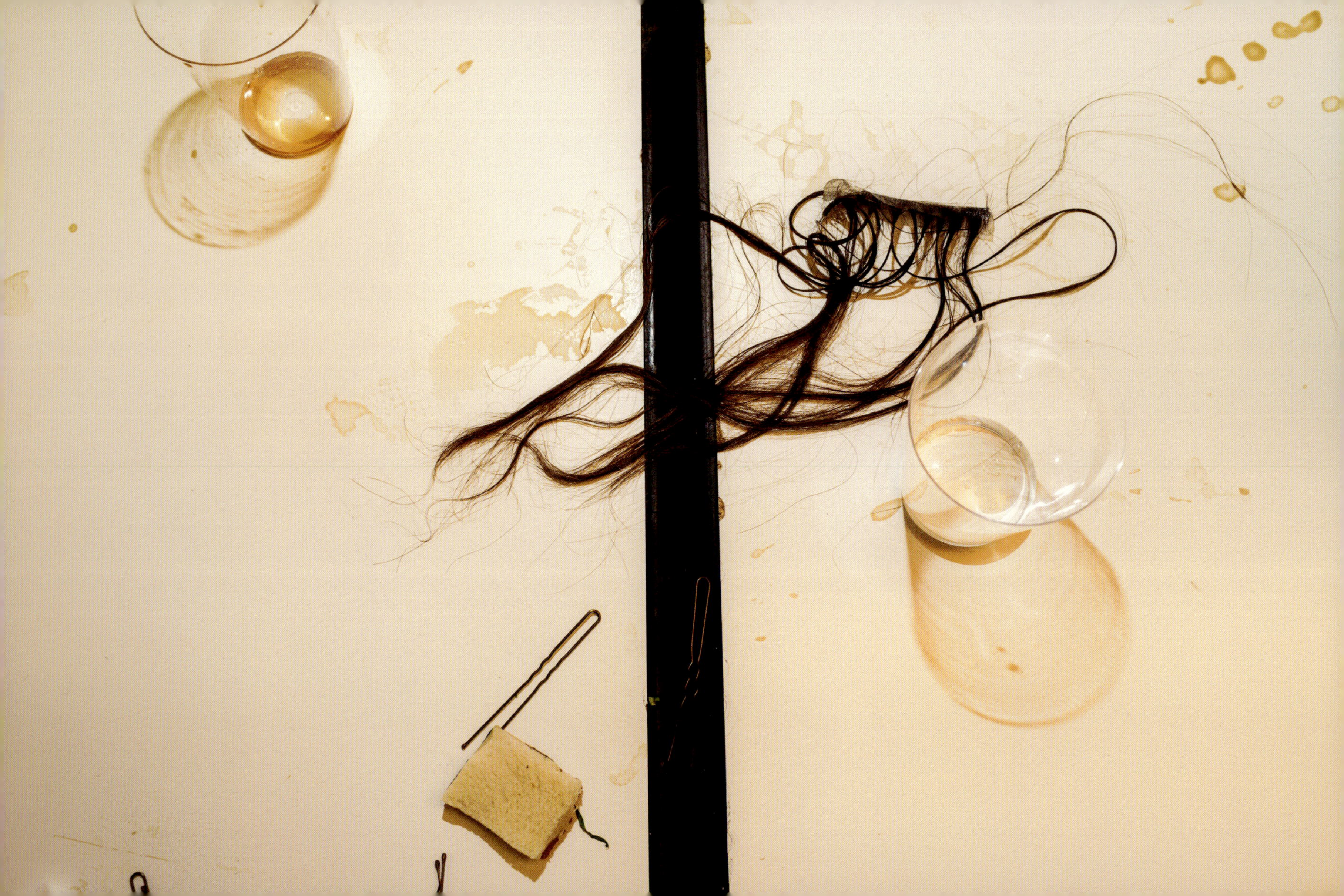

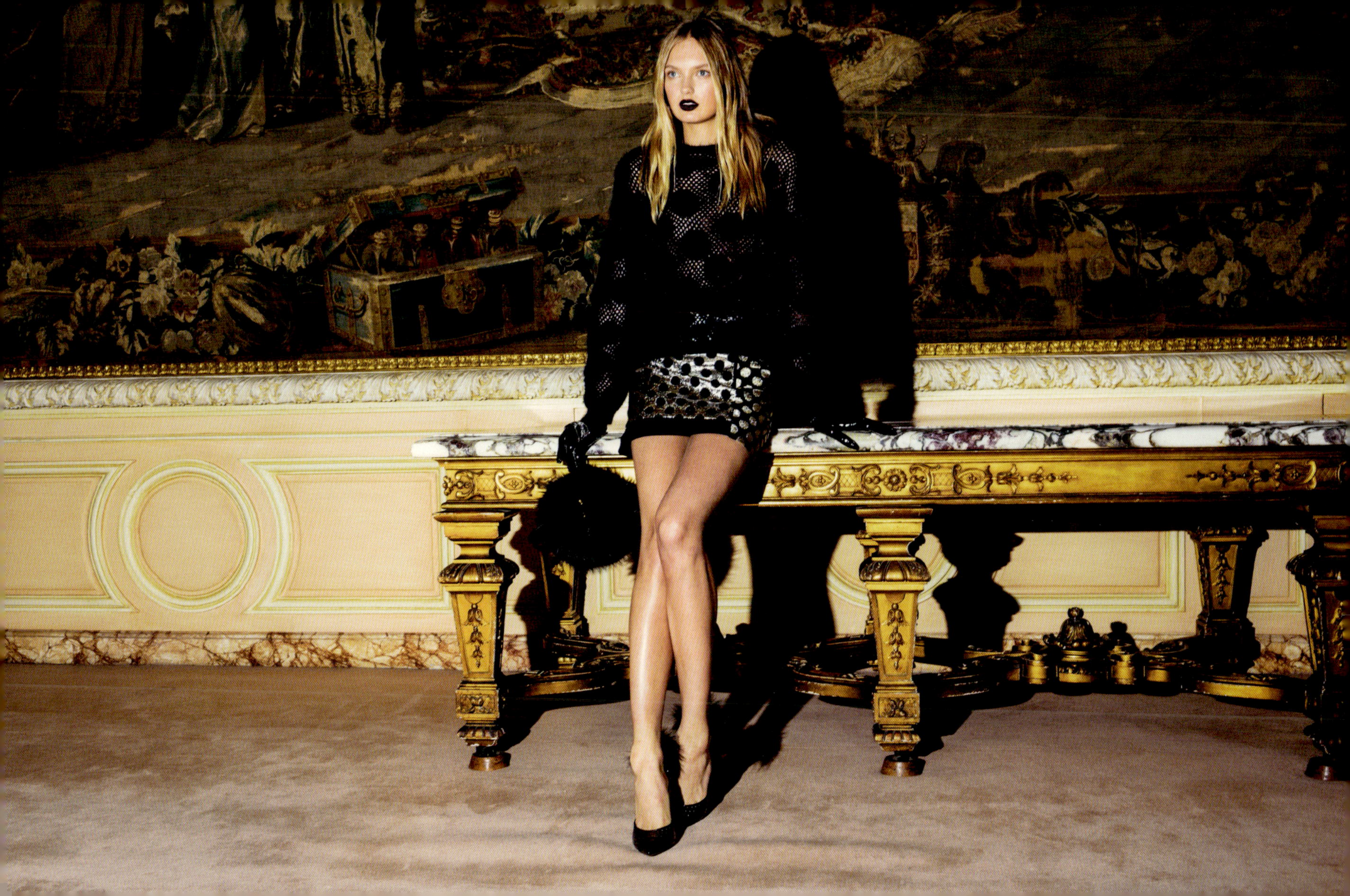

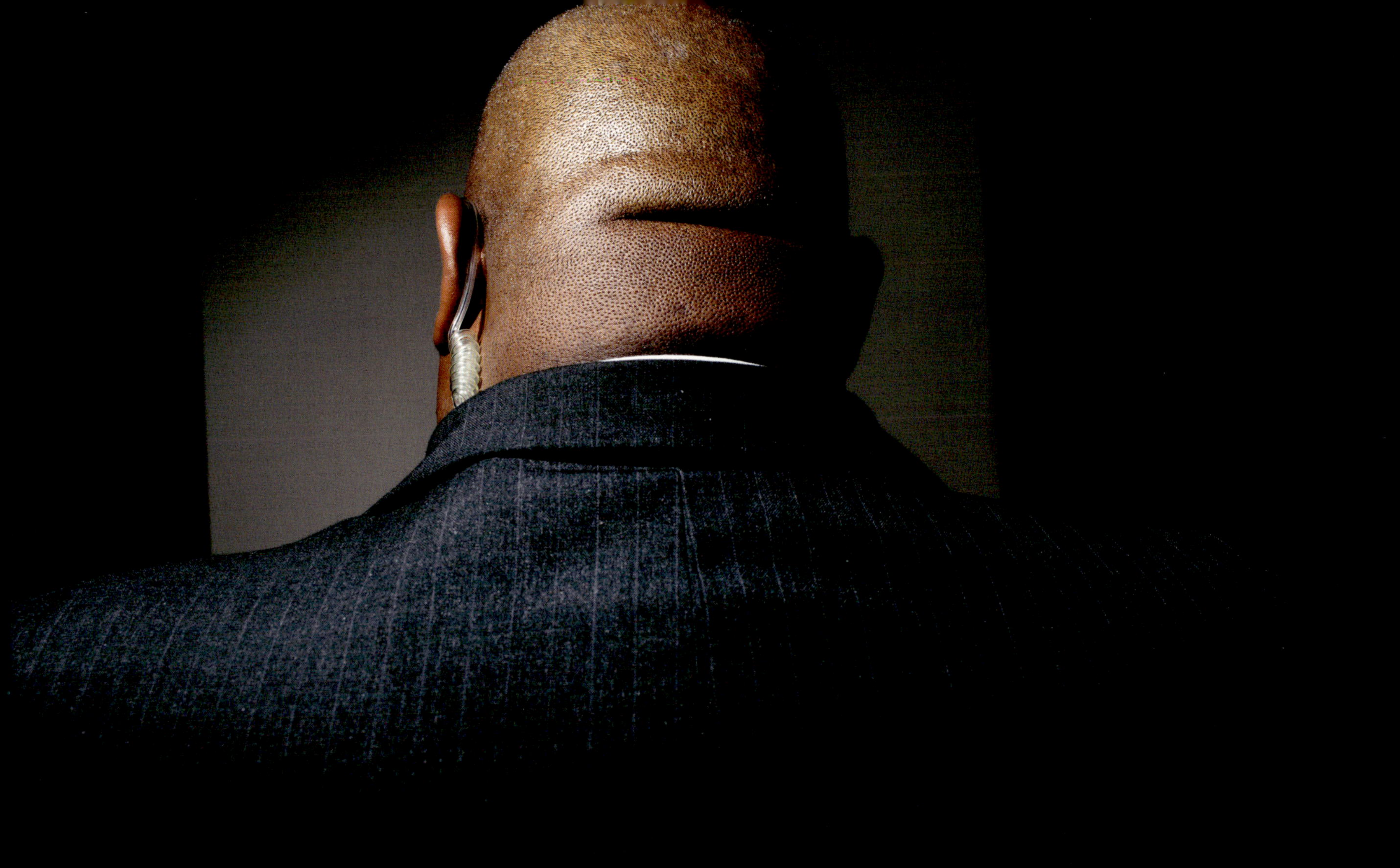

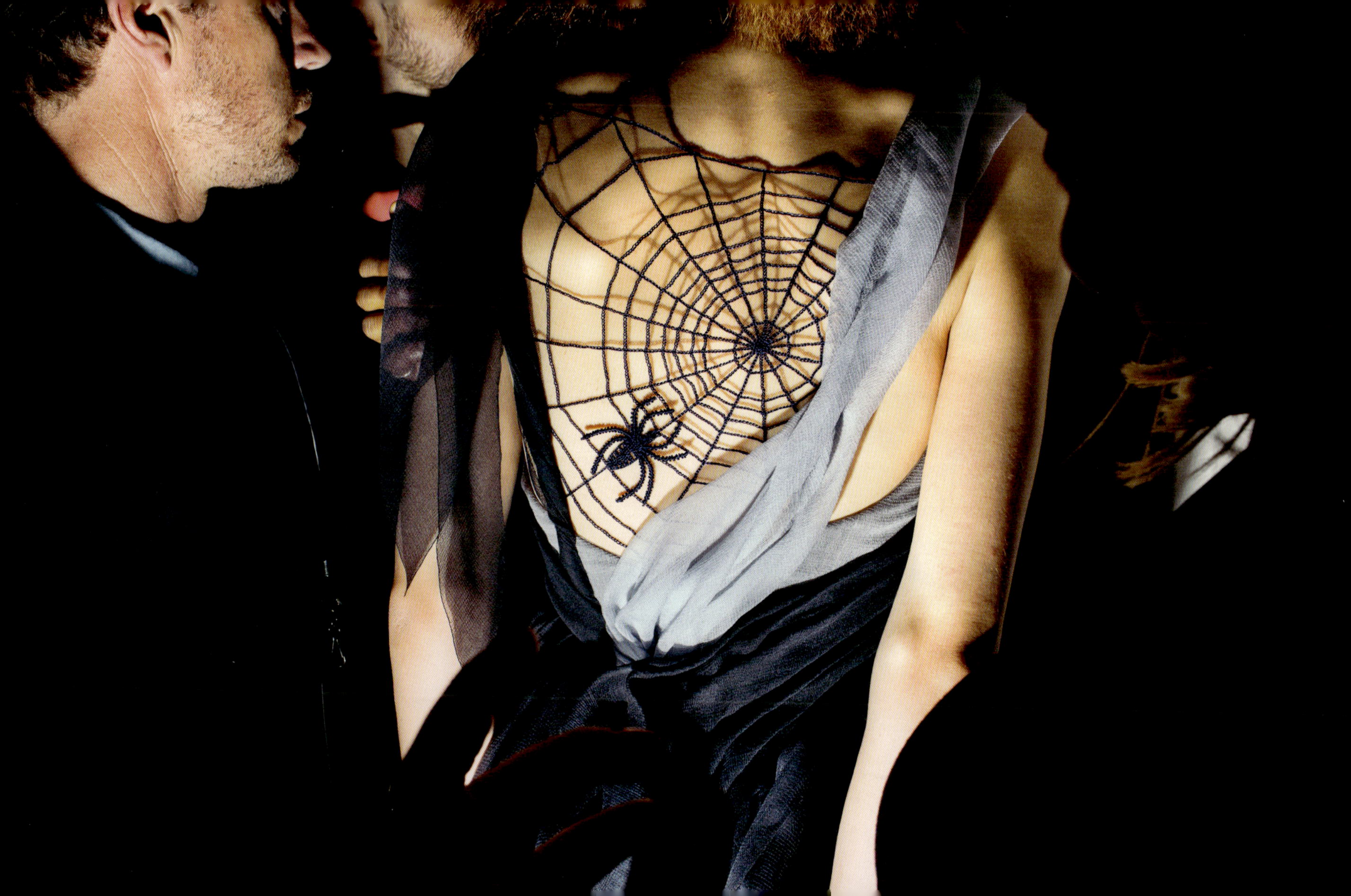

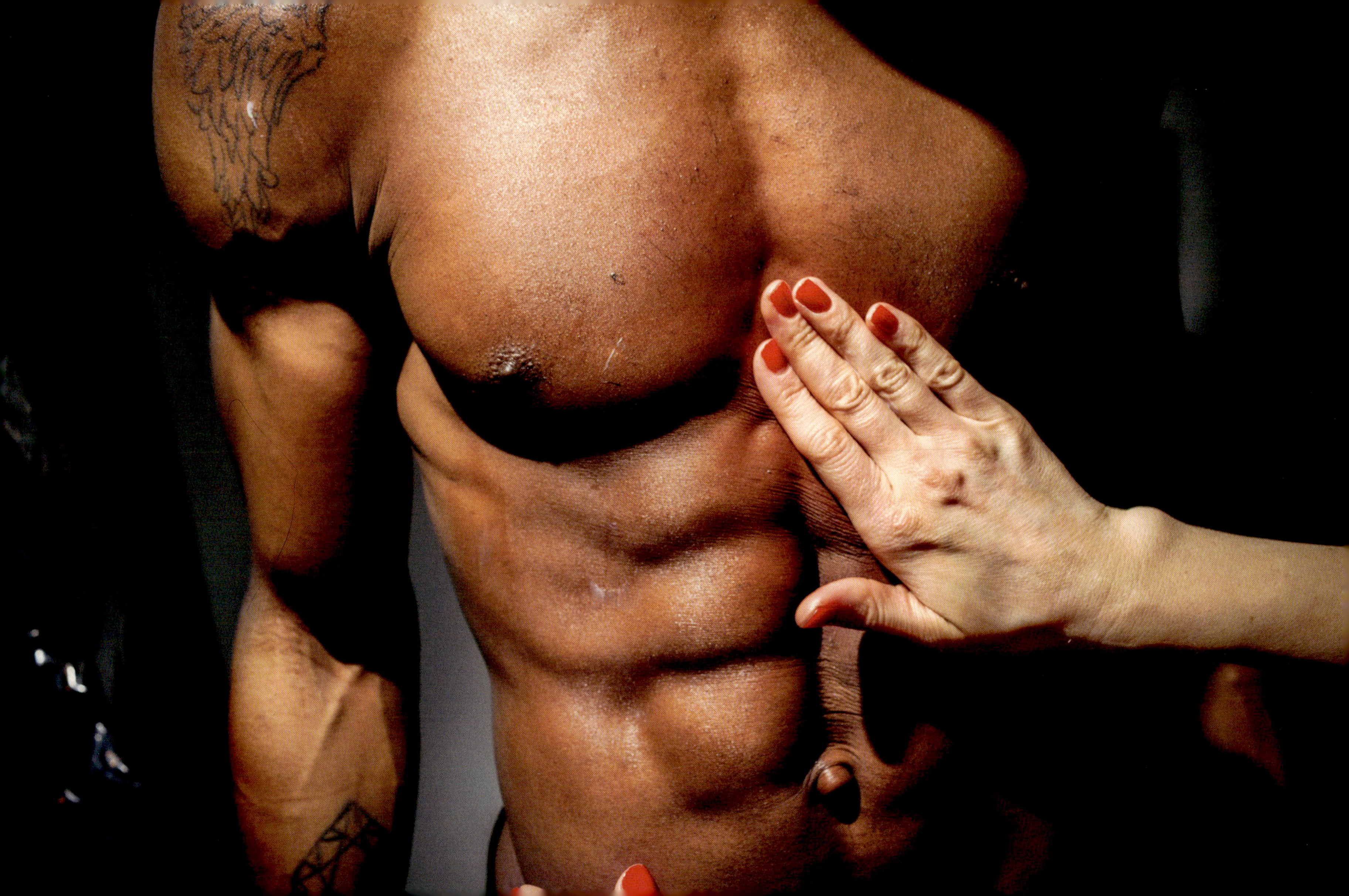

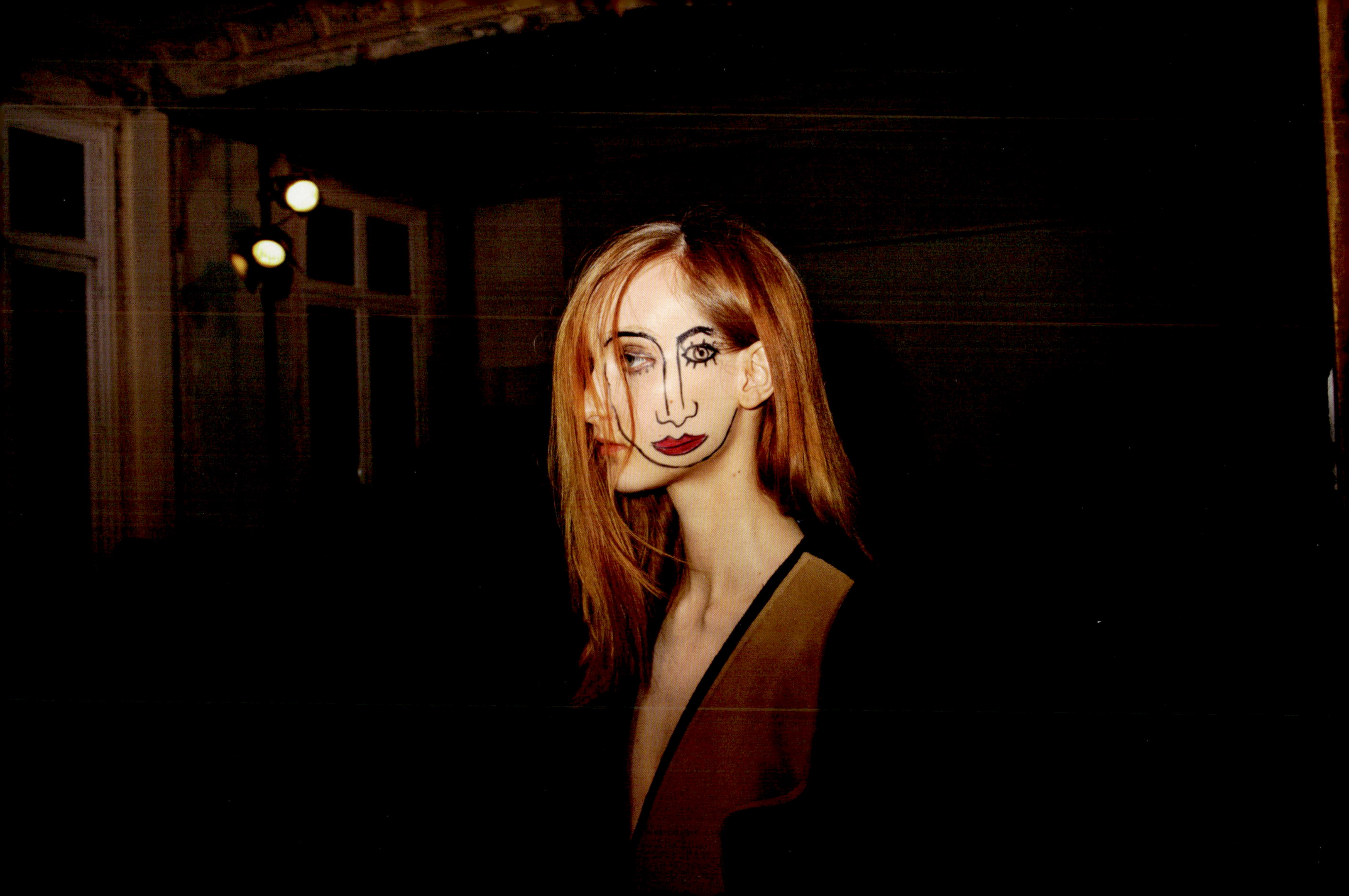

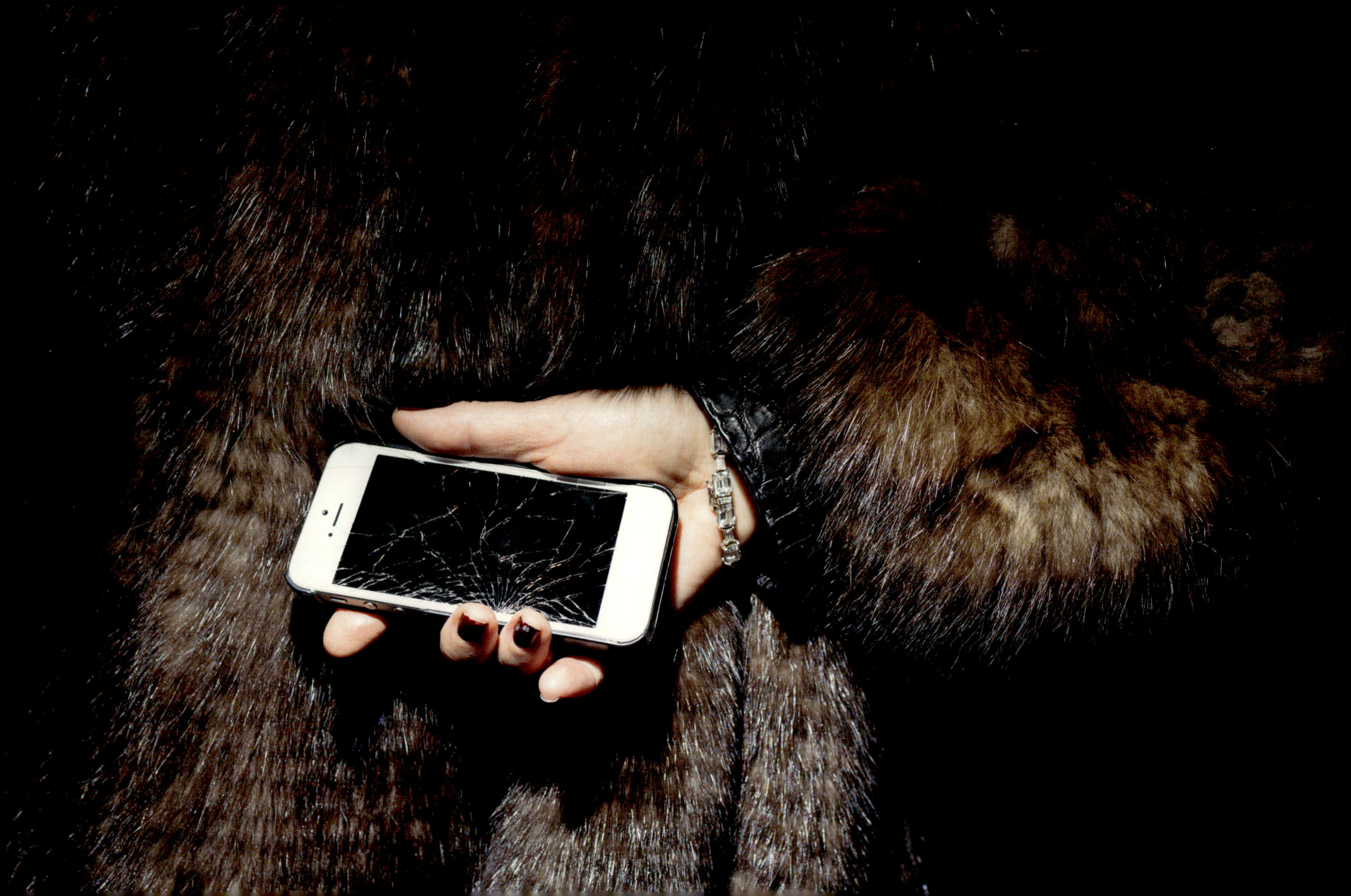

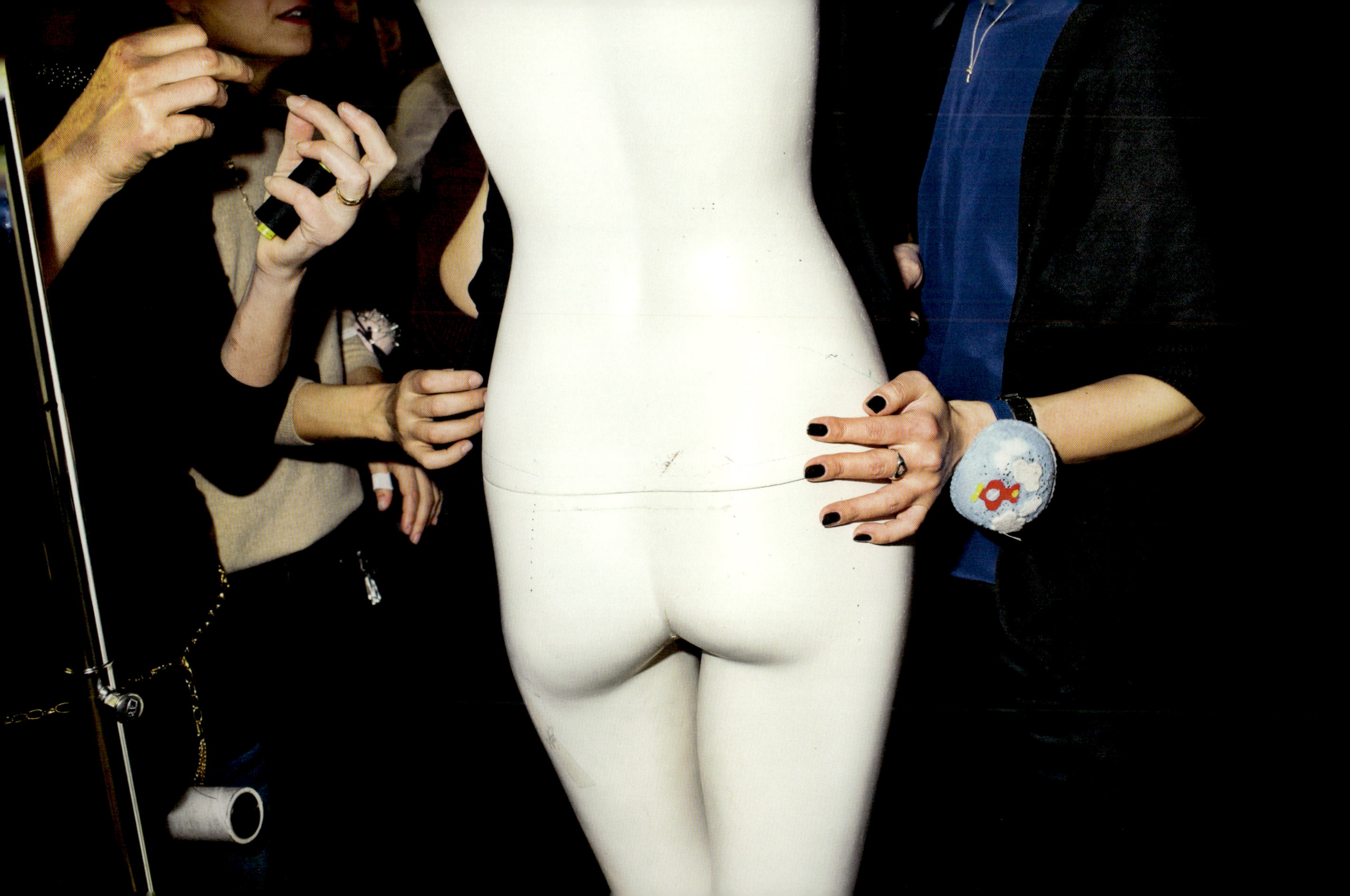

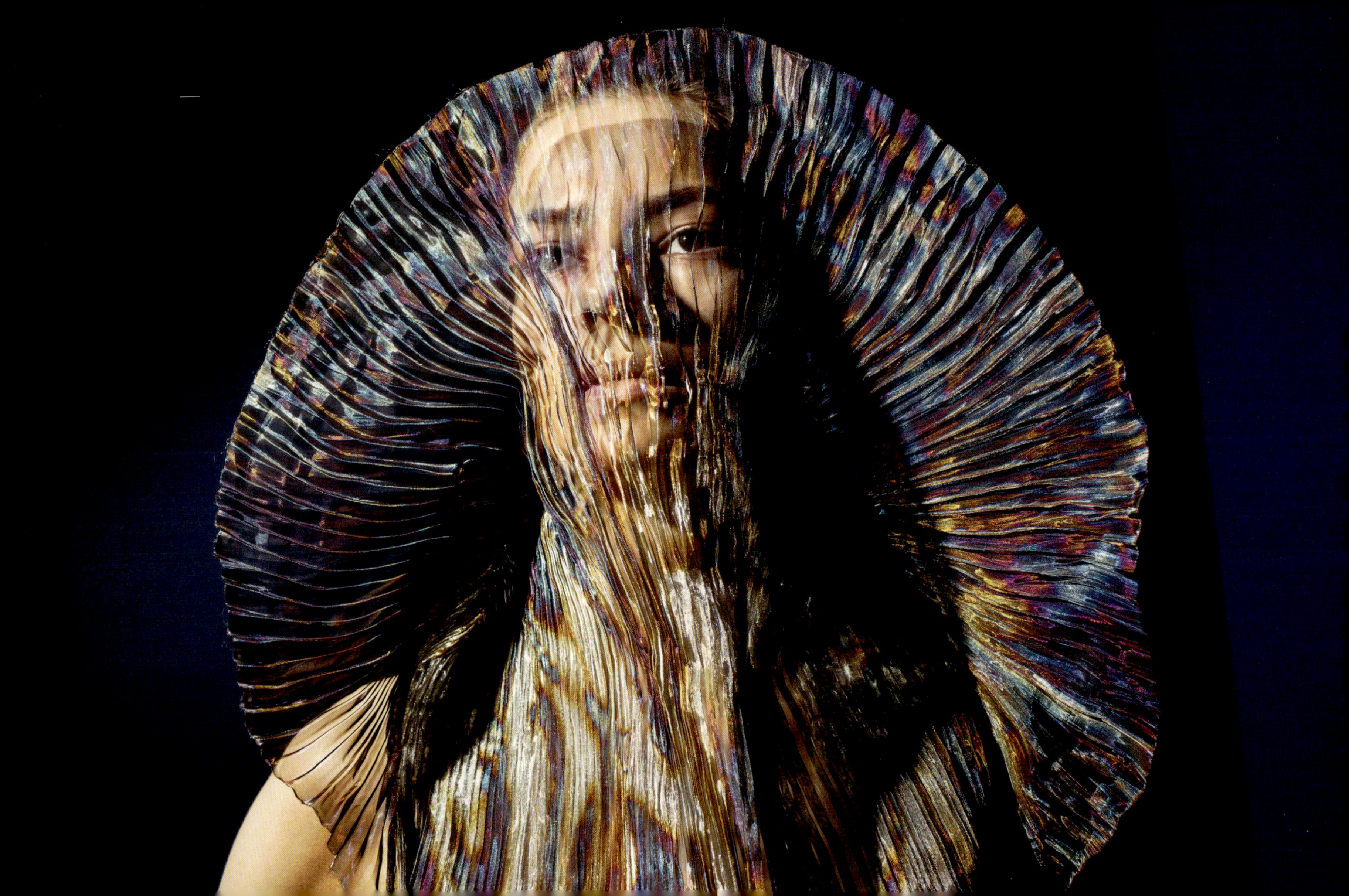

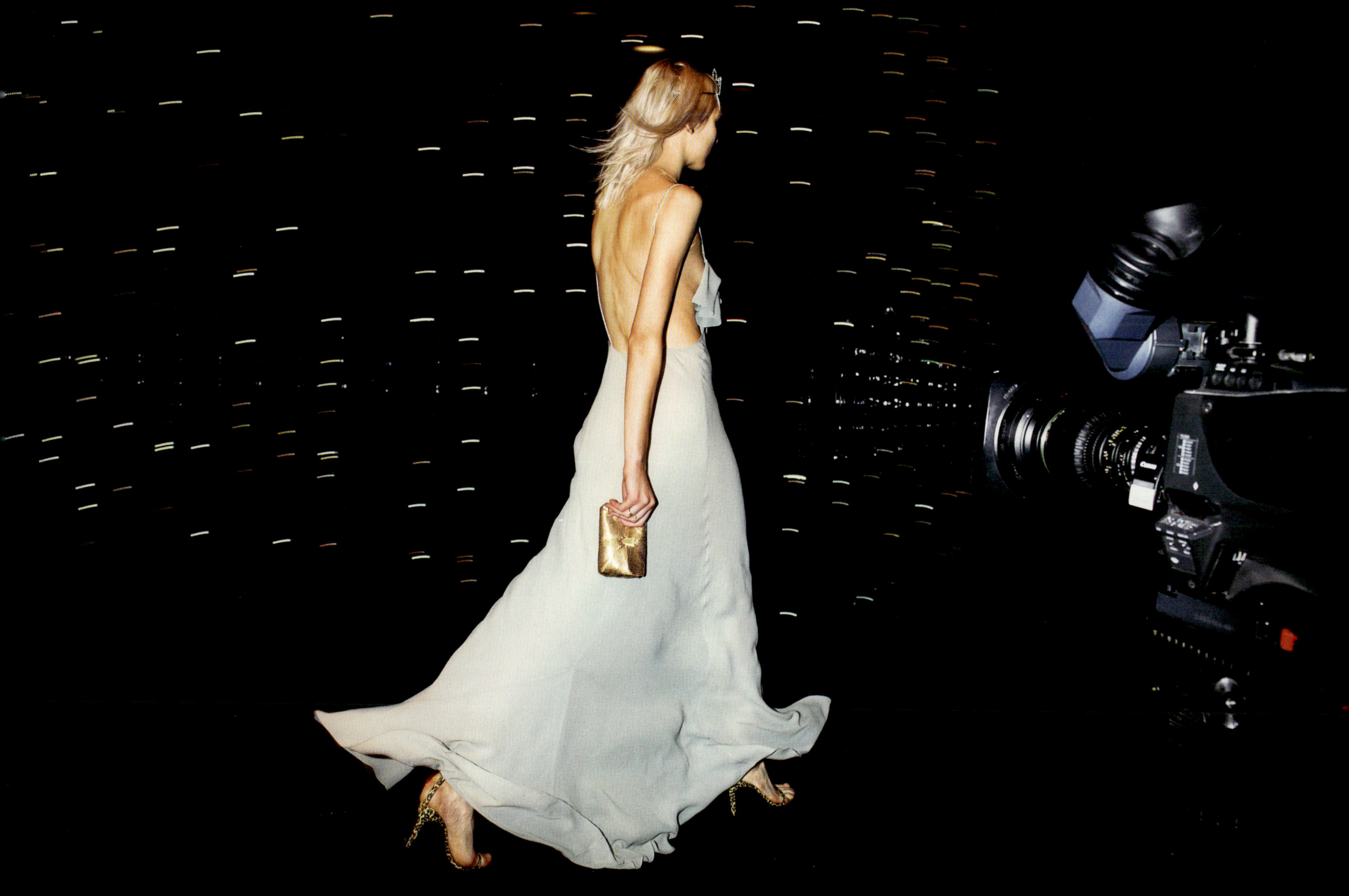

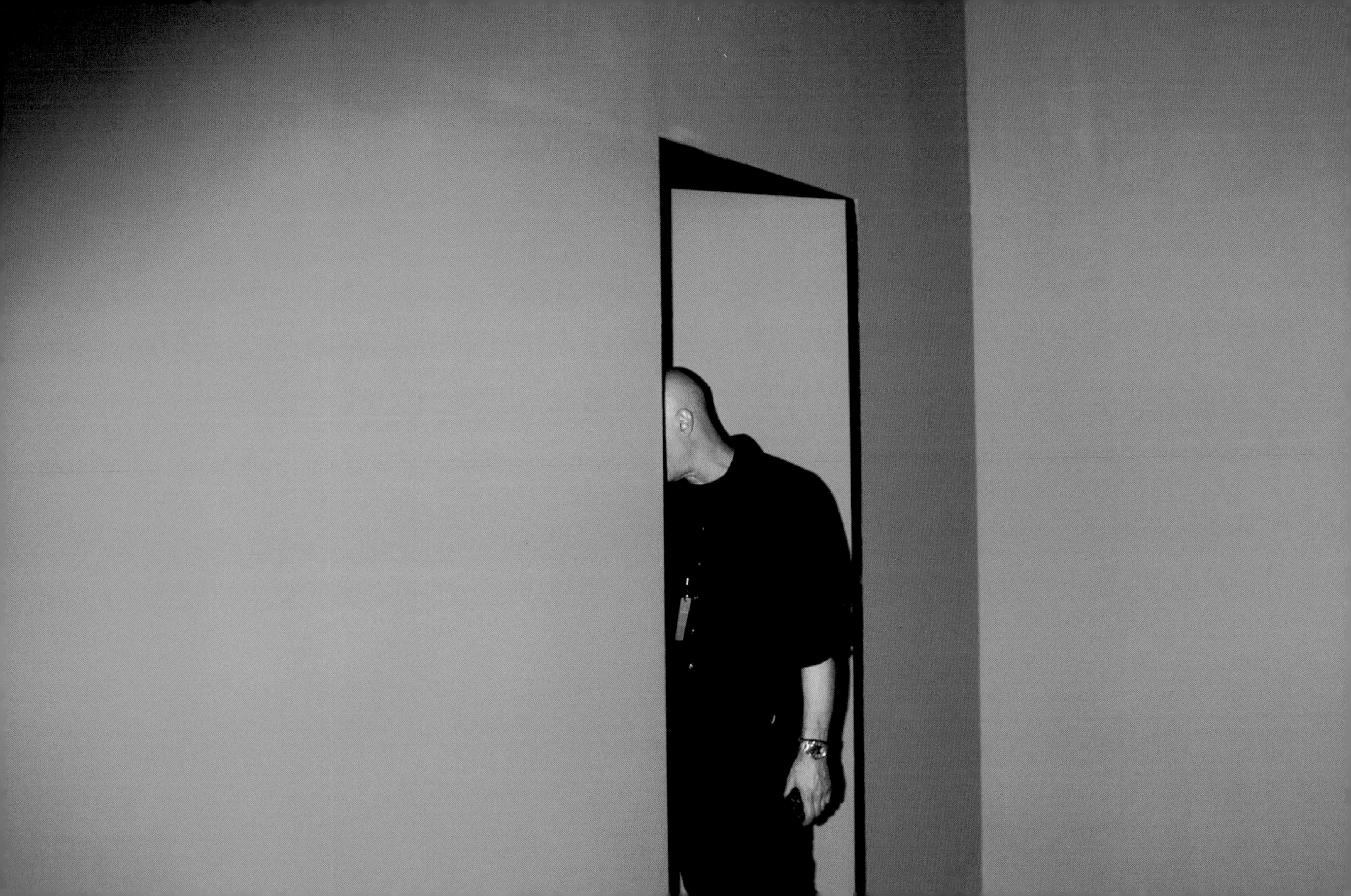

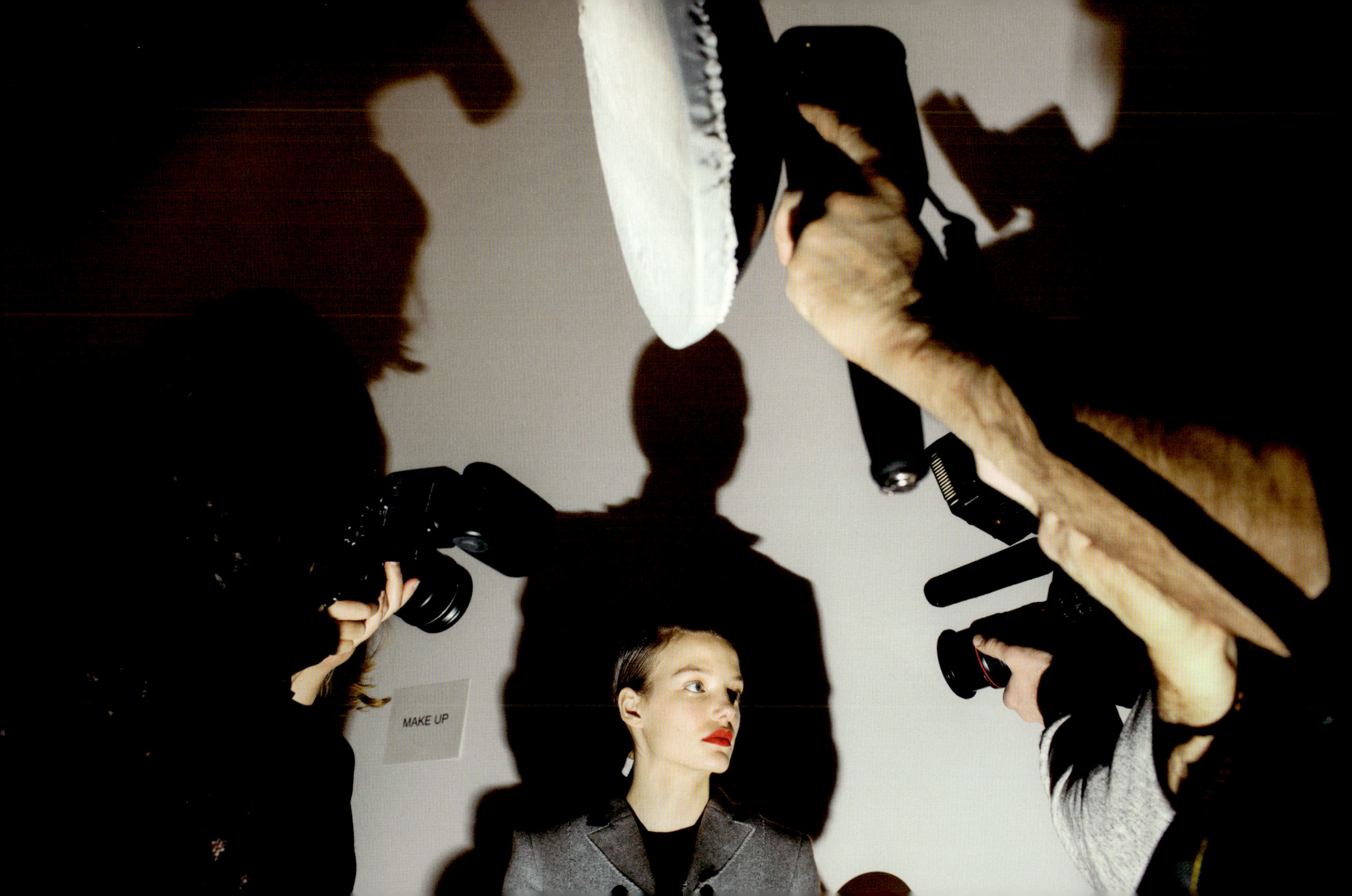
MAKE UP

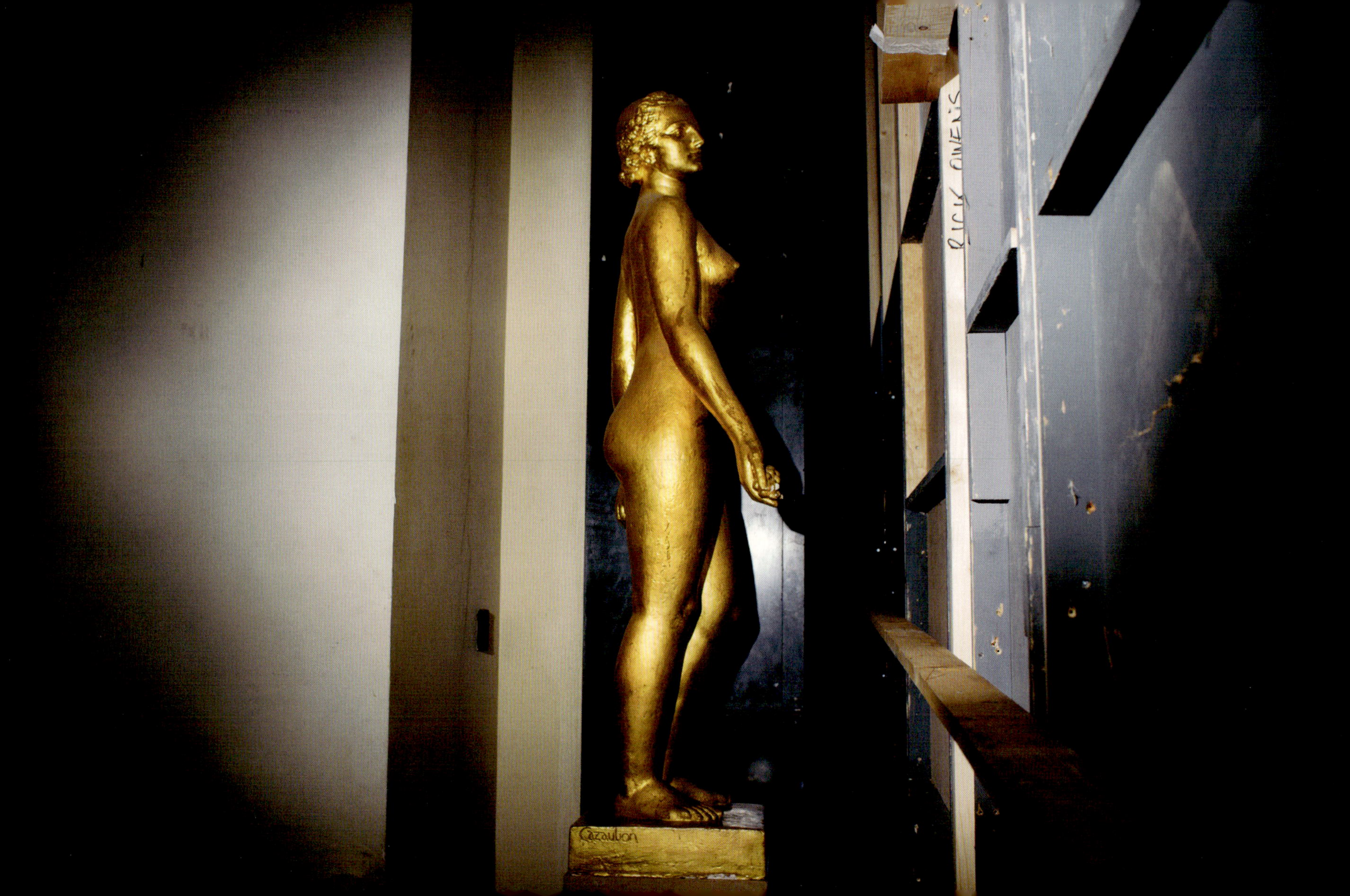
Cazaubon
RICK OWENS

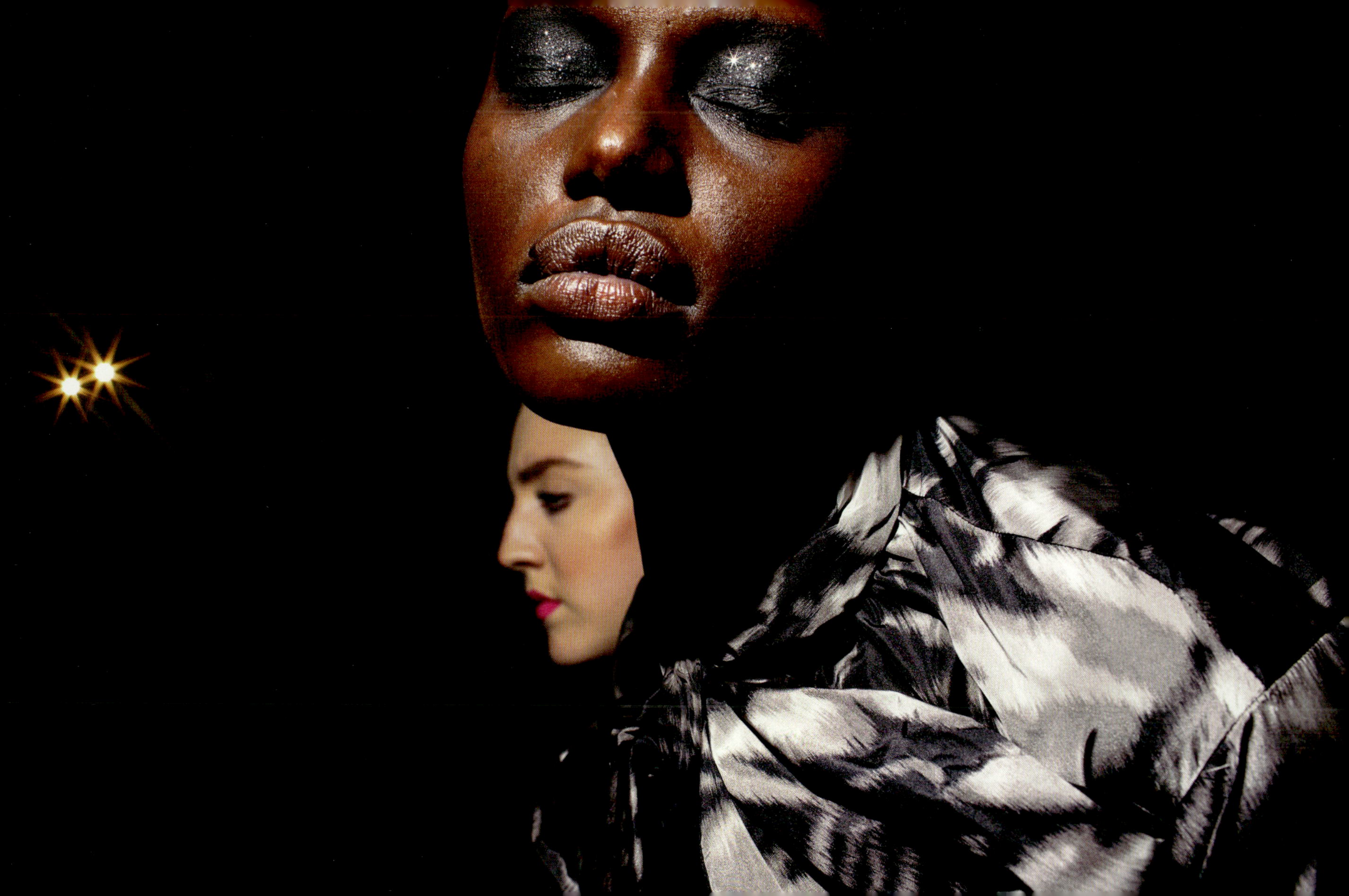

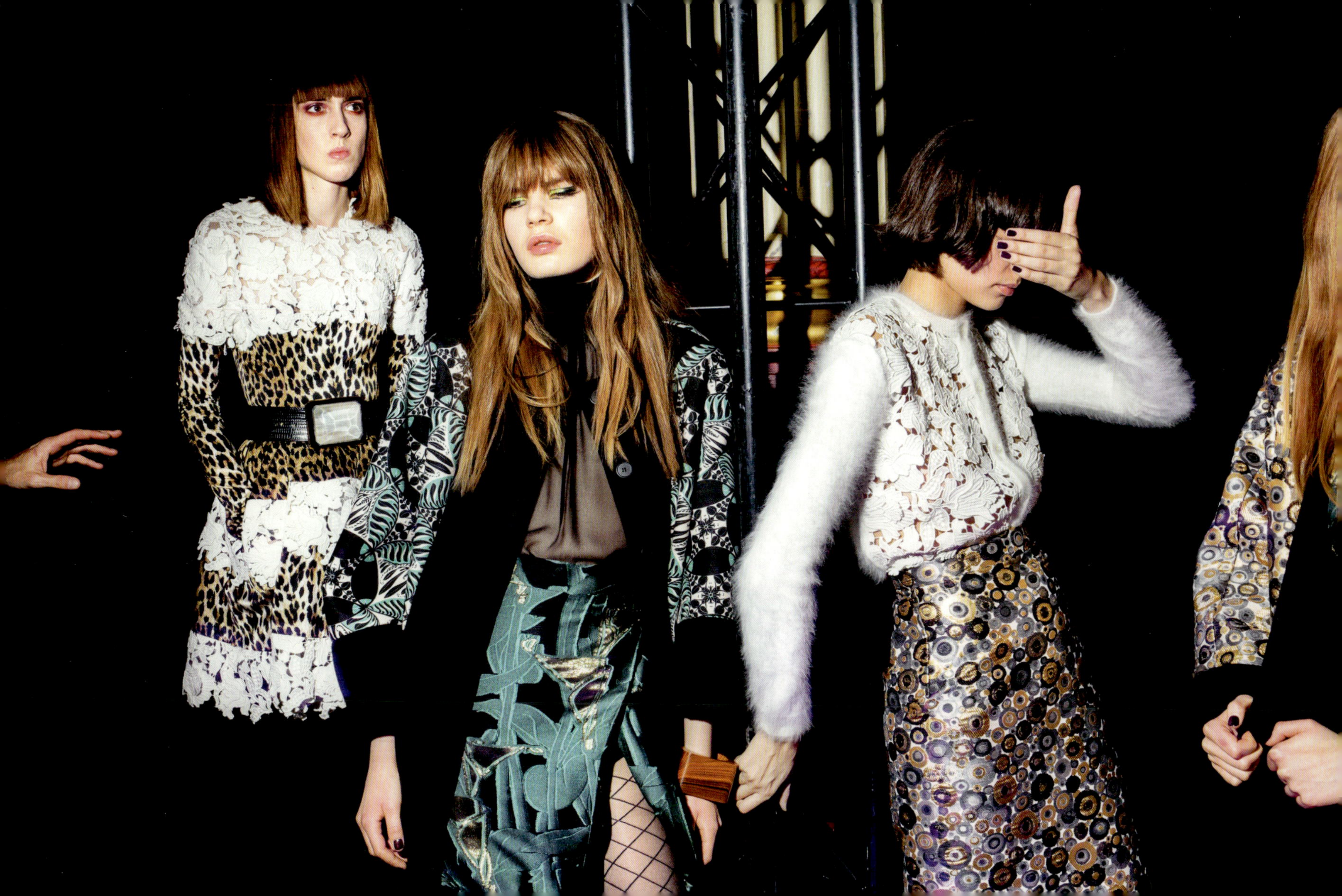

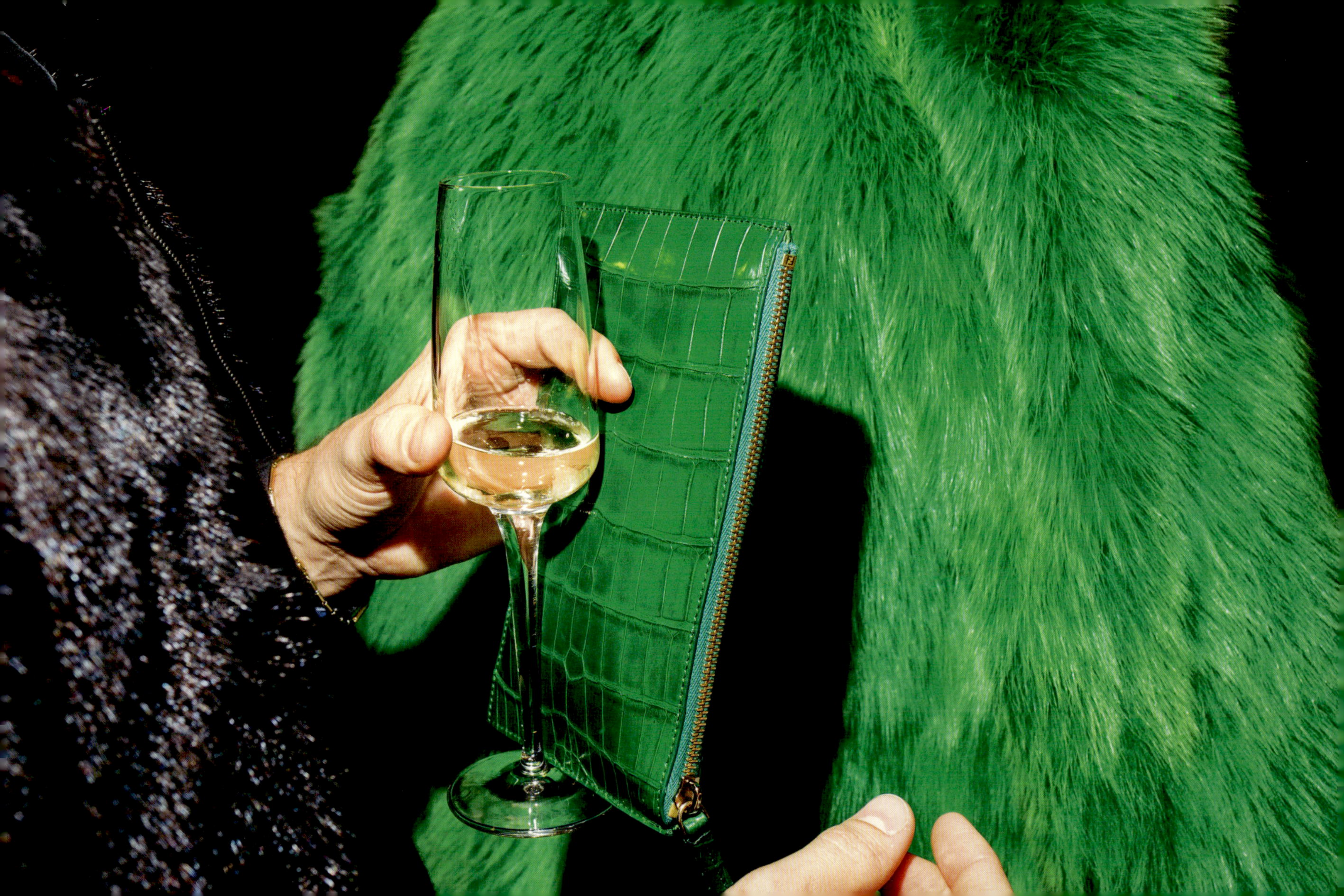

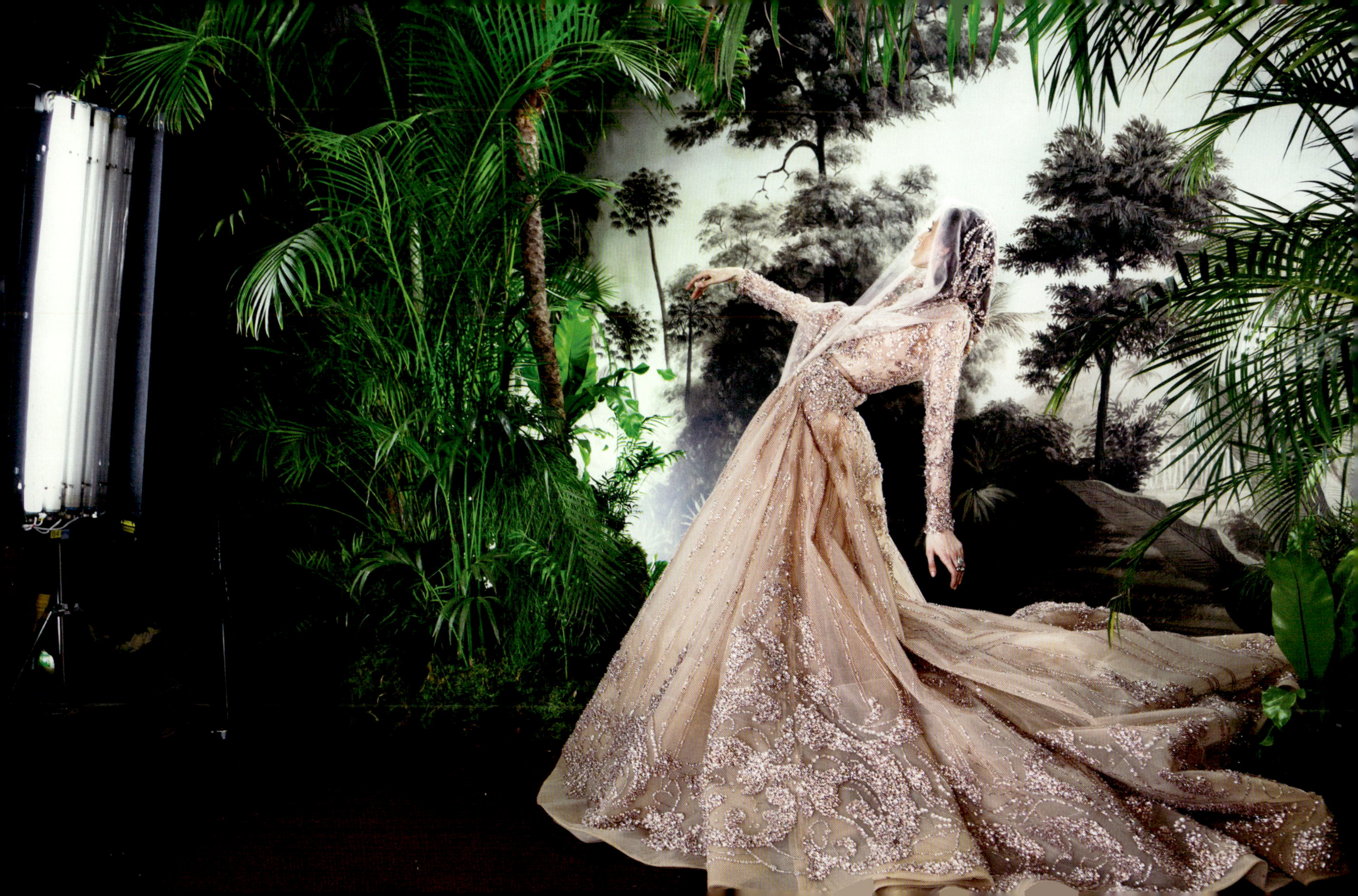

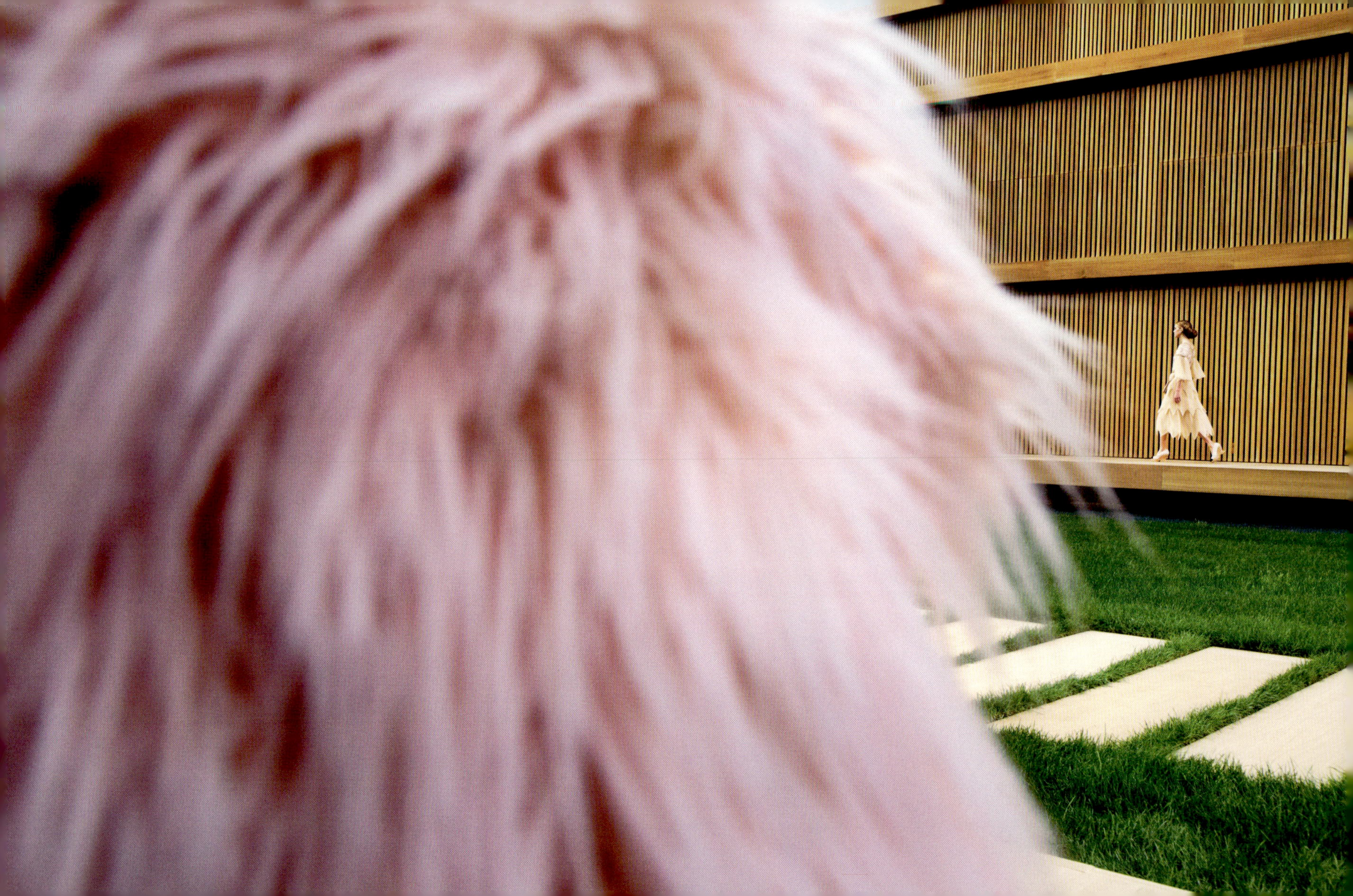

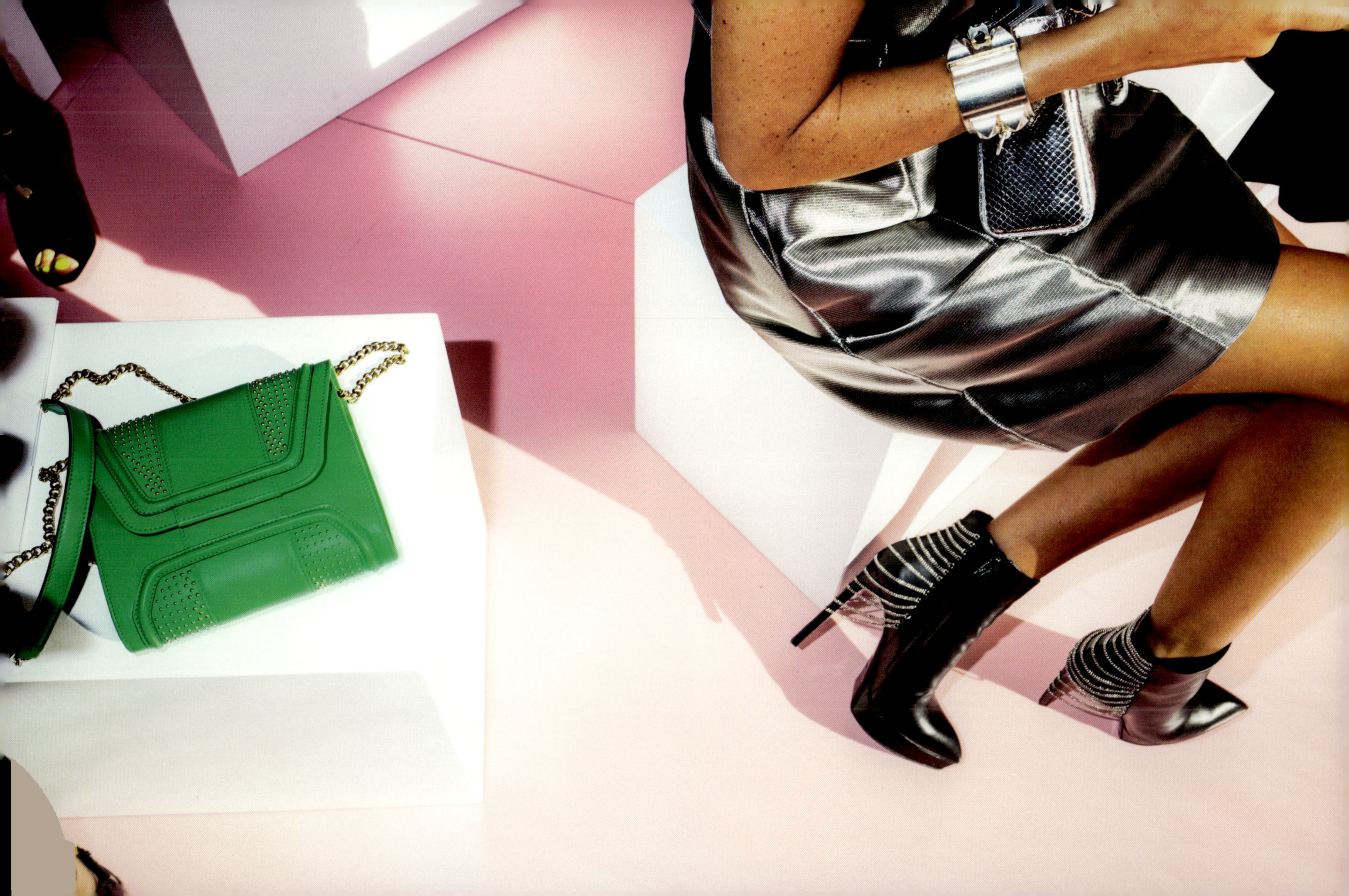

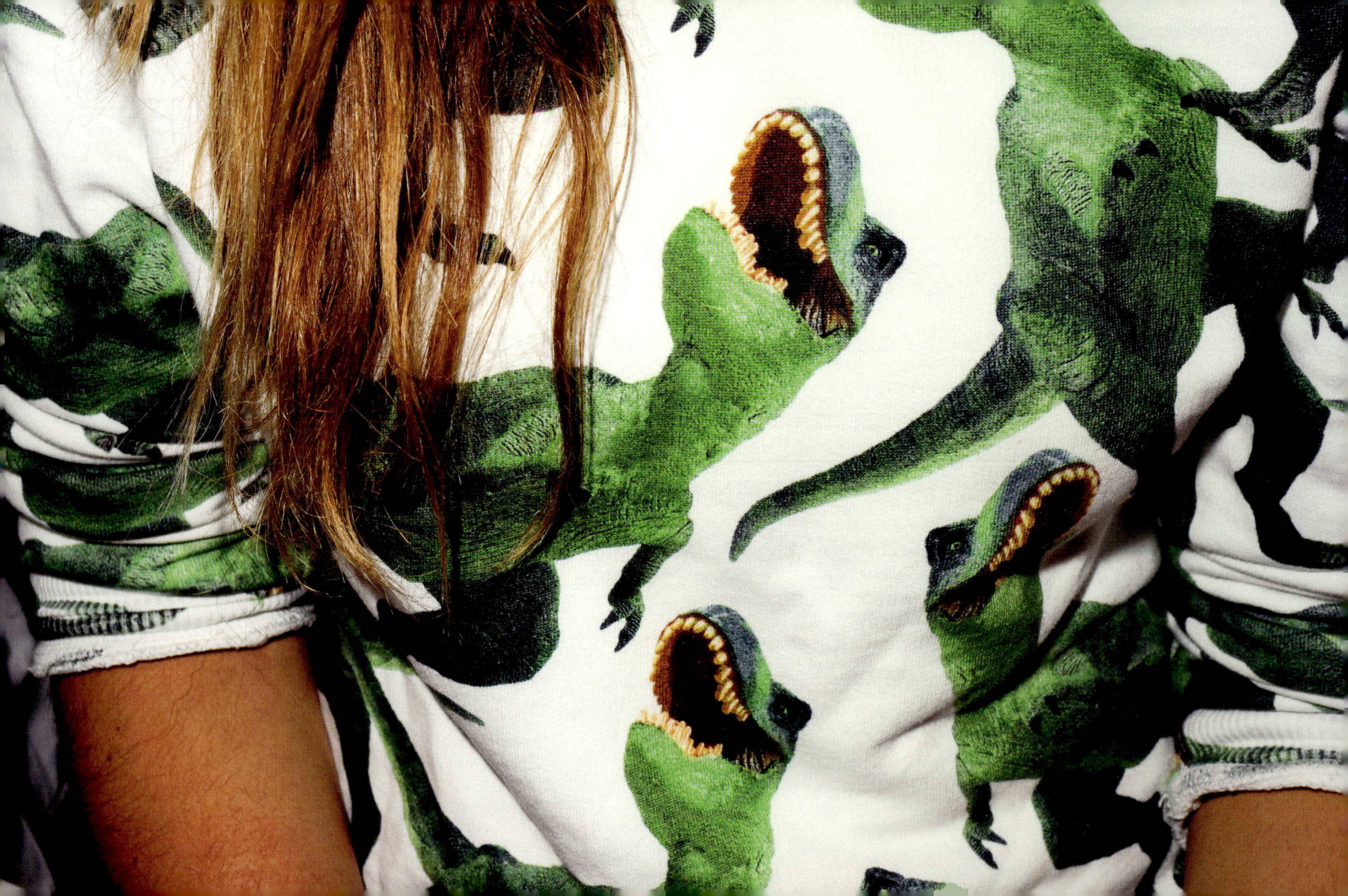

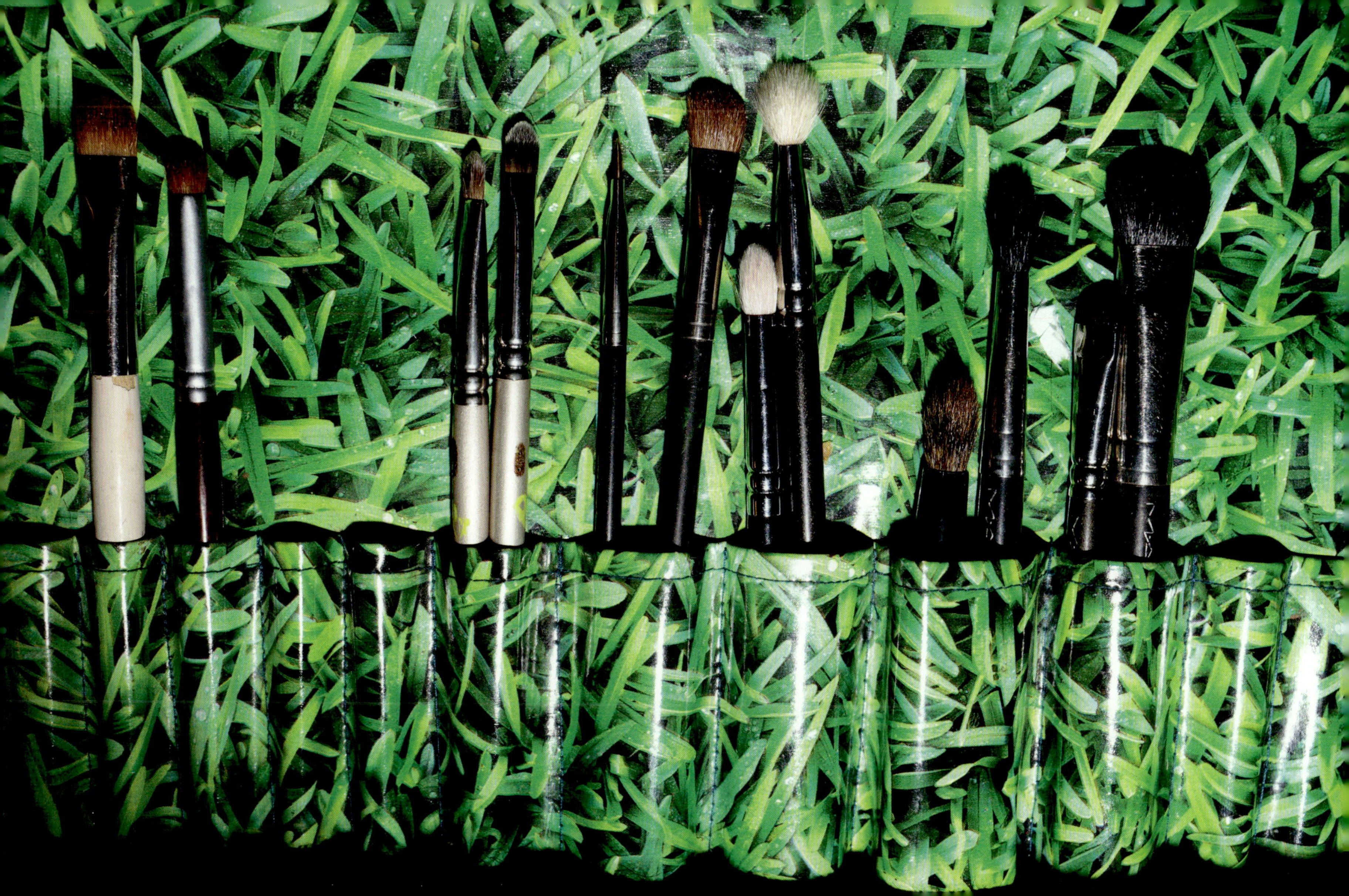

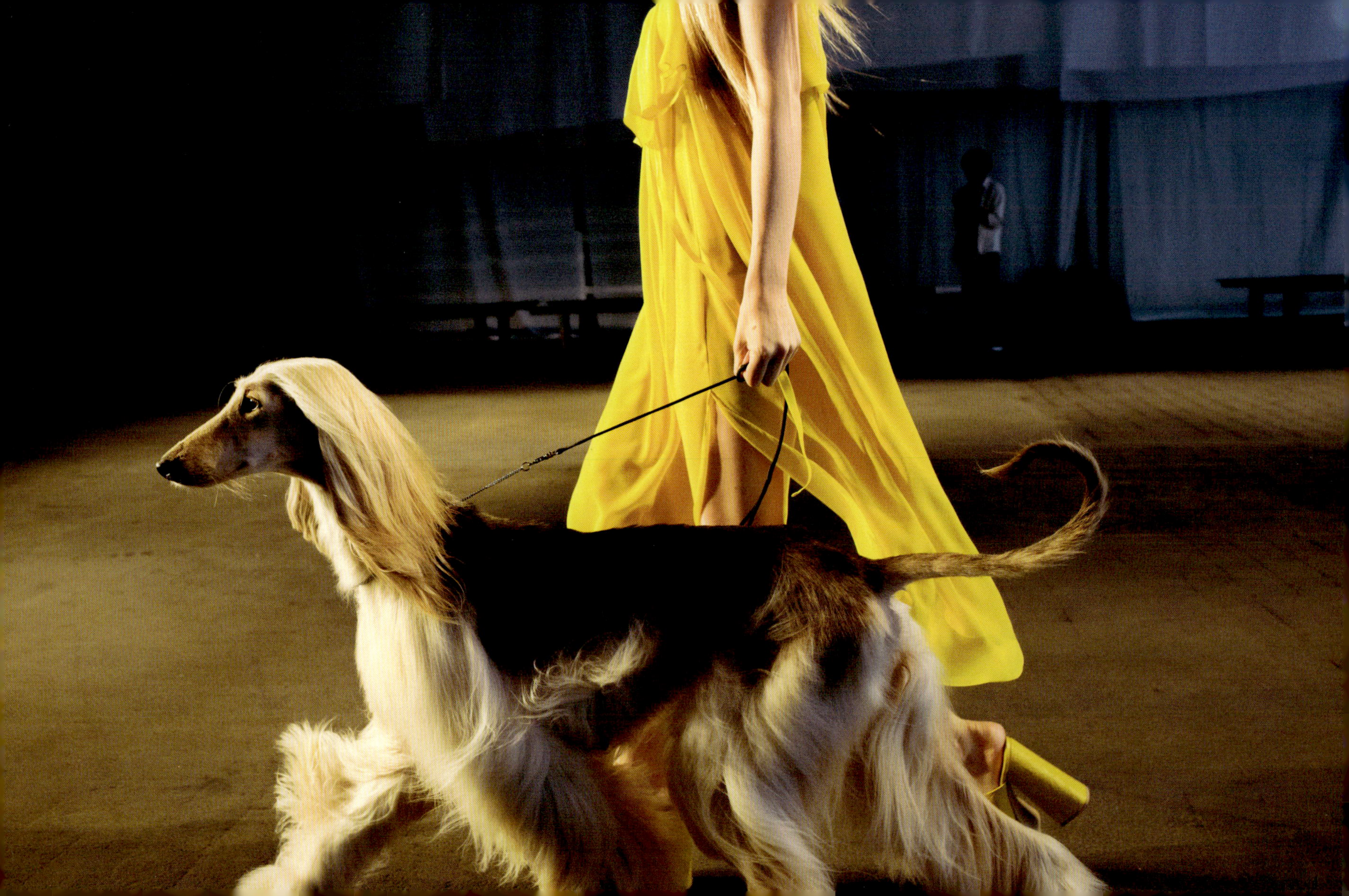

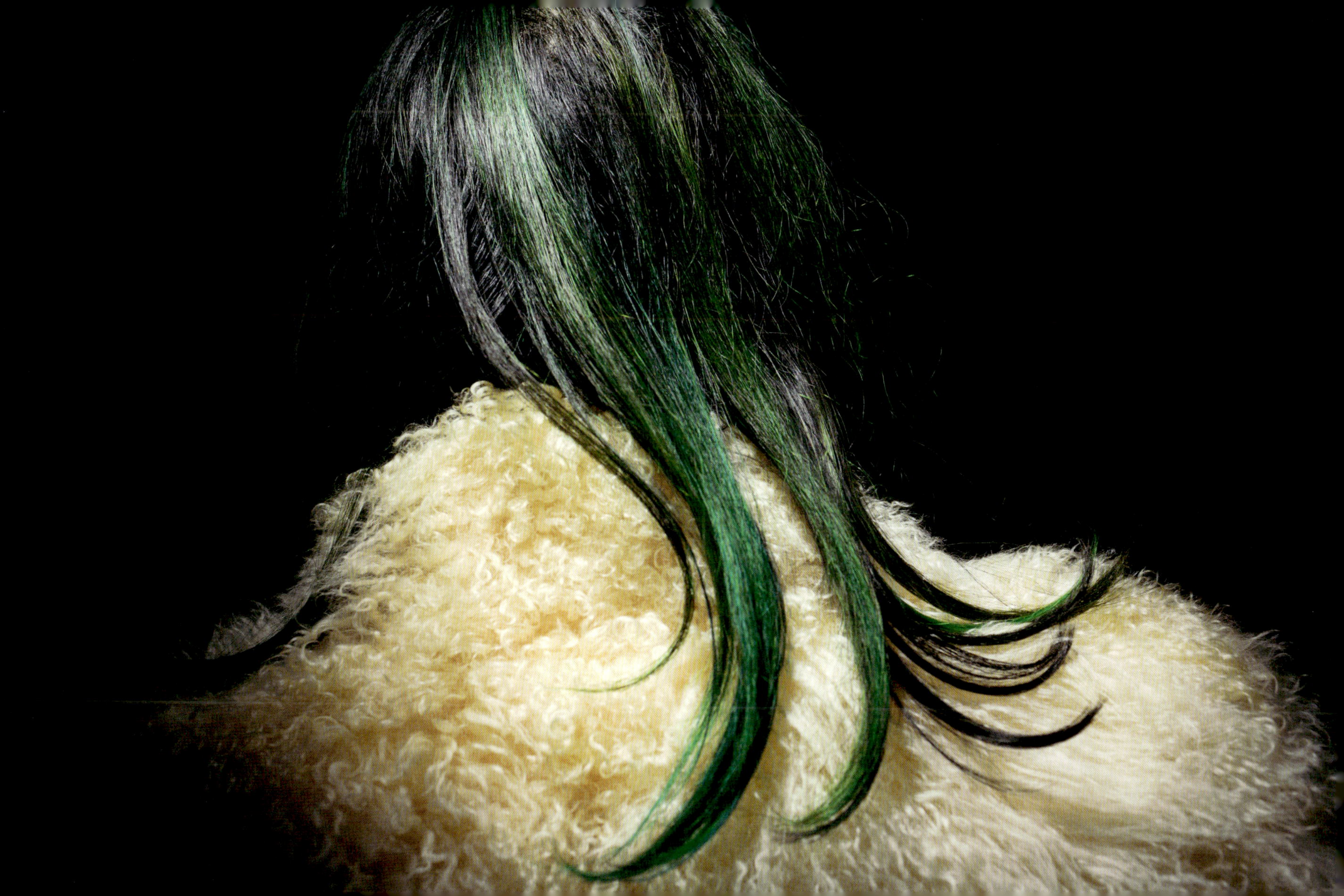

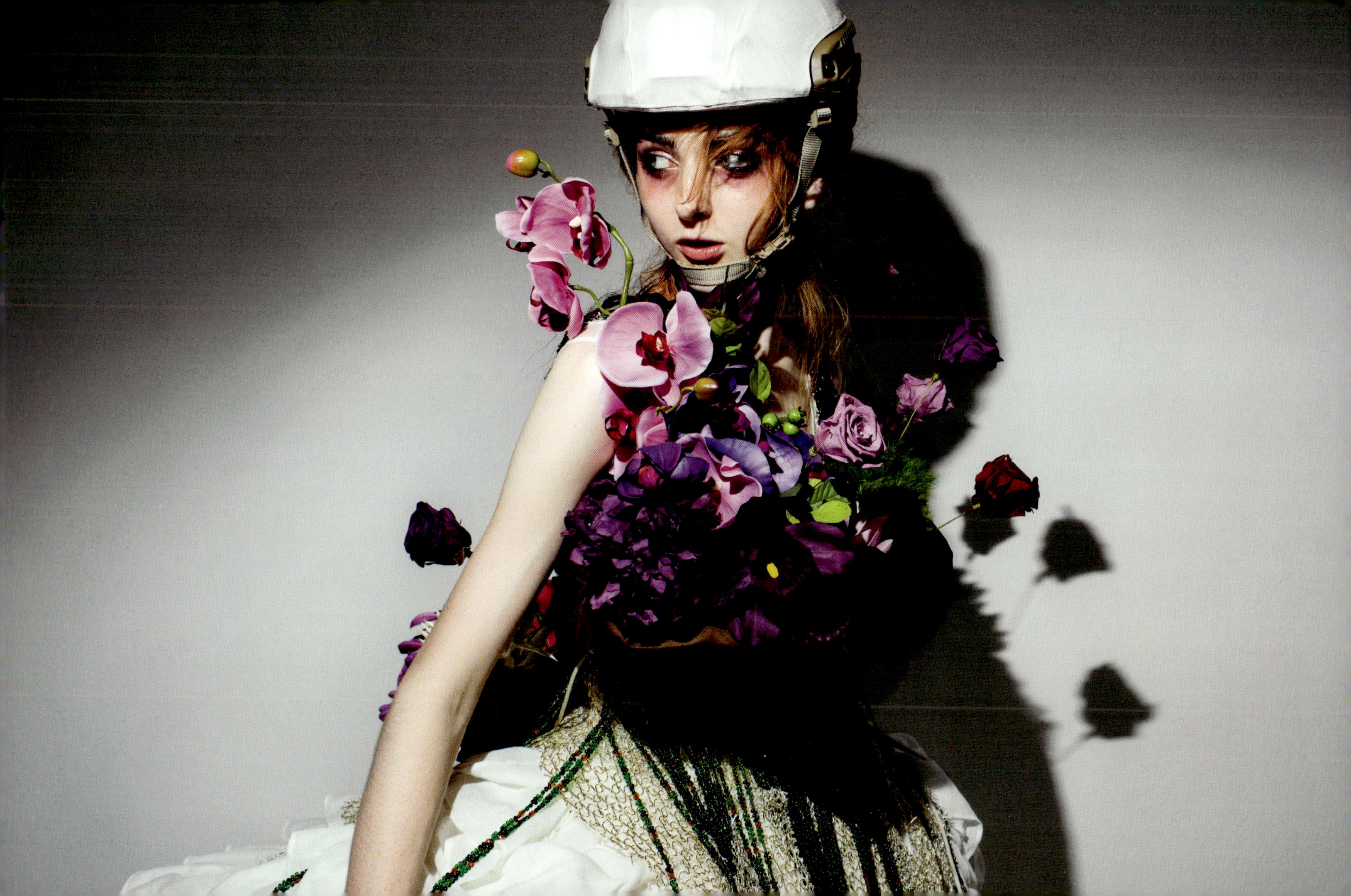

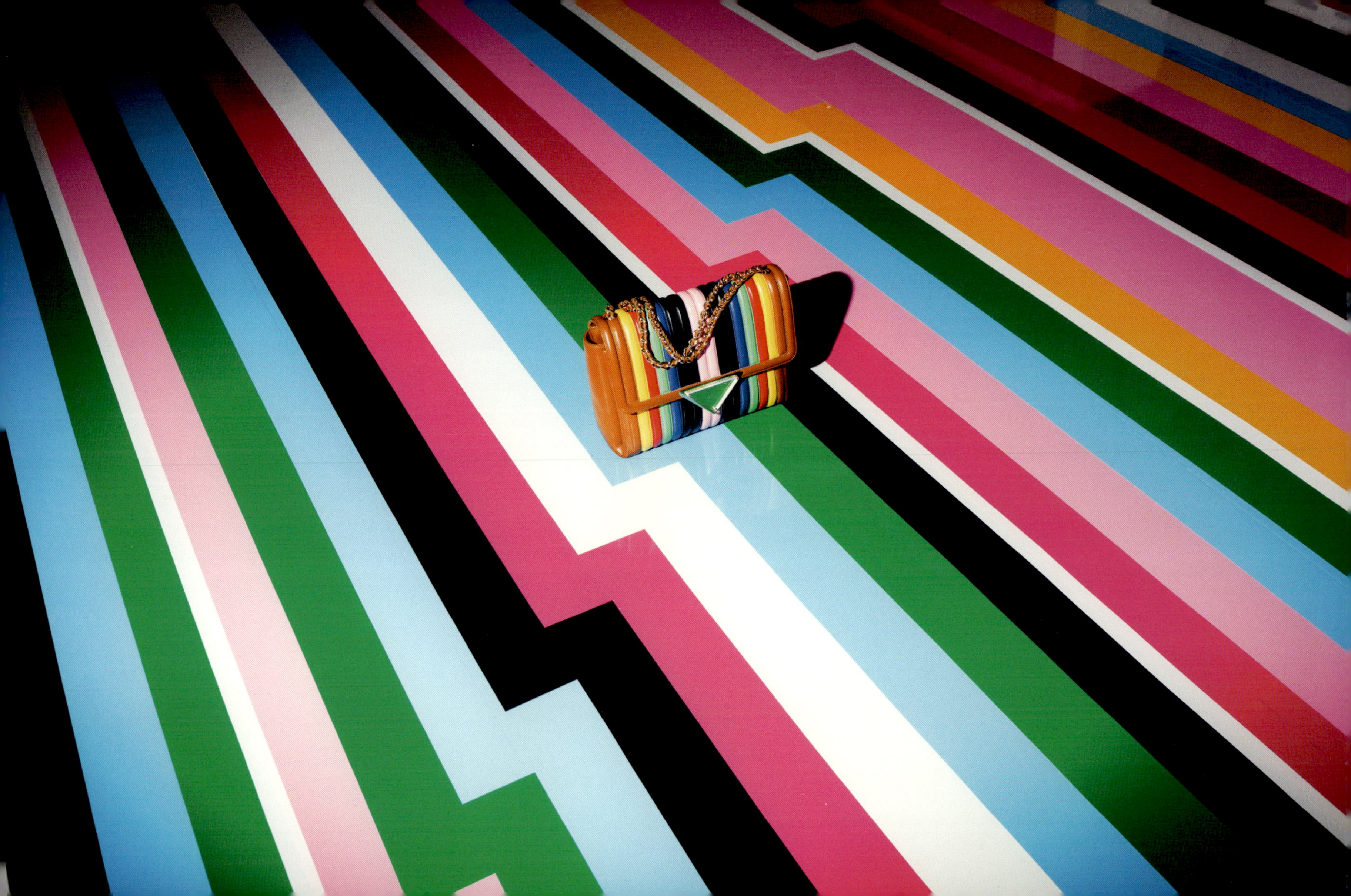

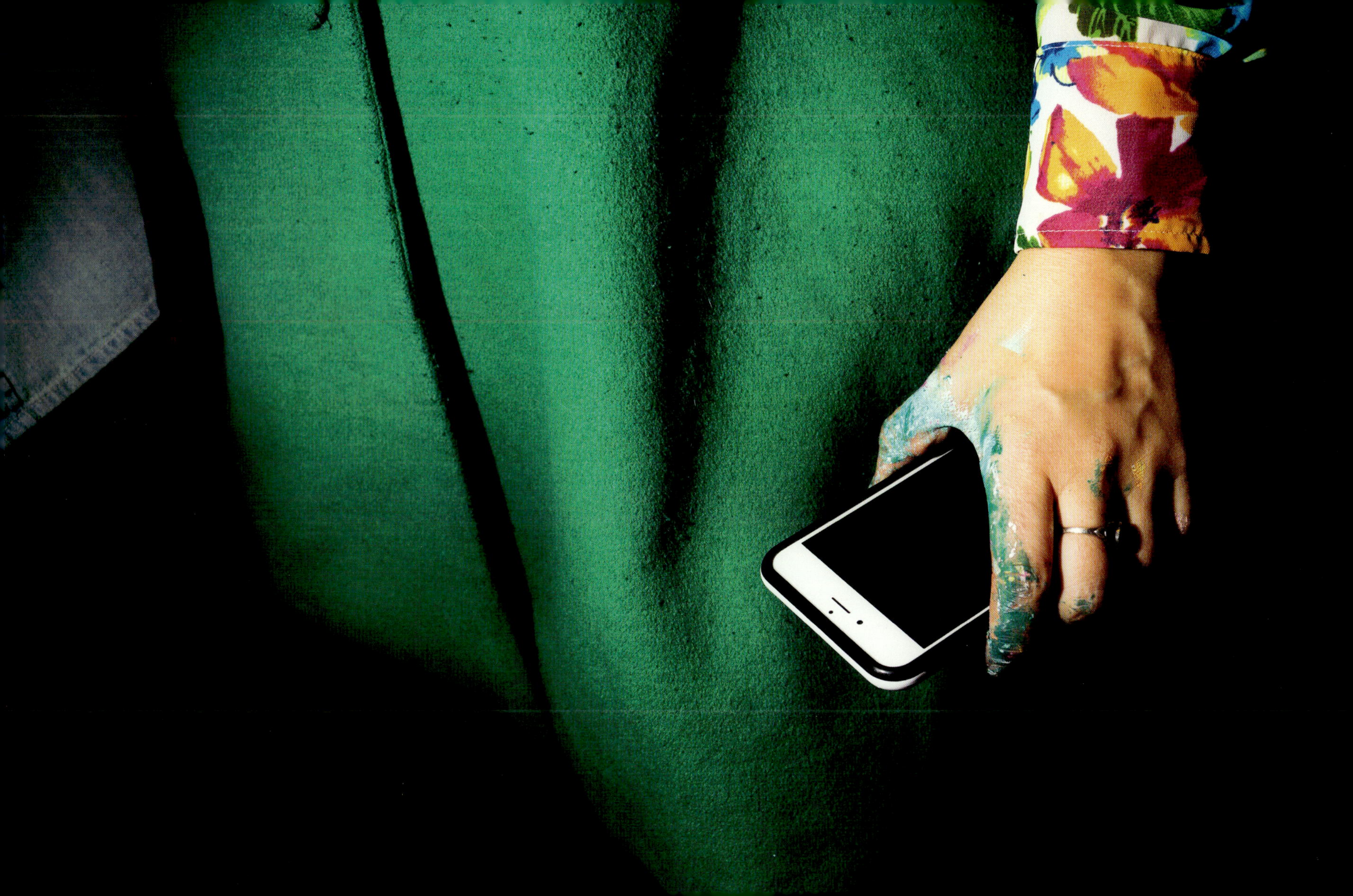

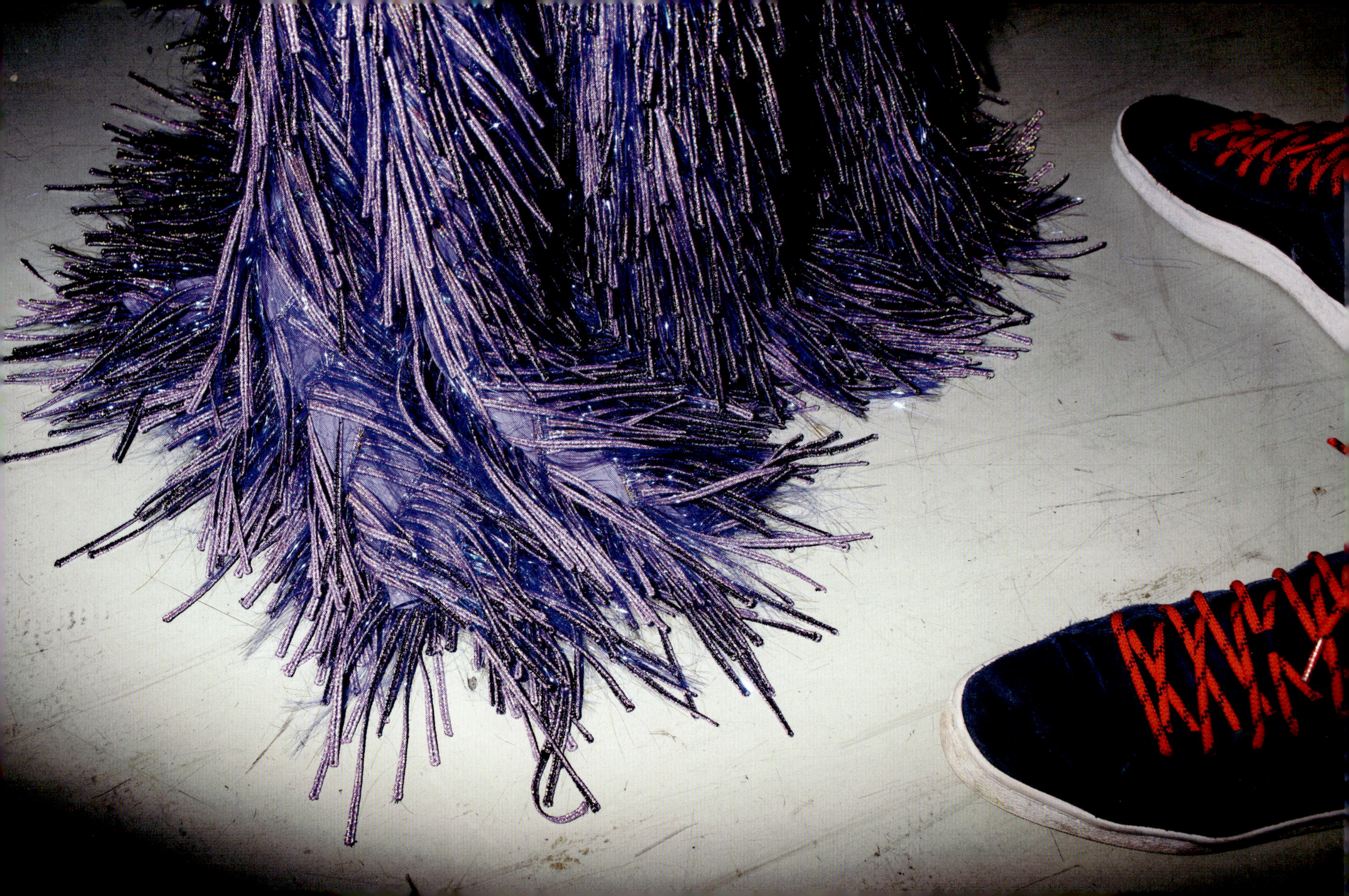

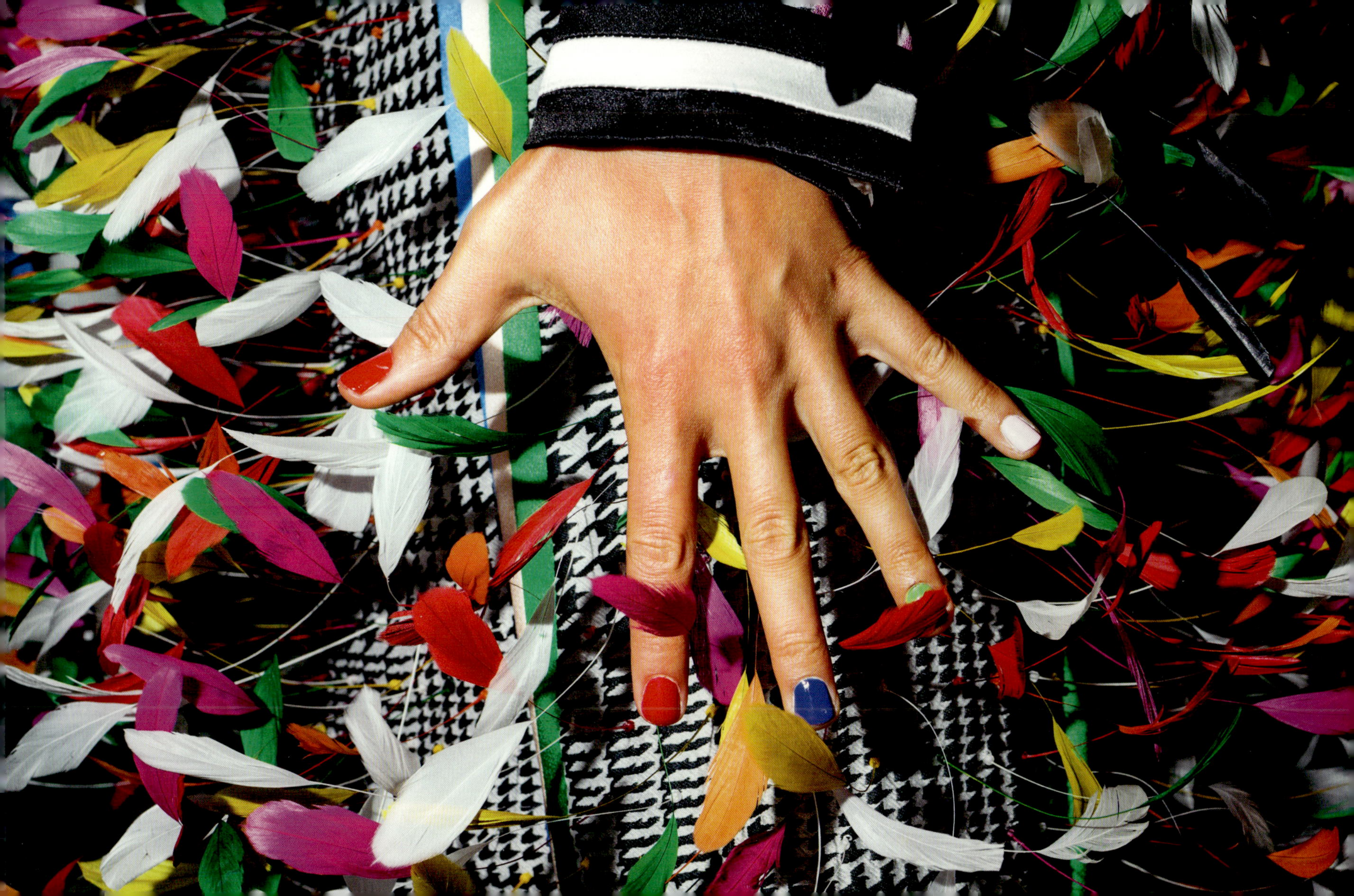

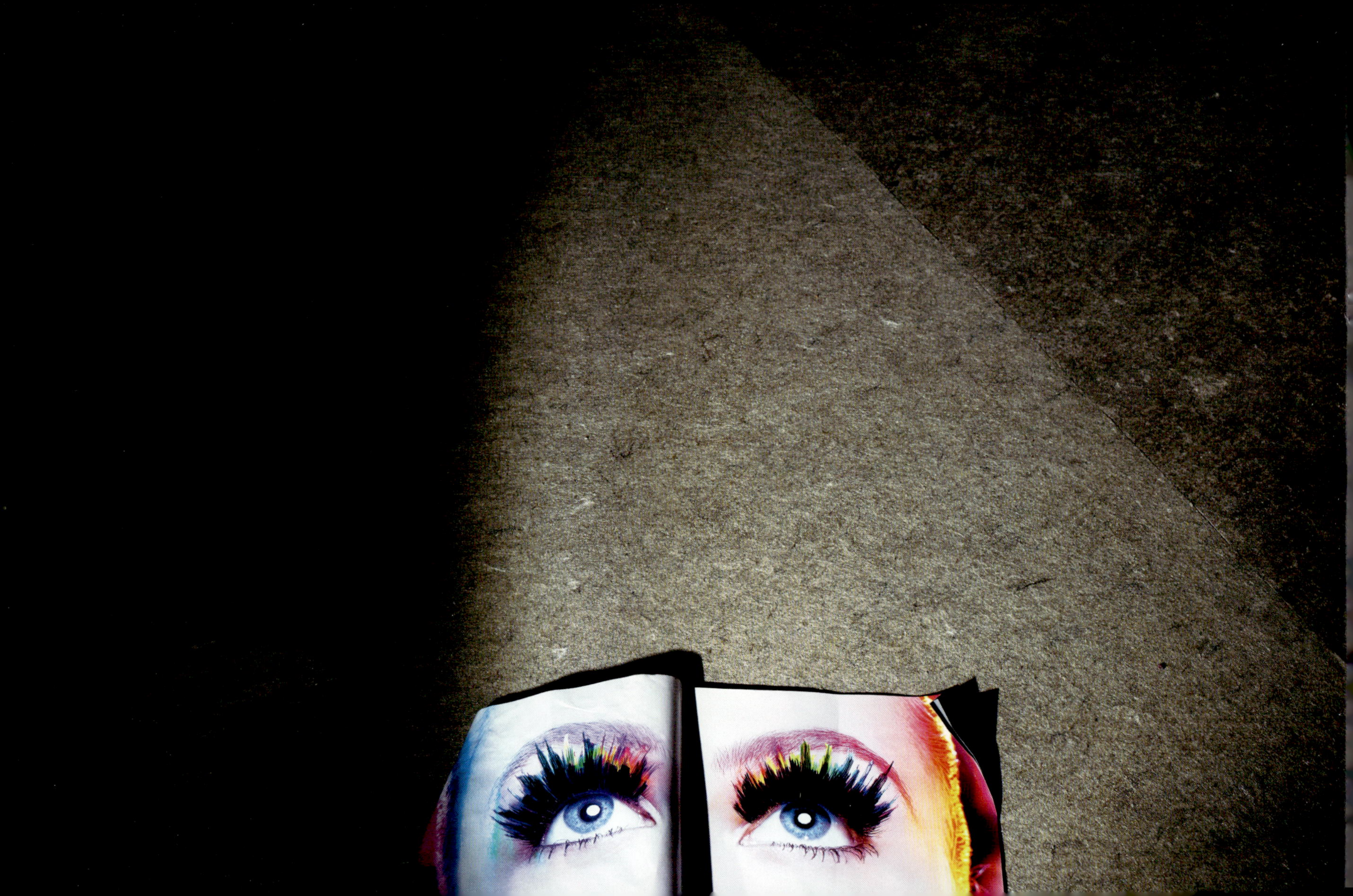

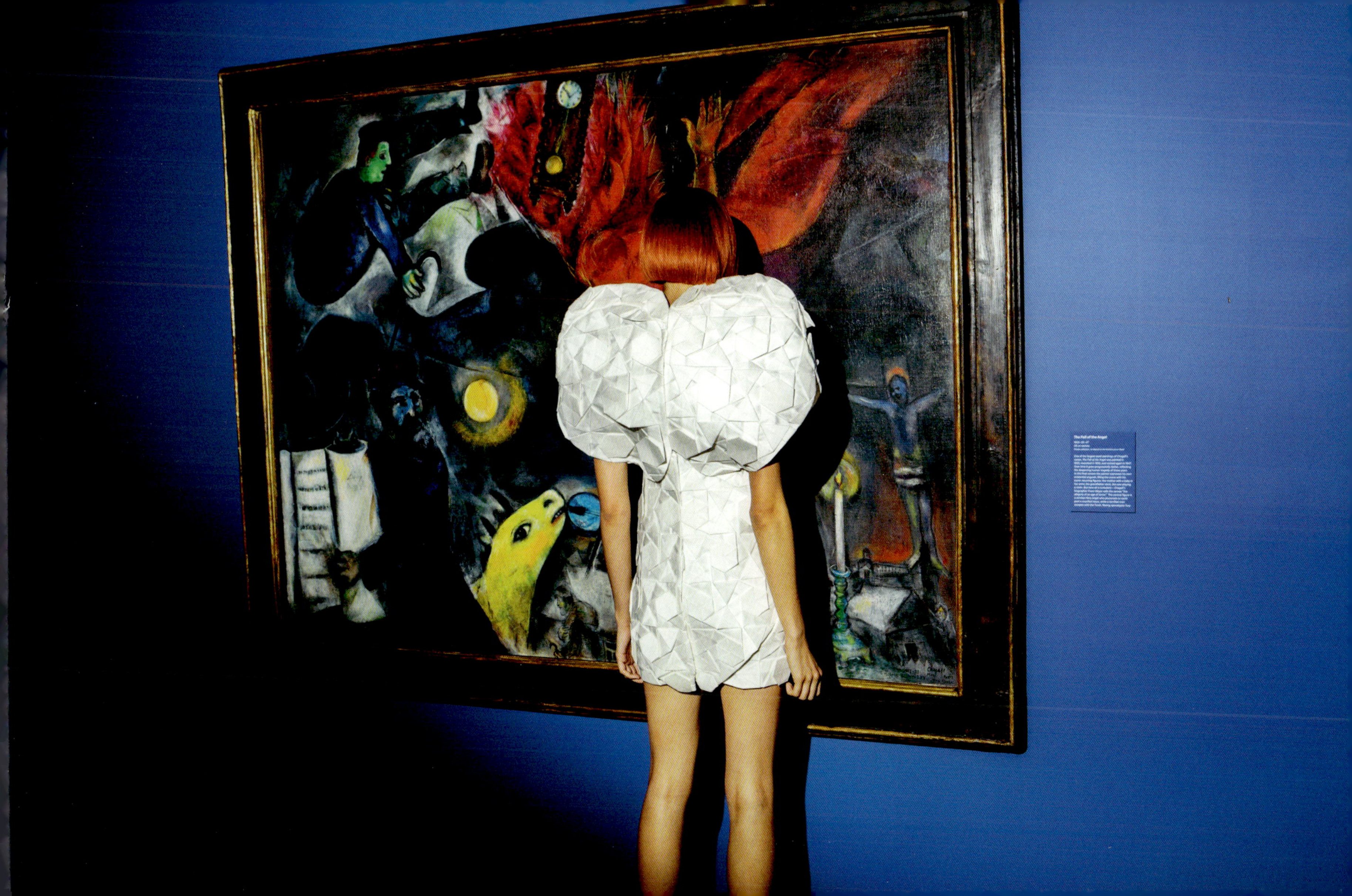
The Fall of the Angel

FROM DOG WALK TO CAT WALK BY ELISABETH BIONDI

What do the Westminster Kennel Club Dog Show and a Marc Jacobs fashion show have in common? They both are great spectacles watched by an adoring crowd, and Landon Nordeman has photographed each of them a number of times. In the case of the Westminster dog show, the cream-of-the-crop show, dogs compete for the prestigious title of "Best in Show." The Marc Jacobs fashion show, attended by fashion insiders and celebrities, is an extravaganza presenting the designer's signature pieces in spectacular settings.

I looked at Landon's portfolio with his wonderful dog show pictures in 2004 when I was the visuals editor at the *New Yorker*. I loved what I saw. This was the beginning of Landon working as a regular contributor to the magazine for many years and dozens of assignments. Several years later a smart picture editor at *New York Magazine* thought that Landon might have the same magic touch photographing fashion shows. Voilà, it was the beginning of a great body of work from fashion weeks here and in Europe, which can be admired in the pages of this book.

In the many years I have been looking at photographs, I must have seen thousands of fashion show pictures. Most of them, more or less successfully, concentrate on models in a zoo-like atmosphere, preparation for the runway, and the audience—invited guests and celebrities and fashionistas. Landon avoids the predictable coverage and instead concentrates on seemingly unimportant situations on the sidelines, or what happens behind the curtain. His eagerly roaming eyes instinctively settle on an overlooked detail, a surprising overall view, the Eiffel Tower looming in the center of the picture, constructivist shapes and patterns, in a way that only Landon can capture. He takes wry photographs of fashion and the fashionable but without malice, he reveals robot-like models, multitasking make-up artists, a woman doing pushups on the sidelines. He truly enjoys the pageantry, the foibles of the style conscious, and the over-the-top displays of vanity—they all make up the spectacle for him.

Many years of working in the documentary tradition have trained Landon to instinctively catch with his camera what visually comes together to make an original picture. It may appear to be effortless but there is nothing arbitrary about his single-minded concentration and in-the-moment observation. Every split second counts and some of his best pictures were made during complete chaos. They are perfectly composed and lively at the same time. They pose questions and seduce the viewer into looking carefully to figure out what is going on. It helps that Landon has a sense of humor, or more important perhaps, the talent to make witty pictures—a rare gift. However, he never makes fun of the people on the fashion merry-go-round—that would be too easy.

Yes, it is hard work in chaotic situations, which demands a go-with-the-flow attitude. While many photographers would be frustrated to work in an often-confined setting—never assured of access and freedom to move around—Landon understands and relishes taking uncontrolled pictures in a highly controlled environment. His pictures never look restricted; on the contrary, they are free, funny, often a little strange, and unconventional. Landon's colors are intense. The images sparkle, which add to their allure. His brightly saturated colors often give the photos a surreal, outer space feeling. Landon's fashion images are fun and super cool while his dog show pictures are witty and heartwarming. Coming full circle, there also is a great dog picture in Out of Fashion. It is a wonderful image of a lissome model wearing a softly floating gown. A gorgeous Afghan hound, as stylish as his mistress for the evening, is leading her down the runway.

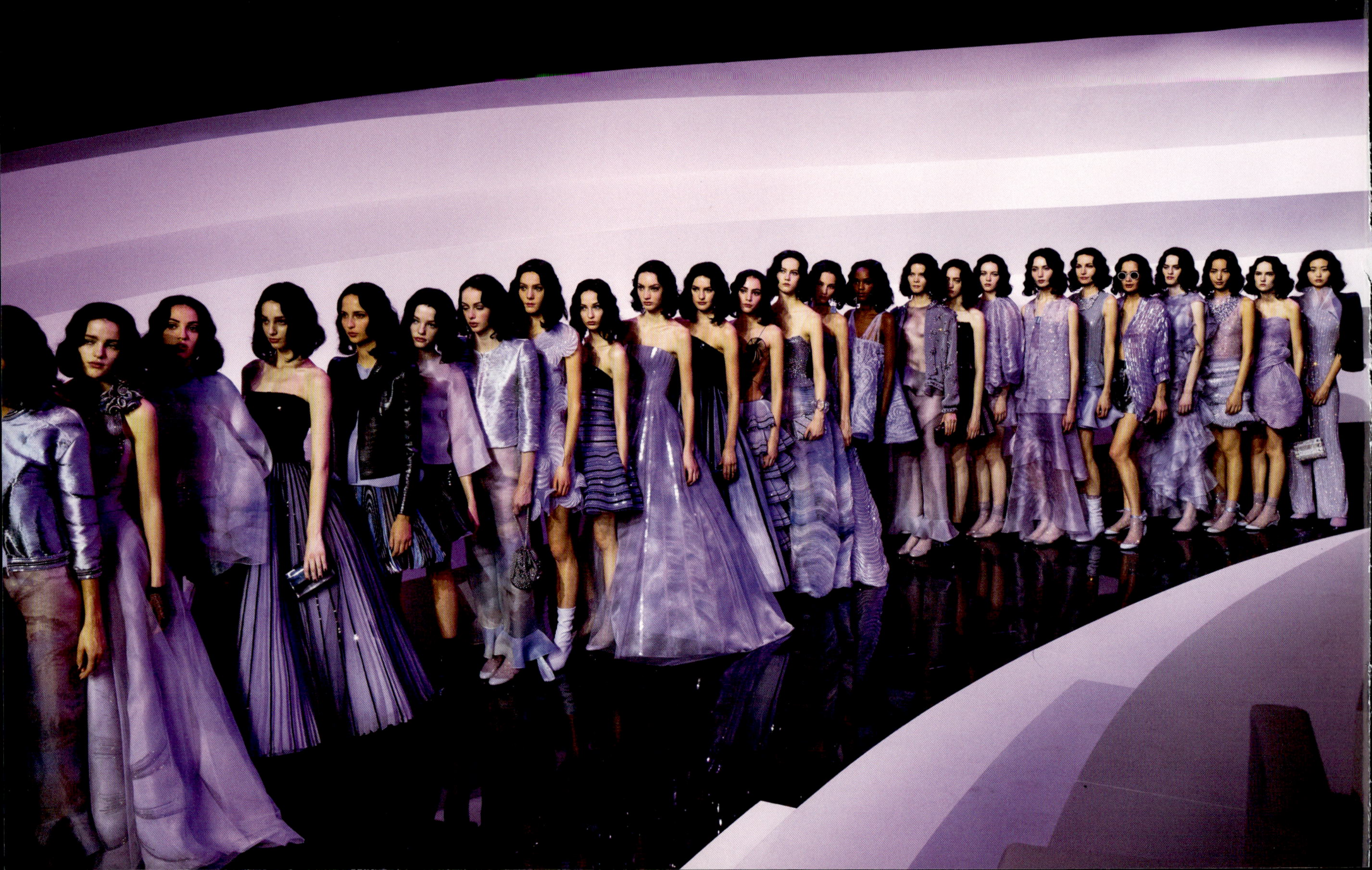

ACKNOWLEDGMENTS

Thank you to Stella Bugbee at *New York Magazine / The Cut* for sending me on this adventure, which revealed something that I didn't know about myself: I love photographing fashion. I am forever grateful for the opportunity.

Thank you to Beth Bristow at the *New York Times* for expanding the adventure to the couture shows in Paris and Paris Fashion week.

Thank you to Emily Shornick for your encouragement and edit, which helped me survive and thrive through it all.

Thank you to Sarah Colton and the Family Nix for making me feel at home in Paris.

To all the kind people at KCD, PR Consulting, Karla Otto, and Black Frame: Thank you.

To all the photographers who helped me navigate the backstage one way or another: thank you. You know who you are.

For the production and design of this book, thank you to the indefatigable Jonno Rattman, Bobbie Richardson, Bonnie Briant, and Yolanda Cuomo. Your energy, wisdom, humor, and camaraderie has made the creation of this book a true joy. Thank you.

Andrea Albertini, same. *Grazie mille.*

Thank you to Elisabeth Biondi for your friendship and counsel—and for contributing your sagacious essay. Woof!

Thank you to Sam Abell, Honor Brodie, Alex Burrows, Eva Chen, Pamela Chen, Bill Clark, Sebastien Clivaz, Aude Debout, Terry Eiler, Allegra Farina, Simone Farinola, Matthew Foley, Genevieve Fussell, Matt Gentry, Alessia Glaviano, Stacy Gold, Lynn Johnson, Nadia Josse, Mary Kalergis, Alice Keating, Michael Kiel, Susan Kismaric, Cecile Lacoste, Sarah Leon, Kerri Mac, Emilie Meinadier, Sarah Meister, Paul Moakley, Nick Nichols, Larry Nighswander, Makiko Onda, Ed Osowski, Andrew Owen, Gary Pinagot, Gus Powell, Sadie Quarrier, Jody Quon, Karen Rabinovitz, Rebecca Ramsey, Alexandre-Camille Removille, Leah Rodriguez, Sabine Rogers, MJ Smith, Brittain Stone, Miwa Susuda, Gaia Tripoli, Benjamin Vu, Kristen Joy Watts, Alex Webb and Rebecca Norris Webb, Sasha Wolf, Denise Wolff, and Rick Woodward.

To my parents and family: thank you for always believing in me.

And most of all to Shannon, my love—thank you for everything. Arthur, Jack, and Townes, I love you.

Out of Fashion
Landon Nordeman

Book Design by Yolanda Cuomo Design, NYC
Associate Designer: Bonnie Briant
Assistant Designer: Bobbie Richardson
Reproduction and Print Preparation: Jonno Rattman

Published by Damiani srl
info@damianieditore.com
www.damianieditore.com

Printed in June 2016 by Grafiche Damiani – Faenza Group Spa, Italy.

ISBN 978-88-6208-496-3